Everyday Credit Checking

Revised Edition

Everyday Credit Checking:
A Practical Guide
Revised Edition

by Sol Barzman

National Association of Credit Management
475 Park Avenue South, New York, N.Y. 10016

This revised edition copyright © 1980
by Sol Barzman

Original edition copyright © 1973
by Sol Barzman

All rights reserved. Except for use in a review, the reproduction or utilization of this work in any form or by any electronic, mechanical, or other means, now known or hereafter invented, including xerography, photocopying, and recording, and in any information storage and retrieval system is forbidden without the written permission of the publisher.

Manufactured in the United States of America

Library of Congress Cataloging in Publication Data
Barzman, Sol.
 Everyday credit checking.
 Includes index.
 1. Credit management. I. Title.
[HG3751.B37 1980]   658.8'8   80–82080
     ISBN 0–934914–36–2

Author's Notes and Acknowledgments

Although the process of credit granting remains fairly constant from year to year, changes do take place. Inflation affects credit lines and high credit; skyrocketing interest rates slow down suppliers' cash flow, as more and more of their customers take longer to pay by, in effect, using their suppliers as bankers. Automation is becoming commonplace. The old familiar bankruptcy laws have been replaced by a Bankruptcy Code that is more beneficial to creditors, and in some ways more restrictive.

A credit manager's two major functions—the granting of credit, and the collecting of monies due—are necessarily influenced by these and other changes that seem to occur with increasing rapidity. Credit management today is far different from what it was only a generation ago. It is both simpler and more complex.

In an effort to keep pace with these changes, it was decided to produce an updated and expanded edition of this book. Like its earlier version, first published seven years ago, *Everyday Credit Checking—A Practical Guide, Revised Edition*, is aimed at the trainee, the newcomer, and the credit manager of the smaller companies, who is often not even a credit manager as such.

For the most part, available texts on credit management are too technical, too theoretical, and too ponderous for quick and easy reference. The average working credit manager, who frequently is the entire credit department of his firm, needs a practical guide that will tell him quickly, in simple language, what problems he will encounter during the course of a given day, and how best to solve them. Therefore this handbook, written for him and for the trainee by a credit manager who has himself encountered these very same problems.

It should be emphasized that this is not a definitive study of credit or credit management, nor is it even a theoretical study. This is, simply, an updated working guide for the many thousands of credit managers all over the country, employed by the smaller manufacturers, wholesalers, and distributors, who encounter the same basic problems every day and who must solve these problems themselves. This book is for them, and for the busy executive who doesn't have time for the training and orientation of his staff.

A credit manager who undertakes the writing of a book of this kind must have more than his own knowledge and experience behind him. He needs the advice and suggestions of his peers and colleagues, and of experts in various fields, for the subject of credit management and collections in today's complicated business world touches upon many areas. The author was most fortunate in having the cooperation and help of credit executives in various parts of the country, and of many others, who gave him the benefit of their knowledgeable counsel, in some cases for the entire book, and in others for specific chapters only. To all of them, I am grateful for their suggestions and constructive criticisms.

I am particularly grateful to Albert E. Bracuti, Assistant Director of Research, Credit Research Foundation, Inc., of Lake Success, New York, to Al Akerblom, Vice President, Credit Clearing House, Division of Dun & Bradstreet, Inc., New York City, and to John McNamara, Credit Clearing House, for their help and advice on general financial and credit matters; to Eugene Barone, General Traffic Manager, Exquisite Form Industries, Inc., of Pelham Manor, New

York, and to Daniel Lorusso, of the Interstate Commerce Commission, New York City, for their invaluable suggestions and information on traffic and shipping problems; to Stephen Smith of ADP—Automatic Data Processing, New York City, for information on computerizing accounts receivable; and to Leonard Schwartz of the law firm of Siegel, Sommers, and Schwartz, New York City, for his clarification and guidance in the preparation of material on the new Bankruptcy Code.

For permission to reproduce their Rating and Credit Keys in Chapter 4, my thanks go to Dun & Bradstreet, Inc., to Credit Clearing House, Division of Dun & Bradstreet, and to the Lyon Furniture Mercantile Agency, H. L. Gomling, Manager.

Finally, I cannot close without a special note of thanks to James J. Andover, director of publications, National Association of Credit Management, for his diligent supervision of this expanded and revised edition of my book.

Sol Barzman

New York City

A Word from the Author

Some years ago, credit management was the exclusive domain of men. But many credit managers today are women, and more and more women are entering the field; they have made rapid advances throughout the entire spectrum of credit management, reaching the same executive levels as their male colleagues. One woman, in fact, Ellen B. Coulam, of Airsco, Inc., Dallas, Texas, recently served as national president of the National Association of Credit Management.

Unfortunately, language has not kept pace with these advances, and we are thus faced with a dilemma. How, for example, does an author write about credit managers without specifying gender? No neutral word, such as "Ms.," has yet been coined to combine "he" and "she."

For the purposes of simplification, therefore, we will refer to credit manager without regard to sex. When we use the words "he," "him," "his," or "himself," such use is simply a literary device, and in no way is intended to convey a masculine meaning.

Sol Barzman

New York City
September, 1980

Contents

1 The Role of Credit 1
2 The Terminology of Credit 7
3 Processing the Order 23
4 Obtaining Credit Information 47
5 The Financial Statement 83
6 Selling Terms 117
7 Shipping Terms 137
8 Deductions and Chargebacks 153
9 Past Dues 185
10 Bankruptcies and Bad Debts 211
11 Letters, Data Processing, and Other Matters 249
   Index 273

1
The Role of Credit

Credit defined
Its significance in the world of commerce
The human element in credit checking
The average credit manager
    In the smaller companies
    His other possible functions
    The fledgling credit manager
    The inexperienced subordinate
    His relationship to the practice of
        everyday credit
Purpose of this book
    As an instructional aid for the credit
        manager of the smaller companies

The very meaning of the word *credit* and its evolution from the original Latin implies belief in the other fellow's honesty. One of the larger credit agencies speaks of credit as "man's confidence in man." The Spanish writer Cervantes maintained that "an honest man's word is as good as his bond." Even the wily Iago, in Shakespeare's "Othello," knew the value of his reputation:

> Who steals my purse steals trash; 'tis something, nothing;
> 'Twas mine, 'tis his, and has been slave to thousands;
> But he that filches from me my good name
> Robs me of that which not enriches him
> And makes me poor indeed.

Iago's point was well taken; once a man loses his good name, he loses the other fellow's trust, and without such trust he is helpless. This is particularly true in everyday business, as we can see from the Latin origin of credit, *credere*, to believe or trust.

Without the use of credit, normal business activities would be impossible. The function of credit as a medium of exchange has long been recognized as a necessary instrument in the history of commerce.

In the beginning, trade between tribes and nations consisted of exchanging one kind of goods for another of like value. But this system of barter was cumbersome. Gradually, over the centuries, barter was replaced, and the practice of credit developed to the point where sellers and buyers conducted their transactions upon paper, relying not upon goods of like value or payment of coin but only upon mutual belief in each other's honesty.

To survive in today's world of commerce, therefore, each of us, like Iago, must protect his good name. "Man's confidence in man" is implicit, yet it must be deserved.

The significance of credit in the phenomenal growth of commerce is a well-known fact that need not be emphasized. Now, because of the increasing use of credit, the role of the credit manager assumes more importance than ever.

On every level of business, from the manufacturer and

supplier to the final seller, someone has to make the decisions on every purchase, whether the purchase be made by a wholesaler or distributor or by the ultimate consumer.

Some of these decisions can be made by machines, and unquestionably are, but machines must be initially programmed and kept up to date. Someone must feed information to them and keep them supplied with the proper data. Machines can't do this for themselves; even the most highly proficient computers are impotent without the human input and human impulse.

Nor can machines make the finely graded decisions that often spell the difference between profit and loss on a given account; they cannot interpret the variables that arise every day.

In credit checking, the human element is still the most vital component.

But, strangely, the credit manager has not achieved the recognition he deserves. Major companies do admit the importance of a credit department. In these organizations, the credit manager may be an officer on a corporate level, and he may participate in corporate decisions. Below him are supervisors bearing various responsibilities under his general direction, with assistants, secretaries, and clerks completing the roster.

What's the picture in the smaller companies, which comprise a far greater percentage of the *number* of individual sellers?

In these organizations, the credit department, if it does exist as an entity, and often it does not, may consist of only one or two people, with the entire responsibility of that department resting upon them.

Who are these people, or who is the one person entrusted with credit and collection?

Perhaps he may not be a credit manager at all. He may

be a controller, with the checking of credit falling naturally into his domain. He may be a bookkeeper who incidentally checks credit. He may be an assistant to the head of the firm—helping out in the showroom, the shipping department, and (again incidentally) in the checking of credit. Or the credit manager may be the manufacturer, wholesaler, or distributor himself. Or he may actually be a full-fledged credit manager.

Whatever his primary function, it is important for the credit manager to know that he is not alone in the performance of that function.

The same applies to a bookkeeper whose duties may include the approval of all orders and collection of all monies due. Such a bookkeeper may sometimes fervently wish for a more completely defined credit department to share his burden.

Let him take heart. He has lots of company.

There are countless thousands like him, of both sexes, conscientiously approving orders, following up on past dues, and resolving the myriad problems that constantly arise to plague the credit department. Every credit manager of a small company frets over the correctness of his decisions, the maddening slowness of certain accounts, and frequently, the lack of appreciation from the front office.

Unlike the giant corporations, with their chain of command pyramiding down from a vice president to dozens of follow-up clerks, smaller companies are notoriously slow to recognize either the importance or need of a credit department; they assign what they consider to be a routine task to the bookkeeper or to an assistant.

But credit and collection are far from routine, as every credit manager knows. More than a minimum of expertise is demanded; how this expertise is acquired and applied can make the difference between a successful credit manager and a failure.

For the purposes of our discussion, it is necessary to understand the basic responsibilities and functions we're talking about.

We are discussing *mercantile,* or *commercial,* credit. There are other types of credit that play a vital role in the day to day course of our normal activity—bank credit, investment credit, and consumer credit. But it is the process of commercial credit that concerns us—the process of a manufacturer or supplier selling goods to someone else for resale to an ultimate consumer. The primary instrument used in this selling process is credit.

The one who extends the credit to a buyer on behalf of the seller is the credit manager. Some purists argue that in its true meaning, the word *credit* refers to the buyer, who offers his promise—in other words, the buyer's credit—to pay for goods purchased. This may be. But language, like business, must be adaptable. Because of popular usage, almost everyone of us now believes it is the *seller* who extends credit to the *buyer;* we use the term in that sense.

The credit manager who has been doing his job successfully year after year reacts with confidence. But it is the credit manager who may be new in the field, or the credit manager still unsure of himself, or the inexperienced subordinate who has not yet received the proper orientation, who needs help. We have therefore set about to offer him the kind of help he needs, and the kind of help he can absorb with a minimum of knowledge. (A note to the overworked credit manager who has just hired a new assistant and doesn't have time to break him in—let this book do the job for you.)

The material in this book has been organized in a simplified form, beginning with a brief discussion of credit and its terminology and then going on to the day by day *practice* of credit.

Our credit manager—the one for whom this guide has been specifically prepared—is the one who decides which orders to ship, how much to ship, what to do about past dues, unauthorized deductions, lost shipments, bankruptcies, etc.

In short, *he* is the credit department.

He may have a secretary or an assistant, and he may even have a separate clerk for collections, or he may be a bookkeeper having other chores, but basically he assumes all responsibility for credit and collections and their resultant problems.

The new credit manager, or the one who is still shaky, wants to know how his colleagues handle these problems. He is not interested in knowing how the job is being done by the vice presidents or treasurers of giant corporations; credit-granting on their level is entirely different.

He looks to his peers, credit managers very much like himself, to see how they go about solving their daily problems. They are the ones who offer him reassurance and aid and, very often, advice, for their problems are the same as his.

What happens in the everyday life of these average credit managers? What are these problems they encounter and how do they resolve them? This book illustrates one such average day, beginning with the opening of the mail in the morning and ending with notations on the credit manager's calendar pad to follow up at a later date.

If the credit manager understands the meaning and the role of credit, and his own role in relation to the entire area of credit, he can perform his tasks as successfully as do his colleagues.

2
The Terminology of Credit

Character, Capacity, and Capital
    Definition of these terms
    Their meaning for today's credit manager
    Their lack of relevance
Computers
    Their importance to the smaller company
The granting of credit
A process of learning for the credit manager
Checklist of credit terms frequently encountered

Like the traditional three R's of elementary education, the words *character, capacity,* and *capital* have long been looked upon as the keystone of credit. Many authorities insist that these three C's, which are sometimes followed by *conditions* and/or *collateral,* lie at the heart of a credit manager's appraisal of his customer. But the words themselves, as interpreted by these same authorities, are sometimes too vague for an accurate judgment. Note, for example, the following definitions, taken from leading textbooks on credit management:

> *Character*. Those mental qualities and actions of a debtor which impel him to pay his debts . . . that sense of obligation to fulfill the payment promise . . . the aggregate of mental and moral qualities which identify (an individual) . . . responsibility, integrity, honesty, punctuality, and consistency.
> *Capacity*. The ability to pay when a debt is due . . . disposition to economize, resourcefulness, and progressiveness . . . a quality of credit worthiness in both personal and business subjects.
> *Capital*. The financial strength of a risk as measured by the equity or net worth of the business . . . those possessions or equities from which payment might be expected when character and capacity become lacking . . . that from which payment may be taken under duress, if necessary.

There can be no quarreling with any of the foregoing; each definition is fundamentally correct. But for the average credit manager today, the credit manager of the smaller company, these are theoretical terms only. How, for example, can he verify the "mental qualities" that will impel a customer to pay his debts? Or how can he prove a customer's "disposition to economize, resourcefulness, and progressiveness"? Similarly, who decides at what point a customer becomes lacking in character and capacity?

For today's credit manager, the three C's have a pleasant ring, as do the three R's, but they all belong to the age of the one room schoolhouse; while their importance should not be minimized, they should be utilized in the light of custom, experience, and technology.

The modern schoolchild has sophisticated teaching

devices his grandparents could not possibly have dreamed of, and the credit manager has the use of giant credit checking agencies to do much of the work he might have had to do himself decades before.

In the early days of *personal* credit checking, when the manufacturer did not have credit agencies to rely upon, character, capacity, and capital were essential tools. The supplier, or his salesman, met his potential customer personally, and based upon his evaluation of the man's honesty, reputation, and assets, then decided whether to ship and how much.

Even so, the guess was often wrong, for how many swindlers impressed their victims with the sincerity of their "character"?

As for capacity and capital, these were easier to verify, but here too, hidden factors sometimes obscured the facts, or later muddied them, so that what appeared to be a cut and dried financial situation was not so at all.

With the growth of technology and the parallel development of the giant credit agencies, personal contact with the customer became both unnecessary and in most cases impossible, so that today the average credit manager never meets most of his accounts, has no assessment of their character, and in fact may not even know the names of the principals.

Does that mean then that character no longer plays a role in the checking of credit?

Not entirely. Though character cannot be precisely spelled out, it can, and often does, influence a credit reporter's thinking. The major credit agencies will send a reporter to visit a subject personally; if that reporter finds anything suspicious, he digs deeper, and perhaps he suggests a "hold" on the account until more complete information can be acquired.

Sometimes a customer visits his supplier's showroom,

and the credit manager has a chance at last to meet him personally.

How does the customer behave? Does he answer the credit manager's questions forthrightly, or is he evasive? What of his reputation and his background? Does he have the proper amount of "integrity"?

Will the credit manager, who believes himself to be an expert judge of other people, size up his customer without prejudice? Or will he convince himself, perhaps for a reason that has no foundation, that his customer is not to be trusted?

No matter what kind of a judge of other people a credit manager may believe himself to be, it would be wise for him to tread warily in this area, for too many bank managers look like convicts, and vice versa.

If you must rely upon character, let it be with all discretion and fairness, and let it be upon verifiable evidence. You can certainly determine what your potential customer's past business patterns have been, and his record as a social and commercial entity. In a different sense, the character or *nature* of your customer's *business* may be what you're really interested in, and may be what you actually investigate.

What about capacity and capital? In essence, they mean exactly what they say—the capacity or ability to carry out the buyer's share of a credit transaction and the capital to back it up.

But here again the credit manager must beware, for capacity and capital may not be what they claim to be, or seem to be. Each is more fully discussed in a later chapter; for the moment, let the prospective credit manager look upon them as potential aids that can help him once he understands their value and their pitfalls.

There is a fourth C that has been coming into wide usage and should, within the foreseeable future, be almost universally employed—*computers*.

The modern system of commerce and its number one offspring, credit, have left in their wake a spiraling demand for more and more paperwork; fortunately, technology has kept pace with our needs, and we have found ways to minimize the vast mountains of documentation that could easily engulf the entire structure. We are even approaching the time when money itself may become obsolete as a medium of exchange; who doesn't now pay for something by check or credit card?

The one tool that has made our rapid advance possible is the computer.

Don't let the term frighten you. The use of computers is not limited to giant companies that either have their own data processing setup or that can afford to spend huge sums on computer services.

More and more smaller companies, and larger ones as well, have come to realize that they must keep pace with modern business methods and techniques, and the only way to do so is to utilize the services of a data processing organization. Some small companies now lease, or purchase outright, one of the minicomputers that have been specifically tailored for their needs, and for their ability to pay. Other small companies prefer to use data processing organizations, who sell their services for a moderate monthly fee. For less than the cost of one full-time bookkeeper, any company can join the future.

If your company is not now enjoying the benefits of computerization, you ought to think seriously about switching over. The uses and advantages of data processing require a more complete discussion and are fully explored in a later chapter.

In the meantime, the credit manager of the smaller company that does not now use data processing should bear in mind that much of the work crossing his desk during the course of an average day has been computerized by someone else—information supplied by credit agencies, orders sent in by his customers' merchandising departments, checks cleared through the banks, and proofs of delivery from truckers and freight carriers.

Data processing is here to stay.

The granting of credit is not at all complicated. When your company sells merchandise on credit, you have accepted your customer's promise (normally unstated) that he will pay for the goods at a future date, within certain terms that you have specified and that he has presumably accepted. And you, as the seller, have presumably allowed any terms your customer may have requested.

Credit is as simple as that. There is no mystique to it.

But there is, necessarily, a process of learning that will bring the credit manager to the point where he understands why and how credit should be granted. He does not require an extensive course in accounting, or even bookkeeping, to learn the fundamentals of credit. But he does have to know the terms he will encounter daily, and the principles of bookkeeping.

We will assume that the reader of this book is familiar with the elementary principle of double entry bookkeeping; if he is not, he would be best advised to undertake a short course to prepare himself for his work. The National Institute of Credit, affiliated with the National Association of Credit Management, sponsors of this book, have excellent correspondence courses for home study. Call your local chapter of the National Association for further information, or write the New York headquarters, 475 Park Avenue South, New York, New York 10016.

There are certain terms that consistently crop up during the course of a credit manager's day. As an aid for the new credit manager, and as a refresher for others, we have prepared a checklist of the most important terms, and the ones most frequently encountered. These terms will be more fully explained in subsequent chapters.

You will note that the checklist has not been arranged alphabetically. It has been set up, rather, in a logical sequence paralleling the relative importance of each item to the credit manager and the probable order in which he will encounter them.

- *Financial statement.* Often called a *balance sheet.* Lists both the resources and liabilities of a business or individual. A financial statement shows the assets of the firm, its liabilities, and its net worth; it is normally dated at the end of the calendar year, December 31st.
- *Assets.* A company's resources, what it owns. Will be in the form of cash, both on hand and in the bank, inventory (merchandise), accounts receivable, equipment, fixtures, real estate, etc. Assets can be either current or fixed: current assets are those readily convertible and available at once to pay debts—cash of course, merchandise on hand to be sold, securities and insurance, and accounts receivable (money owed to your customer by people who purchased from him on credit); fixed assets are those invested in property, equipment, and fixtures.
- *Liabilities.* What a company owes, its debts. Will be in the form of obligations for merchandise purchased (trade debts), taxes, loans, etc. Liabilities are either current or long term: current liabilities are normally the trade obligations, taxes, accrued salaries, interest on loans, and any current portion of a loan; long term liabilities are deferred loans, mortgages, etc., anything that is payable after a year.
- *Net worth.* The owner's share in the assets of the business. Calculated by subtracting the total of all liabilities, both current and long term, from the total of all assets, both current and fixed. What is left is the net worth of the business.
- *Working capital.* Not to be confused with net worth.

Calculated by subtracting the total of current liabilities only from the total of current assets only. What is left is the working capital of the business.
- *Accounts receivable*. Monies owed to you by your customers. To your customer, the credit department of your company is sometimes the accounts receivable department, i.e., the department responsible for receiving monies due. Conversely, to you, your customer's department responsible for paying is accounts payable.
- *Credit checking*. Examining, analyzing, approving, and/or disapproving an order. In everyday credit parlance, to *check an account* normally means to approve an order from that account.
- *Line of credit*. The amount of money you are willing to have an account owe you at a given time. Includes unpaid invoices, merchandise in transit, unfilled approved orders in the house, and new orders. Also, line of credit refers to the total suggested by credit agencies, which may be either higher or lower than yours.
- *High credit*. The highest aggregate amount of credit you've allowed a customer at a given time. It does not mean, as is often supposed, the largest individual order, but includes everything your customer owes you at one particular time. It can be less than his assigned line of credit, or more.
- *Open terms*. Selling on credit, as opposed to selling for cash. When you offer a customer open terms, you have opened a line of credit for him.
- *CIA, CBD, or COD*. *C*ash *i*n *A*dvance, *C*ash *b*efore *D*elivery, or *C*ash *o*n *D*elivery. Used when you refuse to sell a customer on your normal open terms.
- *Credit ratings*. The classification of accounts by rating on numbered or lettered scales, normally beginning with 1 or A. Dun & Bradstreet, for

example, uses a combination of letter and number; other agencies may use letters only, while some agencies do not have specific ratings but offer Recommended for whatever the line of credit will be or Not recommended.
- *Requirements accounts.* Businesses that are eligible for any amount of credit they may require. Not all requirements accounts are alike in capitalization or net worth; some may be infinitely wealthier than others and require much higher lines of credit.
- *Marginal accounts.* Businesses with poor credit ratings and/or questionable prospects. Some credit managers have no problem at all with marginal accounts, since they simply refuse to ship any of them. But most credit managers do ship some marginal accounts, and they have learned to watch these customers carefully.
- *Subsidiary.* A company in which another company owns the majority of the stock, or is wholly owned by the parent. Subsidiaries are responsible for their own payments, except in the case of a guarantee from the parent. A subsidiary can issue a separate financial statement, but usually its figures would be part of a consolidated statement issued by the parent.
- *Division.* A separately functioning unit within a corporation, partnership, or individual proprietorship. It does not issue separate figures, nor is it set up as a separate corporation. A division is part of the parent, and the parent is responsible for payments.
- *Affiliate.* A company in which another company has less than a majority ownership. Neither company bears financial responsibility for the other but there can be intercompany relationship in the form of a loan or merchandise from one affiliate to the other.
- *Personal opinion, or P.O.* A credit analyst's own assessment of an account. The agency for which the

credit analyst is working may not recommend a particular account, but in the opinion of the analyst, the account is worthy of shipment and he will suggest a line of credit. (In some industries P.O. also refers to purchase order.)

- *Credit interchange*. Credit information exchanged with your colleagues in your own industry or in a group of industries. The interchange may be assembled by a credit agency, by a club or council of credit managers organized within an individual industry, or by a larger organization representing many industries, as for example, the National Association of Credit Management, which has branches in major cities all over the country.
- *EOM*. A term frequently employed in the payment of bills—*E*nd *o*f the *M*onth. If payment is to be made in the month following shipment, terms of sale will read, for example, Net 10 EOM, so that a shipment made in December will be paid for January 10th, the tenth day after the end of the calendar month.
- *As of the 25th*. Another phrase frequently used. It is now the custom in some industries to consider that the shipping and billing month end on the 24th; if your customer requests that his invoices be dated as of the 25th,, he is in effect asking for 30 days extra to pay his bill.
- *30x or extra dating*. 30 days extra for your customer to pay his invoice (a variation of *as of the 25th*). Or 60 days extra, and beyond, if you agree to give him that much additional time. The granting of extra dating is the supplier's prerogative alone, although many buyers now make it an integral part of their demands.
- *Net*. The full amount your customer must pay. There will be instances where he will request and receive certain allowances, such as a percentage of the invoice total for a new store opening, or a set amount

for advertising. In spite of such allowances, the terms will still read Net.
- *Discount.* The allowable percentage your customer is permitted to deduct from your invoice total (if freight charges are included, your customer must deduct those charges before computing his discount—discount is figured against merchandise costs only). There are two kinds of discount—trade and cash.
- *Anticipation.* Like the cash discount, a reward for prompt payment, although in this case, ahead of due date. In other words, you are permitting your customer to anticipate the date his invoice is to be paid. Anticipation is based upon the annual interest rate paid for commercial loans and is allowed only for each day ahead of the due date that payment is made.
- *FOB.* Free on Board. The most commonly used term for the shipment of goods. And the most frequently misunderstood. It does not mean *freight* on board, as so many people believe. Simply put, it means the point at which responsibility for the freight charges begins and title passes. If the terms read FOB Destination, the supplier is responsible for all shipping charges to the customer and he still owns the merchandise until it reaches its designated destination. If the terms read FOB Shipping Point, or FOB Factory, or FOB Mill, the customer pays all shipping costs, and title to the goods passes to him at that point.
- *ROG.* Receipt of Goods. Used to calculate the due date of your invoice. If your customer specifies ROG, he wants his payment terms to begin from the date he receives his merchandise, not from the date you shipped it. ROG terms can often give a customer as much as 30 additional days, depending upon the length of time your goods will be in transit.
- *Bill of lading.* A contract for carriage and a shipping

document, normally in several parts (determined by your own needs) and normally numbered. The bill of lading must indicate the full name and address of the consignee (the one to whom the shipment has been consigned), the number of cartons in the shipment, their total weight, and the type of merchandise being shipped. For proper control, an invoice number or order number should be included.

• *Manifest.* Originally, a listing of the goods being shipped; this term is now more often used to list the *stores* being shipped, especially when you ship to a large chain and you are requested to make shipment for a number of stores to one central point on one bill of lading.

• *Consolidating and consolidators.* Consolidating is holding shipments for a customer until you have accumulated or consolidated one large shipment for him; this is then forwarded on one bill of lading (separate shipments require separate bills of lading, one for each shipment, and result in higher freight costs). Or your customer may request shipment to a *consolidator*, who holds smaller shipments until he has accumulated, from other suppliers as well as from you, one large shipment for your customer.

• *Common carrier.* Any individual or organization who offers himself to the public for hire to carry or transport freight. Usually refers to interstate truckers but also includes railroads, airlines, freight forwarders, and express companies.

• *Pro forma.* A Latin phrase meaning *as a matter of form*. In commercial terminology it has come to stand for a document prepared as a convenience, or as a matter of form, in place of or in advance of the official document. For example, you may be requested to send a pro forma invoice, which is no more than a

preliminary dummy copy prepared before shipment is made. A customer's pro forma financial statement is a projection of what he expects his financial picture will be at a future date.
• *Pro no.* A number assigned to the delivery receipt, which has been prepared by the freight carrier making delivery to the point designated by your customer, or prepared by one carrier transferring your goods to another. Originally, pro no. was *pro forma number*, but common usage shortened it to its present form.
• *Proof of delivery.* A signed receipt showing date of delivery to consignee, and signature of consignee or his agent. If you have been requested to ship to a consolidator, you generally will not be required to prove delivery beyond that point.
• *Free and astray.* Sometimes part of a shipment goes astray. If it's the carrier's fault, the missing portion will be later delivered on a free and astray, the carrier's receipt showing delivery to the consignee, without charge, of the merchandise that went astray. If the fault is yours—perhaps your shipping department mislabeled part of a shipment, or mixed up two separate shipments for two separate customers— redelivery charges will be your responsibility, not the carrier's.
• *Back orders.* When orders are not shipped complete, the balance still to be shipped is a back order.
• *Automatic cancellations.* Some accounts prefer complete shipments only and ask that you automatically cancel any balances due. Also, an order may show an outside shipping date; anything to be shipped after that date is considered automatically canceled and will be returned to the supplier at his expense.
• *Invoices.* The bills itemizing merchandise shipped, unit cost, and total cost. Should be numbered in

sequence. They are sometimes included with the shipment, but are more often mailed, either to the designated consignee, or to a paying office.
• *Shipping memo or packing slip*. A detailed listing of the merchandise shipped; if you use style or product numbers or names, colors, or sizes, these should appear on the memo. Also includes department number, order number, packing marks, etc. But should not include prices. Like the invoices, the packing slips should have their own numerical sequence for easy reference and control. Some suppliers use a combination invoice and shipping memo on the same form.
• *Ledger*. A record of debits, credits, and all money transactions; there are subsidiary ledgers that go into greater detail for specialized analysis, but most credit managers are concerned only with the *general ledger*, which is the book of final entry. Whether your general ledger is kept by hand or by data processing, the basic format will be the same, with an individual ledger card or sheet for each customer, and additional cards added as sales with that customer warrant. When you are asked by one of your colleagues for your *ledger experience* with a certain account, check the ledger card itself or an extract.
• *Schedule*. Sometimes called an *aging schedule* or "trial balance." It is a listing, either alphabetically by account name or numerically by account number, of total sales, current sales, monies owing, monies paid, chargebacks, and credits. Computerized schedules are remarkably easy to read and will even include credit ratings and manner of payment; for the credit manager, they are an important tool—another reason to switch over to data processing.
• *Statements*. Forms sent to your customers listing all open items on their ledger cards. These include

unpaid invoices, unused credits, and any chargebacks that you have not allowed. Some customers insist upon statements before they will send you a check; others do not want statements at all.

• *Debit.* Money owed to you by your customer. Each sale you make to your customer, or each item charged back to him, will appear as a debit on the *left* hand side of the ledger and statement. *Credits*, which include payments made to you by your customer, merchandise returned, or allowances for a shortage claim or damaged merchandise, etc., appear on the *right* hand side of the ledger.

• *Past due.* Any invoice that remains unpaid after the date it was scheduled for payment, or past the due date. Most credit managers use a series of reminders as their past due collection letters, with each reminder becoming progressively firmer. Sometimes statements are used as past due reminders.

• *Chargeback or debit memo.* The document or notice used by your customer to advise you that he will deduct, or is deducting from his payment for shortages, allowances, anticipation, freight charges, returns, etc.

• *Insolvency.* Inability to pay debts as they mature, or having more liabilities than assets. A solvent customer is one who *can* pay his bills, although he may run slow.

3
Processing the Order

The language of credit
The nature of the credit manager's accounts
The four major classifications
    Automatic account
    Semi-automatic account
    Average, or non-automatic, account
    Marginal account
The automatic account
    Its composition
    Its behavior in a past due situation
    The credit manager's approach in a past due situation
The semi-automatic account
    Its composition
    Sudden increase in dollar volume
    Possible change of terms
    The small, semi-automatic account
The average account
    Its several subclassifications
    The credit manager's approach to each
    In a past due situation

    The infrequent purchaser
    Flexibility of credit lines
    New accounts in this category
The marginal account
    Definition and composition
    The marginal account as a source of profit
    Credit agency ratings
    In a past due situation
    The small order, automatically checked or analyzed
Rejecting an order
    Wording of your rejection
What to look for in checking an order
    Possible pitfalls for the unwary credit manager

The language of credit, for the most part, is utilitarian and to the point. When a credit analyst at one of the reporting agencies offers his *P.O.* (personal opinion), he is doing precisely that—giving his own opinion about an account, regardless of his agency's position on that same account.

A *financial statement* means exactly what it says—it is a statement of a company's financial condition.

A *requirements account* is one that is eligible for any amount of credit it may require.

And a *marginal account* is one that is on the margin of noncheckability—in other words, investigate it carefully and watch it closely.

With this in mind, the credit manager can now proceed to the opening of his morning mail. What does he normally find? Checks, complaints, excuses, shortage claims, requests for duplicate invoices and proofs of delivery, credit reports, and of course orders.

Of all these, the orders undoubtedly occupy his first attention. Does he separate them? If so, why, and in what sequence?

To discuss the *why*, the credit manager must understand the nature of his accounts. There are four major classifications:

1. The automatic account
2. The semi-automatic account
3. The average, or non-automatic, account
4. The marginal account

The following is based on the assumption that it is the credit manager himself who checks every order. Your company may employ someone else to screen the orders as they come in, or allow all orders to go through a computer, which automatically accepts all requirements accounts and those with high credit ratings. Nevertheless, the following section should be of interest to you because of its relationship to past dues.

The automatic account

First of all, let's define an automatic account. Simply put, it is an account that can be checked automatically as the orders come in, without investigation as to amount of order, credit rating, past dues, or any possible credit problem.

There is only one kind of account that falls into this category—the requirements account. Some authorities insist that certain high rated accounts that are not requirements nevertheless rate an automatic classification.

Not so. These customers may be automatic for some suppliers, but not for others, as we will explain later. They really belong in the following section; semi-automatic.

In the automatic category, therefore, we have the requirements account only. For the credit manager, orders from such a customer are the simplest to handle. If they come from Sears, Roebuck, K mart Corporation, or Montgomery Ward, the credit manager processes the orders without a second thought, regardless of size or dollar amount. These are giant firms, doing business in the billions every year. These customers are shipped whatever they require, and no questions asked.

But are there occasions when a requirements account would not be automatic? You may sometimes think so, yet actually the answer should be no, despite your personal feelings.

Assume that a requirements customer owes you perhaps $10,000, much of this past due for 60 to 90 days, some of it past due only 30 days, and a small part of it owing for as much as 120 days. Most of this involves skipped invoices, coupled perhaps with a perceptible slowing down in the payment pattern.

Assume, too, that you've been trying every way you know how to collect these monies due; you've sent statements, you've written letters, you've dutifully complied with requests for proofs of delivery and duplicate invoices (which you suspect are unnecessary and represent only another delaying tactic), and you've even made long distance calls to your customer's accounts payable department, with no positive results.

What do you do when this particular customer keeps sending in new orders?

In a mood of teeth-gnashing frustration, you may be tempted to say the devil with it and not ship anymore until everything has been cleaned up.

Would this be a proper credit procedure? No, it would not, although it might, under certain additional circumstances, be the right one for you.

A customer doing enough business to qualify for a

Processing the Order

requirements line of credit does not have a money problem; what it probably does have is inadequate or inefficient personnel. It may also have, perhaps recently instituted, an unofficial policy to skip a few invoices here and there so that it will always have a revolving fund of cash that it is not paying to its suppliers and on which it is not paying interest (more about interest in a later chapter; there is also a question of discount involved here, and that can get sticky—see Chapter 8).

You may encounter another type of problem that can be even more disturbing. You may find that one of your requirements accounts is skipping not just a few invoices, but all invoices. This account, with whom you do a sizable volume every month, suddenly starts paying as much as thirty and more days slow, without prior warning, and for no apparent reason.

Now you no longer have a few hundred or even a few thousand dollars in skipped invoices—you have many thousands open for this account, with at least half of that amount past due. You have never really worried about this customer before, since it is a major retail chain, with perhaps a thousand and more stores all over the country. It's always been, in your estimation, a requirements account, and there was no need for you to be concerned about it.

Should you be concerned now? Probably not. Not even when you find, to your astonishment, that your checks from this customer, when they do finally arrive, are dated six or seven weeks previous. In other words, the accounts payable department processed your payments on time, but someone else, most likely on the corporate level, held your checks.

Why? You may never be told the true reason, since the accounts payable department won't know, or won't say, and the one who does know—the corporate treasurer, controller, or financial executive—will never admit the real reason, even if you could reach him, which is doubtful. But you can make an educated guess.

Your customer did not pay you on time because (a) he was using your money for a stronger cash position for his year end financial statement, (b) by holding your money, he doesn't have to go to his bank and thus pay high interest rates, or (c) he invested your money in, let us say, short term notes, and made money on your money. There may be other reasons along the same lines, but these three should give you a general idea.

Does this sort of thing actually happen? Do major companies deliberately withhold monies owing to their suppliers? Evidence gathered in recent years does point to such a trend; an uncomfortably large number of important firms *appear* to be guilty of this practice. There is no definite proof that it has become a precise policy, yet the knowledgeable credit manager who has been dealing with these accounts is aware that his own cash flow has slowed down, and many of his larger customers are taking more and more time to pay.

In effect, they are using their suppliers' money rather than borrow money from their banks. Since they know you will not, or cannot charge them interest, if you hope to keep the account, they save considerable interest charges by using you as their banker.

How do you handle a situation like that? It may only be a temporary condition, as at the end of your customer's fiscal accounting period, or it may go on for a few months.

First of all, gather all the facts on this customer. It's not likely this account is in financial difficulties, but make certain of that. Check with all of your sources (see Chapter 4, "Obtaining Credit Information"), and bring this information to your principals. With major sums of money involved, the decision on this customer should not be yours alone. If this customer is not in trouble, and it probably won't be, you and your principals will decide, correctly, that its past due situation is both deliberate and temporary, and you will continue to ship as you have in the past.

Going a step further, however, you may not be doing enough business at the moment with this requirements account to warrant the expense of allowing it to use you as a banker. If that's the case, and if your company finds itself in a tight money position, or the merchandise you have been selling to this particular customer is in constant demand elsewhere, your company may decide not to ship this customer any longer until and unless it pays everything it owes.

Where demand is involved, you and your principals will also consider the production element—if the demand for this one item grows, can your company's production expand enough to meet the demand? If the answer is no, your decision not to ship a requirements account might then be the right one for you, at least for the moment. But you may regret it in the future, when you will once again need this customer more than he will need you.

In summation, if one of your customers qualifies for requirements, then by all means continue to ship him everything he orders, no matter what he owes you at a given time. But if you see that he's developing a pattern of slowness, or is taking too many unauthorized or unjustified deductions, investigate that account as thoroughly as you can.

Don't take any customer for granted, not even the top rated requirements accounts. The American business world has been badly shaken in recent years by the financial problems of some of the largest corporations in the country, as we saw with W. T. Grant in 1974, and Food Fair in 1978.

Make it a practice to review periodically every account, including the biggest.

The semi-automatic account

(In this category, as well as in the two that follow, credit ratings play an important part. Credit ratings and how to interpret them will be explained in Chapter 4, "Obtaining Credit Information"; the chapter you are now reading deals with credit ratings in a general way only and refers to an account as high rated or as an A account, and so on.)

The credit manager has sorted out his automatic, requirements accounts, and he now has a group of orders from high-rated, non-requirements accounts.

Can any of these be automatic?

Of course they can. You have, as an example, a customer with an average line of credit of $25,000 (as determined by credit agencies, including Dun & Bradstreet, the largest in the field). You consistently receive orders from this customer in the $4,000 to $5,000 category. You know immediately, as soon as you see an order from this customer, that his payments have always been prompt and the account is virtually trouble free. You put his orders through at once, just as you would with Sears, Roebuck.

So do other credit managers, though their line may be considerably higher than yours. One vendor may be shipping this account aggregate orders well beyond its officially assigned line of $25,000, as much as $50,000 and more. To such a supplier, this customer may be as automatic as the requirements account.

You too may consider this customer automatic—as long as his orders remain in the accustomed $4,000 to $5,000 range. But suppose his orders suddenly double or triple, or even quadruple in dollar amount? Would you still treat them automatically? Probably not, at least until you satisfy yourself as to the reasons for this abrupt increase.

If such a customer does suddenly start sending in very large orders, you should ask yourself a few questions:

1. What line of credit does he get from other suppliers in your industry? On what terms?

2. Are your unusually high orders unsolicited, or are they the result of a salesman's visit to the customer?

3. Has your customer decided to eliminate a competitive supplier and transfer more of his buying to your company?

4. Or has he decided to expand and therefore needs more merchandise to fill his expansion needs?

If it's the last point that's involved, you will want to determine whether your customer's expansion has been adequately funded, and where these funds are coming from.

The answers to the first question, and to the last, can usually be supplied by your credit agency. If you're within calling distance, by all means telephone and discuss this account with a credit analyst at your agency. The other questions can of course be answered by your own sales department.

Once you have acquired information that satisfies you, there's no question that you will continue to treat this account automatically—in spite of the suddenly increased dollar amount of his orders. But another note of caution must be sounded.

Take time occasionally to check the terms of your orders; even giant corporations have been known to insert, without prior warning, a new set of terms, such as additional dating, an outrageous allowance for a new store opening, or an equally outrageous dollar penalty for not following instructions. Selling terms are discussed in detail in Chapter 6, and shipping terms in Chapter 7; for the moment, remind yourself to employ constant vigilance in processing orders from requirements and high-rated accounts. You may allow something to slip through that is contrary to your own terms, and you may then have to swallow a chargeback that could have been avoided.

Remember that your major accounts do not automatically assume all the virtues of unadulterated purity and innocence because of their high ratings. A customer of this size may not necessarily embark on a deliberate campaign of deception, but there *can* be occasions when you'll suddenly encounter the unexpected—to your sorrow after the fact, so that you have no defense.

Finally, in the semi-automatic category there is the small account you've been dealing with for years. He may pay promptly, or he may even be slow, but he has been consistently slow in all the time you've known him—so consistent that in effect you have been allowing him extra dating, though it was never officially requested and you never gave it.

Although such an account may not even be recommended by the credit agencies, you've nevertheless continued to ship him, profitably for him and for your company. He has always paid, within the same time pattern he has been following for many years; the account is relatively trouble free—he does not make unauthorized deductions, and when he claims a shortage, you can be certain it is justified.

For you, an account of this kind can be as automatic as your high-rated customers, provided he keeps his dollar volume within the credit line previously established. Any sharp variation upwards calls for immediate investigation. So does a noticeable slowdown in his payments. And it would be prudent to keep a close watch upon him during an economic slowdown, or if the patterns of his community change for the worse.

Until then, continue shipping him, even though a new supplier may regard him with skepticism.

The average, or non-automatic, account

With the first two categories out of the way, the credit manager next faces the orders he has received from his non-automatic accounts. These fall into several subclassifications:

1. The customers you have been dealing with for years who order on a fairly regular basis.
2. The customers you have been dealing with for years but who order only infrequently, perhaps once every twelve months or so.
3. New customers who are well established.
4. New customers who have just gone into business.

The last two can themselves be subdivided, as either solicited by your salesman or unsolicited. An unsolicited order should be examined carefully. How did this customer happen to pick your company? Have his normal sources dried up?

How does the credit manager handle orders that fall into any of these classifications? Does he check a ledger card for possible past dues? Does he consult, or create, a credit file for these customers? Does he work with a schedule supplied either by his bookkeeping department or a data processing service?

Whatever method the credit manager employs to process his non-automatic accounts (he is to be envied if he has time to create, update, and consult a file for each of his customers), he must determine certain facts about them.

If it's an old customer, does he owe money? If so, how much and for how long?

And what does the debit represent?

If it's a disputed chargeback, or a deduction you did not allow, it may not be important enough or large enough to warrant holding up a new order, even though your customer may have ignored all your correspondence on the matter. That may be his way of getting an extra little edge or he simply may not have the personnel to answer letters, so he takes the easy way out and replies to nothing.

If it's a past due invoice, how long has it been past due, and how much is it?

Together with his new order, your customer's past due invoice may represent less than the line you would normally assign him. As an example, if you had received an order from him for $1,500, you may have processed it without question, since his line of credit is $2,500. But now he owes you $500 and he sends in another order for $500 for a possible total of $1,000, far less than his line of credit and even less than the $1,500 you would have okayed originally.

Should you approve his new order without waiting for payment of the past due invoice?

You can, if you know him well enough—not personally, but if you've been dealing with him for many years, you may feel secure enough in your relationship to continue shipping even when he owes you money.

On the other hand, if he places orders with your company only infrequently, and this particular past due is the first time he's run slow, you may want to find out why he is now running past due. A courteous letter explaining your company's policy regarding past dues, and advising that you must hold his new order until his balance has been cleared, will probably bring a check by return mail, and perhaps an explanation for his tardiness.

Even if the explanation appears to be plausible, by all means keep an eye on this account; if he continues to run slow, you may want to dig deeper and find out a little more about him. You would be particularly interested in his current position—as current as it can be; the available information may be as much as a year old. If that's the case, and it usually is, the credit manager will have to rely upon the trend of his customer's financial affairs, and other pertinent facts such as working capital, net worth, current ratio, and so on—see Chapter 5, "The Financial Statement."

What about the account that is past due to the limit of his line who then sends a new order before clearing his balance?

Here again your relationship with this customer might well govern your action. If you have determined from various sources available to you that your customer is not in financial difficulty of any kind, you might correctly decide that your past due invoice is an oversight; even though the money owing and your customer's new order total more than his assigned limit, you might be tempted to go beyond his line. Very often, the line of credit one credit manager assigns is unrealistic and less than the line assigned by someone else. The same holds true of credit agencies. They may well recommend less than you are willing to ship.

Remember that credit lines can be flexible and should be applied to your particular situation; and remember, too, that one past due invoice does not have to spell trouble.

This is especially true of the A-rated accounts, even those with a modest net worth. If they have been rated A as long as you have known them, it isn't likely they would go bankrupt overnight. But again, continuing slowness might evidence some kind of deterioration, and it may well be that, before the year is out, a former A account will have to be downgraded. A downgrading, even to the next category, calls for watchfulness.

If you receive an order from an established account who owes you nothing, you will probably review your records—whether it be individual ledger cards or an aging schedule—to determine his payment pattern.

Prompt payments of course mean that you will process his orders immediately (provided they remain within his normal line of credit).

If occasional slowness is indicated, you may want to verify his present rating to make certain he hasn't been downgraded.

And if this is the first order for some time—perhaps a year—you will certainly want to investigate his current condition, either through your agency or your industry interchange (see Chapter 4, "Obtaining Credit Information").

What about new accounts? First of all, you would check with your credit agency. Dun & Bradstreet issues reference books that give you the current rating on any established account. It takes only a moment to verify the rating for a new customer. If he's in Column 1 or A and his order is well within the indicated dollar amount, you can ship him without worry.

An entry in Column 2 or B might call for closer investigation, especially if the opening order seems rather large for his rating. But the B listing may not be bad at all, and may indicate nothing worse than an occasional slowness, perhaps 15 to 20 days, or even a rare 30 days past due. This, in itself, should not be enough to turn him down.

If, however, your new customer is listed in either the third or fourth column, you should not approve his order until you have made a thorough investigation (see the next section, *the Marginal Account*).

A *newly established business* requires additional analysis:

1. What is its opening capital (or investment)?
2. How much of this is a loan?
3. Is it secured?
4. By what?
5. How much of an opening inventory does your new customer hope to have?
6. What is his projected sales figure for the next twelve months?

7. What is his personal history?

8. In the case of a partnership or corporation, who are the principals and what have they done before?

9. Is management experienced in this line?

Your credit agency will generally supply their own thinking about such an account. If, in the view of the agency, your prospective customer is undercapitalized or lacks the proper background, you will get a Not Recommended or a negative response. A Not Recommended should spell caution; examine with care and proceed with discretion.

At the same time, it should be remembered that on occasion a new business will, for its own reasons, not submit an opening financial statement to any credit agency. But it will forward a statement to a prospective supplier who asks for it. If your agency does not recommend because no opening statement was submitted, write to your customer and ask for a copy. He may send it, and you can then make your own analysis.

Of course if he refuses your request, and your other sources are not able to supply information, you have no option but to reject his order. Such an action on the part of a new business would be either quixotic or ignorant; it fortunately doesn't happen too often, but it does happen.

Sometimes a newly established business may not be all that new. It may be a reorganization under a different name, or a reshuffling of partners, or a move from one community to another. And it may be that the principals, who might have come together from two other separate businesses to form the third, have simply never issued statements and still refuse to do so. They rely upon the good will of their former vendors for their new merchandise.

In an instance of that kind, the agencies would officially have to offer a Not Recommended, but you or your colleagues might have sold one or both of the principals in the past. Despite the lack of an opening statement, there may nevertheless be enough confidence to warrant an adequate line of credit.

The marginal account

Aside from the major account that has gotten itself into trouble, the most vexing customer for the credit manager is the marginal account. Remember our definition at the beginning of this chapter—a *marginal account* is one that is on the margin of noncheckability—in other words, investigate it carefully and watch it closely.

More specifically, the basic characteristics and risk factors of a marginal account can be listed as:

1. Unsatisfactory finances
2. A poor payment record
3. Incompetent or inexperienced management
4. Insufficient credit information
5. Continuing losses from operations
6. Inadequate working capital
7. A deteriorating trend in financial condition

All of the above were cited by some 500 credit managers, in a survey conducted by Credit Research Foundation, Inc. of Lake Success, New York, as being the most important elements in the evaluation of a marginal account. These 500 were employed by commercial and industrial firms and financial institutions ranging from "Apparel, Banking, Building Materials" to "Tobacco, Transportation Equipment, Watches & Jewelry."

One fact stands out, from this survey as well as others—marginal accounts can be profitable and therefore should not be rejected simply because they *are* marginal.

This point is stressed by every authority on credit management, without exception.

Marginal accounts increase the risk of incurring bad debts, but the credit manager who refuses to run that danger or who boasts that he has never had a bankruptcy will necessarily have thrown away much valuable business for his firm.

It is true that marginal businesses constitute the largest percentage of bankruptcies, but it is just as true that *not all marginal businesses fail.* Most of them continue, perhaps struggling, but they manage to survive, honorably, with the trust and cooperation of their suppliers.

If you subscribe to a credit agency service that furnishes ratings, your task is simplified. The credit ratings of marginal accounts will always be either 3 or 4 (on a scale of 1-2-3-4), C or D (on an A-B-C-D scale), or Fair or Limited if precise terms are used.

The 4, D, and Limited ratings are rarely assigned; if you come across an account in that column, you can be sure he's in desperate trouble, and you'll want to stay away. More often, the marginal account is in the third or C column, and it is with these C, or Fair, accounts that this section is primarily concerned.

If such an account owes you money, you would probably not ship his new order until his past due invoices have been paid. Your own experience will no doubt parallel those of your colleagues or that of your industry; prudence is therefore indicated, and your course of action should be influenced by the extent of slowness that your own records show, as well as by the payment pattern reported by others. It may be that your customer has been generally reported to be as much as 60 days slow. In a case like that, by all means hold every new order until he has paid all past due invoices.

Once his indebtedness to you has been cleared, you of course still have the option of rejecting his new orders. You may no longer feel confident of his ability to continue meeting his obligations, or you may have new information that indicates further deterioration of his affairs, or you may simply not care to wait that long for your money.

In the latter instance, you must determine first of all how much of a loss this account will represent to your company. No one likes to lose business or deliberately turn it away, but if your principals prefer a conservative approach, you'd be better off advising this particular customer, with your regrets, that you can no longer accept his orders on your normal open terms.

On the other hand, if your company policy is more flexible and you are expected to make all credit decisions, a slow paying account should not be rejected out of hand. At the least, you ought to weigh the pros and cons very carefully:

1. How long has the customer been running 60 slow?
2. What's the reason for his slowness?
3. Is it a poorly turning inventory, too much competition, bad management, inadequately financed expansion?
4. How close is he to real financial difficulty? If you do decide to ship him, but on an order to order basis only—in other words, ship him only one order at a time and do not ship anything else until his first order has been paid for—what are your chances of getting caught, eventually, in a business failure?
5. Based upon the amount of sales you've had with this account over the years, how much would it hurt to be caught with one unpaid shipment? What effect would such a bad debt have upon your *total ratio* of bad debts (see Chapter 10, "Bankruptcies and Debt Losses")?
6. Conversely, what are this customer's chances of turning his business around and developing into a substantial, well-rated account?

Whatever decision you reach, bear in mind that the decision is yours alone to make, although what your colleagues or competitors are doing will of course help to influence that decision, especially if other suppliers are not shipping. In that case you can be certain your customer will not have a proper flow of merchandise, and without the right goods to sell he can't remain in business (as happened with W. T. Grant, and more recently with Food Fair—specifically, the J. M. Fields subsidiary of Food Fair). But in the final analysis, you alone must decide what this account means to your firm, and your decision will be based upon that evaluation, whether the account owes you nothing or there is a balance due.

Similarly, you will apply the same yardstick to new accounts in the marginal category—with one added element. First of all, you must determine if their orders were unsolicited. If they were, why did a new account happen to choose you? Is it possible he can no longer get merchandise from his normal sources? This question applies as well to solicited orders. It may be that your salesman has called upon this account in the past without success, yet now he places an order with your firm.

Why? Perhaps, again, his previous suppliers refuse to ship, and your new customer turns to other vendors, to anyone who will ship. But here, too, you must not jump to conclusions. The orders may have been placed with your company simply because the customer likes your merchandise and wants to sell it.

In short, make certain of all the facts before reaching an irrevocable decision on a new marginal account. It may be that your company (or you) may have a loosely defined policy to accept without investigation any order from anyone that falls below a certain dollar total—say $200, or $300, or perhaps more. In that case you would approve some marginal accounts automatically. But if it is your pattern to review all orders no matter how small, then you owe it both to your company and to your prospective customer to investigate carefully and completely.

Rejecting an order

Rejecting an order is never easy. Nor is it easy to find the right way to tell your customer.

No matter how diplomatically you have worded your letter, you are in effect telling the recipient of that letter—whether it be an old customer or a prospective customer—that he is not worthy of credit on your normal open terms. Some people will resent such a letter immediately, even though it's written with the greatest skill and tact. Others may take offense because they disagree with your findings; in their own view, they are indeed worthy of credit, and your rejection therefore may sound to them like a compound of poor taste and worse judgment.

So what do you do?

First of all, you must be aware that the moment you mail a letter of rejection, whether it be to a specific individual or, in a more general way, to the company itself, you run the risk of losing that account for all time. Are you prepared to take that risk, or do you feel that you must, after reviewing and analyzing all available facts?

Once you've reached a decision that it is in the best interests of your company to reject an order, you must then transmit the basis for that rejection. If you don't care how your customer may react, you can of course be blunt and to the point.

"Sorry. We don't like the looks of your financial statement, and we'd rather not ship."

Such an approach is simple and direct, and conceivably solves a few headaches—you don't have to worry about composing a conciliatory letter and you'll never again hear from a troublesome account.

But if you're like the overwhelming majority of credit managers, you do care about other people and you do care about protecting possible future sales for your firm. The marginal account you reject today may develop, tomorrow, into a profitable customer.

So you don't choose the blunt approach; you prefer to be more tactful, even though, in the end, it comes down to the same thing. Most people appreciate consideration and will respond in kind.

When rejecting an order, try to put the blame on your company rather than on your customer. In other words, it is your company's long-established policy that has motivated your rejection, not your customer's history. It's a small point, but some people may appreciate a face-saving device of that kind.

We now come to a knotty question—after you say no, what then? Do you ask for cash, either in advance or on delivery, or do you leave it up to your customer to make some kind of an offer?

The second choice is unbusinesslike and shifts your burden to the other fellow. If you'd rather avoid the mention of cash, you can write your customer a *provisional* or *tentative rejection* and give him an opportunity either to submit recent financial information or to discuss your terms of sale.

This tactic sometimes has exactly the effect you want—your customer won't answer, because he has no recent financial information that can help him or his payment record is far too spotty to invite confidence.

Or you may accomplish what you really don't want. Your customer does respond, and he promises faithfully to abide by your terms. You're fairly certain he won't, but once you've given him that opening, can you back away? If you've committed yourself to listen to his promises and/or explanations, you may find yourself shipping against your better judgment. So be definite in your mind as to how you will proceed if your customer accepts your invitation for further discussion. Don't just hope that he won't answer.

Once you've decided on an outright rejection, you leave yourself one final alternative—to request a prepayment, or cash, either before delivery or on delivery. (For a fuller discussion of prepayment terms, see *CIA, CBD, or COD* in Chapter 6.)

Few people like to be told that the only way they can buy merchandise is with cash. But there is a device that may have a soothing effect.

Offer a hard-pressed customer the right to anticipate on his cash payment. If your normal terms are EOM, allow him to take a full month's anticipation at whatever the going rate of interest might be—provided, of course, that you permit anticipation—some suppliers don't—and provided, too, that the interest rates are not excessive. When the prime rate reaches a very high point, as it did in the latter part of 1979 and in the early months of 1980, and other interest rates are raised accordingly, it may be that anticipation may become too expensive for you. But if the total anticipation on a cash payment is a relatively small amount, even with very high current interest rates, you may be willing to allow your customer the few dollars involved, and he will appreciate the gesture.

You might also be willing to split the risk with him. For example, if his order totals $1,000, you could ask him to send half of that in advance. In that way, you would each be investing $500. (But don't permit anticipation on this amount unless he specifically asks for it, and don't ship any of his order until you're certain his $500 check has cleared.) If he's willing to invest $500 with your company before having any of your merchandise to sell, the chances are he'll be good for the rest of it.

It may also be that he's desperate for merchandise, and he has just enough cash on hand to pay what you've asked, and it may be he won't be able to pay for the rest of it.

Is it worth the gamble to you? You've shipped $1,000 worth of merchandise, and you've been paid for half of that. The loss may not be all that onerous, assuming there *is* a loss. Bear in mind that, as an ongoing business, your new customer will be generating cash; your gesture of splitting the risk with him may impress him enough so that he will go out of his way to pay the rest of your bill on time.

What to look for in checking an order

Approving an order on the basis of your customer's credit standing comprises an integral part of your work, for your knowledge and expertise play a major role in your decision. But sometimes there's much more to do than simply initialing the order, or signing it, or whatever method your company utilizes to signify your approval.

You must, in addition, examine each order carefully for possible traps, not placed there deliberately (although that's been done, too), but perhaps in all innocence. Whether innocent or deliberate, any variation in terms will almost always become your responsibility. If you accept an order that does not conform to your terms and if you do not advise your customer of the proper terms and wait for his acceptance, you leave yourself open for possible charge-backs or incorrect payments.

Here are some of the things to watch for:

1. Payment terms
2. Allowances, new store and advertising
3. Discounts
4. Home office allowance, or warehouse allowance
5. Shipping terms and instructions
6. "As had" terms

7. Invoicing instructions
8. Confirmations and signed orders
9. Penalties for violating instructions.

All of the above are more fully discussed in Chapters 6 and 7, "Selling Terms" and "Shipping Terms."

This is by no means a complete list of possible pitfalls for the unwary credit manager. Others have undoubtedly been encountered, and still new ones crop up with depressing regularity. It is almost as if some of your accounts were constantly at war with their suppliers; they keep searching for ways to benefit themselves, usually to the disadvantage of the vendor.

For some credit managers, accounts of this kind may be rarely encountered; for others, they may represent a large share of their daily volume. Whether you fall into either category or somewhere in between, you would be wise to add one more word to your lexicon of credit terminology—

Vigilance.

4
Obtaining Credit Information

The seven areas of credit information
Credit reporting agencies
    Their operation
    Dun & Bradstreet
        Its rating system
    Other specialized agencies
    Various agency services available
Industry interchange reports
    Their value to the credit manager
        National Association of Credit Management interchange
            Its operation and functions
            NACIS reports
Group interchange
    Its value to the credit manager
    Its operation
    Methods of group interchange

        Case history of a failure
Banks
    Their value to the credit manager
    How to obtain information from a bank
        The customer's bank
        The credit manager's bank
Your salesman
    His role explained
    His reluctance to provide information
    His possible value to the credit manager
References
    Their validity
    How to follow up on references
Your customer
    As a last resort
Negative credit information
    Legal digests and collection agency lists
How much to ship
    Setting a line of credit
    Requirements accounts
        Their relationship to the shipper's policy

After processing the bulk of his orders, the credit manager has left himself with a segregated batch containing new accounts, marginal accounts, one major customer he is no longer sure of, and established accounts who have reordered for the first time in a year.

He now faces the problem of making a decision on each of these segregated orders. He must therefore determine:

1. Shall he ship?
2. How much?

To help him answer the first question, he has a number of sources of information available to him. For some of his accounts, he may need only one of these sources, or perhaps a combination of two or three; in rare instances, as in the case of the major account he is no longer sure of, he may have to employ most of them so that he can reach a decision proper for his company.

Whatever the credit manager's needs, he can find his answers from the following list:

1. Credit reporting agencies, both general and specialized
2. Industry reports
3. Group interchange
4. Banks
5. His salesman
6. References
7. His customer

Credit reporting agencies

A prime source of information for the average credit manager is the credit agency. There are many credit reporting agencies operating all over the country, most of them specializing within given industries. The services they offer are varied, but are usually limited to the following:

1. Reference books
2. Ratings
3. Recommendations
4. Reports

Some agencies, such as Dun & Bradstreet, provide all these services, while others offer perhaps only one or two.

Where recommendations only are offered, you have, in effect, a *credit checking* agency, for the agency concentrates its best efforts upon furnishing enough information within a specific recommendation so that the credit manager's task is reduced to a minimum.

In the other three services, the entire decision is left to the credit manager (as it is even with a recommendation). When he uses a reference book supplied by his agency, he finds the credit rating of his customer and then makes his decision based upon that rating. Sometimes his judgment will be strengthened by a report, which may or may not contain a recommendation and/or a rating.

This reliance upon credit reporting agencies is often deplored by authorities who specialize in the *theory* of credit management. They minimize the value of these agencies for the average credit manager; they emphasize, rather, the need to develop an independent profile and analysis of each customer.

While it is true that the average credit manager should not rely solely upon his agency, we must face an uncomfortable truth—most credit managers of smaller companies simply do not have the time and/or the personnel to work up the kind of detailed study advocated by the experts. By necessity, they have to be more dependent upon their agencies, for they cannot possibly handle the many tasks that face them every day without agency help.

Of all the credit reporting agencies a credit manager might use, the best known and largest is Dun & Bradstreet.

For the average credit manager, Dun & Bradstreet's particular value lies in its bi-monthly general reference books, its rating system, and its credit reports.

In its rating system, Dun & Bradstreet uses a combination of numbers and letters to signify Estimated Financial Strength, and has four columns under Composite

Credit Appraisal—High, Good, Fair, Limited—with 1 denoting High in all ranges, 2 for Good, and so on, as shown in Table 1.

Table 1. Dun & Bradstreet Credit Rating System

Estimated Financial Strength				Composite Credit Appraisal			
				High	Good	Fair	Limited
5A	$50,000,000		and over	1	2	3	4
4A	$10,000,000	to	$49,999,999	1	2	3	4
3A	1,000,000	to	9,999,999	1	2	3	4
2A	750,000	to	999,999	1	2	3	4
1A	500,000	to	749,999	1	2	3	4
BA	300,000	to	499,999	1	2	3	4
BB	200,000	to	299,999	1	2	3	4
CB	125,000	to	199,999	1	2	3	4
CC	75,000	to	124,999	1	2	3	4
DC	50,000	to	74,999	1	2	3	4
DD	35,000	to	49,999	1	2	3	4
EE	20,000	to	34,999	1	2	3	4
FF	10,000	to	19,999	1	2	3	4
GG	5,000	to	9,999	1	2	3	4
HH	Up	to	4,999	1	2	3	4

ABSENCE OF RATING DESIGNATION FOLLOWING NAMES LISTED IN THE REFERENCE BOOK
The absence of a rating, expressed by two hyphens (--), is not to be construed as unfavorable but signifies circumstances difficult to classify within condensed rating symbols. It suggests the advisability of obtaining a report for additional information.

Now compare the Dun & Bradstreet chart to the rating symbols published by the Lyon Furniture Mercantile Agency in its *Lyon Red Book*, which is issued semiannually.

In each system, we have a combination of numbers and letters used to indicate financial strength and method of payment, although the Lyon key goes beyond Dun & Bradstreet's in the variety of letters and numbers em-

Table 2. Lyon Credit Key

CAPITAL RATINGS
Estimated Financial Worth

A	$1,000,000	or	over
B	500,000	to	$1,000,000
C	300,000	to	500,000
D	200,000	to	300,000
E	100,000	to	200,000
G	75,000	to	100,000
H	50,000	to	75,000
J	40,000	to	50,000
K	30,000	to	40,000
L	20,000	to	30,000
M	15,000	to	20,000
N	10,000	to	15,000
O	7,000	to	10,000
Q	5,000	to	7,000
R	3,000	to	5,000
S	2,000	to	3,000
T	1,000	to	2,000
U	500	to	1,000
V	100	to	500

Z-No financial basis for credit reported.

INDEFINITE RATINGS

F — High financial worth indicated.
P — Moderate financial worth indicated.
W — Small financial worth indicated.
Y — Limited financial worth indicated.

The omission of a rating is not unfavorable, but indicates that sufficient information is not at hand on which to base rating.

PAY RATINGS
Based on suppliers' reports

1 — Discount.
2 — Prompt.
3 — Medium.
4 — Variable, prompt to slow.
5 — Slow.
6 — Very Slow.
7 — C.O.D. or C.B.D.
8 — Pay rating not established, but information favorable.
9 — Claims to buy always for cash.

SPECIAL CONDITIONS

12 — Business recently commenced.
13 — Inquire for report.
21 — Buys small, usually pays cash.
24 — Name listed for convenience only.
29 — Rating undetermined.
31 — Financial statement declined, or repeatedly requested and not received.

SYMBOL INTERPRETATION

● or 12 — Business recently commenced.
+ or 116 — New Statement recently received.
▲ — Indicates information of unusual importance.
☉ — Sells on installment plan.
(?) — Sells from residence, office or catalogue.

---

ployed. And the Lyon ratings are far more precise in the lower ranges.

A number of specialized agencies other than Lyon publish reference and rating books for a given industry. You have, for example, the Produce Reporter Company and its *Fruit and Produce Credit Book,* and the Jewelers Board of Trade and its *Red Book.*

A division of Dun & Bradstreet, Credit Clearing House, which services only apparel manufacturers, has its own rating key (see Table 3). You will note that this chart, which employs a combination of letters and numbers as do the other systems, has an additional column for "payments appraisal." Because of this additional information, and because of the Apparel Trade Books, reference directories published for the apparel industries four times a year, many apparel manufacturers buy this service from Credit Clearing House in addition to their regular subscription from D & B.

Table 3. Credit Clearing House Rating Key

		ESTIMATED FINANCIAL STRENGTH		PAYMENTS APPRAISAL				COMPOSITE APPRAISAL			
B-	A	Over	$1,000,000	1	2	3	4	A	B	C	D
		....See Note............		1	2	3	4	A	B	C	D
	C	Over	500,000	1	2	3	4	A	B	C	D
F-	D	Over	300,000	1	2	3	4	A	B	C	D
	E	Over	200,000	1	2	3	4	A	B	C	D
		....See Note............		1	2	3	4	A	B	C	D
	G	Over	100,000	1	2	3	4	A	B	C	D
K-	H	Over	50,000	1	2	3	4	A	B	C	D
	J	Over	30,000	1	2	3	4	A	B	C	D
		....See Note............		1	2	3	4	A	B	C	D
	L	Over	20,000	1	2	3	4	A	B	C	D
	M	Over	10,000	1	2	3	4	A	B	C	D
S-	O	Over	5,000	1	2	3	4	A	B	C	D
	R	Up to	5,000	1	2	3	4	A	B	C	D
		....See Note............		1	2	3	4	A	B	C	D

Note: The letters B, F, K, and S in the Estimated Financial Strength column, indicate in a general way what is considered relative in size. To illustrate: the letter B indicates size comparable to concerns classified in the range A to C inclusive; the letter F, comparable to those from D to G inclusive; the letter K, comparable to those from H to M inclusive; and the letter S, comparable to those from O to R inclusive.

Other specialized agencies offer only recommendations and/or reports. Some examples in this group are Feakes Mercantile Agency for leather and allied trades, the Lumbermen's Credit Association for the lumber and woodworking industries, and Credit Exchange, Inc. for the apparel industries.

Reports vary with each agency; some go into greater detail than others, but generally, when a report is furnished to you, either at your request or automatically as part of your service, it contains enough pertinent data to help you lay the groundwork for a proper decision.

Some of the important elements that most reports contain are:

1. Your customer's antecedents
2. His financial resources and current condition
3. His buying and paying habits
4. His history
5. His type of operation

In certain cases, reports might provide only ledger card experience of other suppliers, or perhaps more complete ledger information, including terms of sale, high credit, amounts owing, past dues, and manner of payment.

As for the type of service you can buy, the recommendations and/or reports supplied by some of the specialized agencies are most helpful, but it is the combination rating in the reference books that provides a quick and simple method of checking for the credit manager.

An agency, for example, in response to a telephoned or written request, may answer "Recommended for up to $5,000," or "Recommended as a slow payer for up to $2,500," or perhaps, "Not Recommended—30 to 60 slow, unbalanced condition, financial statement lacking." On the other hand, if a credit manager receives an order from a new account, one glance at either the Dun & Bradstreet chart or the Lyon Credit Key could conceivably give him enough information to warrant an immediate decision without phone calls or correspondence.

Assume the order is for $3,000, and the new account is listed as BB1 in the D & B reference book; a glance at the D & B chart shows that his $3,000 order falls well within a checkable range. A BB1 account shows an estimated financial strength of $200,000 to $299,999 and could easily absorb not only an order for $3,000, but up to $10,000 and perhaps more. (Methods for establishing a line of credit are discussed in Chapter 5.)

Under the Lyon Credit Key, this same account would be rated D1, again well within a checkable range. In the Apparel Trades Book, the rating would be E1A, or perhaps E1B.

The same process would be applied to any order, regardless of dollar amount. Whether the credit manager relies upon an agency that offers recommendations only or whether he consults a rating book, most orders should give him little trouble. Any account listed either in the first or second column, or shown to be "prompt to occasionally slow" can be checked without difficulty, assuming the dollar total remains within defined lines of credit.

Now let's alter the ratings of our new account. In the D & B book the account is no longer listed as BB1; it is BB3. The comparable Apparel Trades Book rating is E3C, and in the Lyon Book it is D5. We have, therefore, not a High rated account, but one that is only Fair and obviously slow in its payments.

With this type of rating, a $3,000 order cannot be approved without additional investigation. Since the credit manager is now faced with a marginal account, he has a difficult decision to make, and he must look to other sources of information. His credit agencies can help him no longer.

Industry interchange reports

Ranking perhaps as high as the agencies in importance to the credit manager are industry reports. These can cover a variety of industries or perhaps only the one industry the credit manager is working in. They offer him the ledger experience of his colleagues from all sections of the country; properly utilized, such industry reports or interchange can supply a picture of a given account's paying habits, his exposure with other suppliers, and terms of payments.

There are many localized groups that offer a limited interchange of credit information. They are generally clubs or councils organized within a given industry, and usually within a specific geographical area. (See the following section, *Group Interchange*.) But there is a national organization that has been offering countrywide credit interchange for most of the twentieth century.

The National Association of Credit Management was formally founded in Toledo, Ohio, in 1896, when a group of credit executives, representing about a hundred of their colleagues, convened for the purpose of organizing themselves into a national association of credit managers. Today, the NACM has more than 44,000 members in 87 chapters across the country.

Early interchange was conducted through the medium of local bureaus, a number of which were organized during the first decade of the twentieth century. It was soon discovered that local or regional information wasn't enough; some kind of national coverage was needed. In 1912, therefore, a central interchange bureau was established in St. Louis; the other bureaus, still independently operated, channeled their requests and their information through St. Louis.

The National Association of Credit Management assumed control of the central bureau in 1919, and two years later created its Credit Interchange Bureau Department to service the many local bureaus, with the St. Louis unit as the clearing office.

The NACM now has 58 reference bureaus in both major and minor markets all over the country; these local bureaus cooperate with each other in the compiling of credit information so that it is possible for any participating member of the Association, in any part of the United States, to secure national exposure on one of his customers through the medium of the Association's interchange program.

The Association's national interchange has a number of advantages for the credit manager:

1. It can tell him whether his own experience with a given customer is unique, or whether other suppliers have encountered a similar pattern.

2. It can provide a composite portrait that will help him to reach a proper decision on his customer.

3. It can operate as an "early warning system" by alerting him to a possibly deteriorating trend.

There are certain disadvantages as well:

1. The mere mechanics of compiling information from all over the country (or even within a specific territory) can take at least two or three weeks or more.

2. Some credit managers, afraid that negative information might harm the customer and thereby slow down his flow of merchandise, may offer only partial ledger experience so that the pattern that emerges may not tell the entire story.

But these disadvantages are far outweighed by the positive contribution an interchange can make. If a few credit managers withhold information, most do not; the overwhelming majority of credit managers who participate in interchanges supply complete and honest ledger experience.

As for the time lapse, it is the rare order that cannot be set aside for at least two or three weeks until a proper evaluation can be made. If your customer is in such a big hurry for your merchandise that he must have it at once, and if his background requires extensive investigation, perhaps he cannot survive a careful scrutiny, and he doesn't deserve your credit.

It is just as possible that a marginal customer does legitimately need your merchandise or supplies immediately; if you're satisfied that's the case, you can speed up the clearance process by authorizing the interchange to be conducted by long distance telephone, or by requesting a NACIS report (see the section that follows). This may cost you a few dollars, but if the size of the order warrants it, it would well be worth the expenditure, if only to retain the good will of your customer.

A credit interchange properly conducted will provide information in these basic areas:

1. How long sold
2. Date of last sale
3. Highest recent credit
4. Amount owing
5. Amount past due
6. When due
7. Terms of sale
8. Paying record

You will also find a column on the interchange report for any comments you or your colleagues may care to make; these comments in themselves can be revealing; "Takes unearned discount." . . . "Makes unauthorized returns." . . . "Skips invoices." . . . "Placed for collection."

Although the interchange conducted by the National Association of Credit Management is nationwide, not every major city participates in the program. For example, New York City does not, but there is enough coverage in nearby cities for the New York market to have an ample clearance; this is just as true in other parts of the country.

The NACM interchange is handled through the 58 local bureaus. Each bureau has a set annual fee for its interchange service; the fee varies from one section of the country to another, but in each case the cost per interchange is very small. For more complete details, contact your local branch of the Association, or Credit Interchange Bureaus, National Association of Credit Management, P.O. Box 1398, St. Louis, Missouri 63188.

A subscribing member begins the interchange process with a credit inquiry card sent to his local bureau, or a telephone call placed with the bureau's interchange department. (Each subscriber is given a supply of inquiry tickets—see Figure 1.)

The local bureau checks its files; if the requested information is available, it will be forwarded to the inquirer. If the information, however, is more than 120 days old, the bureau then canvasses possible credit grantors within its own territory through the medium of an inquiry sheet, individual requests for credit experience (see Figure 2), or telephone calls to determine whether more current data can be locally obtained.

If the local information is still not sufficient, or if its files have nothing on the customer, the bureau then requests a clearance from the NACM chapter where the account is located (provided of course it's not the same as the supplier's). The second bureau checks its own files and if it finds that inquiries have been received in the past from other parts of the country on this particular customer, it then asks for a credit clearance from these other bureaus.

Information funneled back to the second bureau will

FORM 1

NATIONAL ASSOCIATION OF CREDIT MANAGEMENT

MEMBER INQUIRY

NATIONAL CREDIT INTERCHANGE SYSTEM

P. O. Box 2606, Spokane, Wash. 99220 326-3420

SEND US A REPORT ON DATE ______

NAME ______

TRADE STYLE ______

STREET ADDRESS ______

______

TOWN STATE ZIP CODE

TYPE BUSINESS ______

MEMBER	CHECK FOR AUTOMATIC REVISION ☐ 4 MONTHS ☐ ___MONTHS	☐ SEND PRELIMINARY REPORT ☐ SEND ONLY COMPLETED REPORT	REVISING FILE ☐ 1st ORDER ☐

LIST ADDITIONAL REFERENCES ON REVERSE SIDE

IMPORTANT

List other sources of supply below. The bureau will endeavor to obtain their information.

PRO. NO.

NAME	ADDRESS

BANKS WITH ______

SUBJECT HAS BRANCHES AT: ______

______

______

______

Figure 1

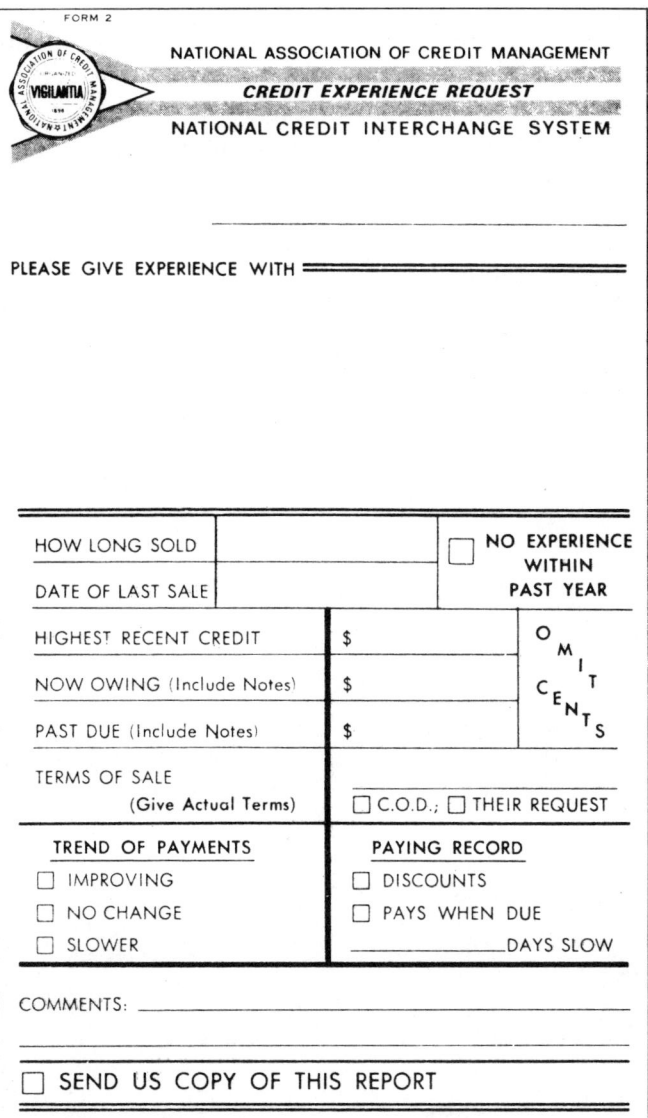

Figure 2

be collected and forwarded to the original inquiring bureau, which then collates the national clearance on a credit interchange report (see Figure 3); this report is sent to the inquiring member, and to any participating member who requests it.

	NATIONAL ASSOCIATION of CREDIT MANAGEMENT							
	Credit Interchange Report							
							OFFICES IN PRINCIPAL CITIES	
ABC Construction Co.			Pittsfield, Ind.				Feb. 4	

The accuracy of this Report is not guaranteed. Its contents are gathered in good faith from members and sent to you by this Bureau without liability for negligence in procuring, collecting, communicating or failing to communicate the information so gathered.

BUSINESS CLASSIFICATION	HOW LONG SOLD	DATE OF LAST SALE	HIGHEST RECENT CREDIT	NOW OWING INCLUDING NOTES	PAST DUE	TERMS OF SALE	PAYING RECORD			COMMENTS
							DIS-COUNTS	PAYS WHEN DUE	DAYS SLOW	
CONN. NEW YORK										
NATIONAL CONSTR. DIV. (101-853)										
*NC-1263	yrs	Oct.	51000			½-10-N30			30-60	Secured by Contra-a/c
		CREDIT INTERCHANGE REPORT DATED DEC. 21								
ST. LOUIS 1109-17										
*838 Mach	6 mos	Nov.	15	15		N-10-Px				N/P/E
820 Mach	yrs	Oct.	630	125		N-10		x		
818 Mach	yrs	Oct.	23000	5713	5200				1-4mos	
846 Mach	yrs	Aug.	9800	1200	1200	Var			60	
1521 Aacc	2 yrs	Sept	70			2-10-Px		x		Dep. account low five fig. Credit accom. med. five fig. Loans secured total med. five fig. Satisfactory
*854 Contr	1 yr	Oct.	60	15		N-10		x		
*KANSAS CITY 1116-501										
184 Mach	2 yrs	Nov.	3000	1000	450	1-10-30		x	30-60	
*WICHITA - KANSAS 1213-522										
256 Inds	2 yrs	Sept	3500			N-30			30-120	
-OMAHA NEBRASKA 1115-38										
192 Bldg	6 mos	Aug.	800			N-30		x		
155 Mach	1 yr	June	619			N-30			30	

Figure 3

The information thus gathered, as can be seen in the accompanying illustration, covers a wide range of suppliers in a number of industries countrywide, so that the inquiring credit manager now has a valid profile of his customer (the name and address are fictitious, as are the areas reporting, but the data has been taken from an actual case).

Examination of the illustrated report reveals a definite pattern of slowness, running from 30 to 120 days. There are also prompt payments shown, but for the most part these are small amounts. Where higher lines of credit have been allowed, the slowness is marked, indicating an inability to meet major commitments within specified terms.

Taken together with his own experience, and added to the report from his credit agency (which has an additional clearance, although not as far-ranging as the NACM report), the national interchange can provide a current picture that will immeasurably help a credit manager in his analysis of a troublesome account.

NACIS reports

As an adjunct to its National Credit Interchange System, the National Association of Credit Management not too long ago installed a new computerized service called NACIS (National Credit Information Service). With thousands of subscribers, and a directory that currently lists, in alphabetical order by state, over 5.2 million business names, NACIS can be a valuable addition to the credit services you may now be buying, and can be another important tool for you in the gathering of credit information.

Operated by TRW Business Credit Services for the National Association of Credit Management, NACIS provides immediate and up-to-date computerized reports on the payment pattern of each business listed in its directory. Thousands of manufacturers, wholesalers, and distributors, as well as banks and factors, contribute accounts receivable information to NACIS. These NACM members represent many industries, ranging from "Apparel & Other Related Products" through "Travel and Transportation."

NACIS reports incorporate all the features to be found in the reports supplied by NACM's National Credit Interchange System. But unlike that earlier, non-computerized service, NACIS has a number of features not found anywhere else. In addition to the industry category of the subscriber contributing ledger information, date of the last sale, terms, recent high credit, and account status, a NACIS report includes as well the percentage of those contributors reporting current payment, and percentage reporting days beyond terms, from 1-30 days slow, to over 90 slow.

There is also a column for "Comments," as you have in the National Credit Interchange System, which alone can be worth the price of the report. Finally, your NACIS report will list the name and address of your customer's bank; these can be helpful when you reach category four of your credit information sources—"Banks."

The trade payment information in NACIS reports usually covers a broad spectrum of suppliers, so that, while your own industry may have a strong representation, a NACIS report will frequently include secondary and peripheral suppliers as well. This can be significant for you, since it will enable you to tell where else your customer trades, and how he behaves with other industries. This kind of composite coverage, which will indicate the actual categories of the participating subscribers, is not presently available in credit agency reports, which give only the number of suppliers offering information, not their category or industry.

As with Dun & Bradstreet reference books, you must first consult your NACIS directory to see if your customer is listed. If he is, you can then request your report either by mail or phone. Hooked into TRW's central computer in Anaheim, California, participating NACM associations can forward a report to you immediately. If needed, you can even request information from that report by telephone, so that your decision need not wait on the mails.

Perhaps your customer is not listed in the current NACIS directory. This does not mean that no NACIS report on him is available. NACIS data files are continuously being added to and updated; most of NACM's Affiliated Associations will inquire of the NACIS files to see if a report is available. Unless such a report is available, and unless it consists of a minimum number of information lines, no charge to the inquiring member is made.

It should be noted as well that the strictest security is applied to the inquiring procedure. As a NACIS user, you will have an access number and assigned security code, and both must be employed in order to obtain a report.

If you can afford it and if your volume requires it, you can rent a desktop terminal from NACIS, and have instantaneous information available, relayed in seconds from the central computer in Anaheim to your office, anywhere in the country. Once your request has been entered, the information you have asked for is extracted from TRW's vast files, the report is teleprinted, and reaches you within two minutes. If you already have a terminal, it may be compatible with TRW's equipment. This can be a savings for you.

NACIS is available to any NACM member, whether or not he contributes information for the NACIS directory.

And if you're only using the National Credit Interchange System, you can still request NACIS reports through your NACM affiliated association.

The importance of NACIS, whether you subscribe to the regular service, or use a terminal as well, is the availability of constantly revised and current payment history on your customer supplied by the thousands of participating NACM subscribers. As you request a report, the latest information has already been compiled and collated into your customer's file, so that what you receive is as up-to-the-minute as modern technology can make it.

Credit agency reports frequently list information as much as one year old, and the information furnished by NACM's National Credit Interchange System, while thorough and completely reliable, is slower than the computerized NACIS reports, which can reach you in a matter of minutes if you have your own desktop terminal hooked into TRW's central computer in Anaheim, California. Even without your own terminal, the NACIS service is much faster than any other. In this respect, NACIS has benefits not readily available from credit agencies, or from other interchange services.

If your funds for credit services are limited, however, your first choice will probably be a Dun & Bradstreet subscription. The data supplied by D & B's three R's—Reference books, Rating charts, and Reports—can make it possible for you to process a large percentage of your orders without looking further.

But if you do need additional help, and if your budget will permit it, by all means buy the NACIS reports. Not only do they tell you how your customer is behaving at the moment, they also help to pinpoint trends, and can alert you to possible danger. All of this in the fastest possible way—in minutes if you need it.

(To find out whether NACIS can be useful to you, get in touch with your local NACM association. Or write to

National Credit Information Service, P.O. Box 1420, Long Beach, California 90801.)

Group interchange

In addition to its national interchange, NACM conducts credit clearances on a local level through industry credit groups. Other local groups are sponsored by credit agencies or trade associations, or have established themselves independently, with no affiliation to other organizations.

NACM industry groups number about 1,500, with some of them organized on a regional or national basis. The average credit manager, particularly in a smaller company, would most likely limit his participation to a local interchange group; our discussion is therefore concentrated in that area.

Local interchange groups operate in much the same way as the NACM national clearance, with two important differences:

1. They are limited to their own membership, which usually is made up of credit grantors within a specific industry in a specific market or city.

2. The groups hold regularly scheduled meetings, as often as once a week, or perhaps only once a month, to discuss either a mailed interchange or additional names raised at the meeting itself.

National or regional groups may meet less frequently, once every two or three months, and the city for meeting can change each time to accommodate the scattered membership.

Although a group interchange lacks the comprehensive coverage of an NACM national clearance, which can include a number of industries, it nevertheless can be of inestimable value. Very often, such an interchange, conducted within one industry and one market, can offer enough information to permit a member of the group to reach a crucial decision on a troublesome account.

A local group interchange provides credit information in the same basic areas as does the NACM national clearance:

1. How long sold
2. Date of last sale
3. Highest recent credit
4. Amount owing
5. Amount past due
6. When due
7. Terms of sale
8. Paying record

And again, as in the national interchange, the group interchange has a column for comments. Here, too, these comments can sometimes tell you as much as any of the other columns: "Will never sell this account again" or "Holding orders, will sell only for cash."

There are two methods of group interchange—by mail, or orally, at a meeting. Many groups will use both methods; some use only one.

In the mail method, each member of the group is asked to submit a name or names he is particularly interested in investigating. The names sent in by the entire group are then collated onto one inquiry sheet, which is then sent to each member, who indicates his own ledger experience for any account he may have shipped.

One sheet, in the meantime, has been prepared for each account submitted. When the members of the group return their general inquiry sheets, the information they supply is extracted from the general sheets and transferred to the individual sheets, so that the members now have an interchange report on each account that looks very much like the NACM interchange report illustrated earlier.

If the group is sponsored by a credit agency, the agency may offer its own thinking on the submitted accounts by way of an oral report at the group's regularly scheduled meeting. Or the members may feel that one of the names submitted deserves a more thorough investigation, and they will therefore discuss this account at their meeting. Also, other names will be raised for discussion—perhaps an order was received too late for inclusion in the mail interchange. Sometimes, a few of the members may know the name but not be too certain of their ledger experience, so they ask the inquiring member to give them a call and the account is then discussed by telephone.

This face to face and personal method of credit interchange is one distinct advantage a group interchange has over a national clearance. A credit manager meets and gets to know his colleagues personally; when he discusses an account with one of them, he knows that the information he is receiving is accurate and up to the minute. And he has a constant source of references to call upon.

It is not often that a credit manager is blessed with an absolute currency of information, as he can get from his group interchange. Reports from his credit agency may have information that is many months old, including a financial statement from two or three years before. And interchange clearances may be missing one vital fact that might save a credit manager a bad debt.

This latter point was vividly illustrated by a case that involved a pair of small but highly profitable northern California stores specializing in ladies' wear. For years the owner had placed orders only for her normal needs, usually in the $500 to $1,000 range. She dealt with many of the top New York ready to wear manufacturers, without difficulty of any kind. She paid her bills on time, never made unauthorized returns or deductions, and behaved, from the suppliers' point of view, in a most exemplary fashion.

Her last statement reflected a healthy condition: current assets, $41,013, and total assets $45,283; current liabilities, $5,076, and net worth $40,206. Sales volume for a six months' period totaled $100,520, with a net profit of $8,751.

The following spring season she came to the New York market and began to place orders beyond her previous amounts. In itself, this would not have aroused suspicion, for her credit rating and her long history of prompt payments, together with the extremely liquid position shown in her last statement, should easily have supported an increase in the dollar volume of her individual orders.

But she made the mistake of approaching too many new suppliers, as reported by the San Francisco office of a leading credit agency:

> Investigation discloses that as of June 20, subject had placed over 200 orders in amounts totaling over $230,000 with suppliers located mainly out of town. A complete check is not available; however, it is reported that the majority of the orders being placed are with new suppliers and have not been solicited.

The report was correct. Most of the orders had not been solicited.

Fortunately for a number of her new suppliers they were members of an industry interchange group. Some of them, as a matter of course, began to ask questions of their colleagues and of their credit agency. It was only then discovered that she was placing orders all over the market, mostly in amounts double and triple what she had previously requested. An investigation, quickly instituted, revealed that she was opening a substantial number of additional stores, at least nine, *without investing additional capital*. She was relying solely upon the good will of her former suppliers to capitalize her expansion and to act as references for her new suppliers.

Telephone calls went out to all members of the interchange group; as it happened, she had visited and placed orders with almost all of them. Most of them held up her orders. But she did receive a great deal of merchandise from other manufacturers who did not have the benefit of the fast-breaking information provided by the interchange group.

Despite her new inventory, she was operating precariously. Above all, she needed capital, which she did not have. Within a few weeks, on August 8th, she called a meeting of her creditors, and reported that as of July 15th, she had:

Cash, $856; inventory, $314,368; fixed assets, net, $5,480; or total current assets of $320,704.

Accounts payable, $503,060; bank overdraft, $3,768; payroll and sales tax, $23,342; or total current liabilities of $530,170.

Less than a month later, on September 6th, the court in the Central District of California judged her to be bankrupt. The new stores she had managed to open went down the drain with her original two, along with the claims of many creditors.

In this case, reported here as it actually happened, it was only the vigilance of an interchange group that saved a large number of New York suppliers from certain involvement in a business failure. For fail she did and fail she would have; expansion, she learned to her deep regret, requires adequate funding as well as the good will of suppliers.

On the other side of the coin, there are far more examples of successful conclusions to group interchange, both for the customer and the credit grantor. Most accounts do not behave as did this unfortunate woman from northern California. If they plan to expand, they do so in the proper and approved manner, with the required financing of their own. Only favorable reports about them will reach an interchange group and be passed on to its membership. The result is a mutually profitable and pleasant relationship for all concerned.

For the average credit manager, a local group interchange can often be a satisfactory substitute for a national clearance. Nor should the *immediacy* of information be overlooked. In some cases, time can work against the credit grantor. He can occasionally avoid an unfavorable situation through the vigilance and cooperation of his group. For this alone, membership in a local industry club or council would be warranted.

When should you request a clearance on one of your customers, either through the NACM national interchange or through a local industry group?

1. For a new marginal account. If his rating is unsatisfactory, as is the credit agency report, try to find out if any of your colleagues are dealing with this customer, or have dealt with him in the past.

2. For an unusually large order that doesn't seem warranted by your customer's rating.

3. When an old customer begins to slow down.

4. When a major account starts skipping invoices—if he's doing the same with your colleagues, it might be a deliberate pattern.

5. For an established customer whose payment record is sporadic. Sometimes he's prompt, and just as often he's slow; a clearance at your group may reveal that his irregular pattern is simply a reflection of seasonal fluctuation—not an entirely healthy situation, but not really that bad either.

6. For any account that proves troublesome in some way, either through unauthorized returns or deductions, or chargebacks that you refuse to allow but that he refuses to

repay, or unreasonable demands for allowances and excessive extra dating.

Banks

As a valid source of credit information, banks play a vital role for the credit manager. What they can tell him can sometimes make the difference between acceptance or rejection of an order. Yet, strangely, banks are too often neglected in the credit manager's search for information or are utilized as an afterthought only.

A bank can be approached as a credit source either directly or through your own bank. Going through your own bank presents at least one advantage—a fellow banker may reveal more to a colleague, even one in a distant city, than he would to a trade supplier writing to him out of the blue. Also, as a financial institution, your bank may be in a better position than you are to determine the extent of loans outstanding for your customer.

If you've learned the name of your customer's bank (you can get it directly from him, from your credit agency, from a NACIS report, or from checks he's sent you in the past), and if you've decided the account requires additional investigation, by all means write to his bank and explain exactly why you're writing and what information you'd like to have.

Tell the bank first of all the reason for your request:

You've received a first order from this account for X number of dollars; or

You've been dealing with this account for some time, but you now have an order considerably higher than any he's placed in the past; or

The account is beginning to run slow, and you wonder whether it may be due, perhaps, to a change in his bookkeeping procedure or conversion to data processing (it's best to put the blame on something like that, rather than point an accusing finger at his paying habits).

Once you've established the reason for your letter, you then ask the bank for answers to the following:

1. How long has the bank had the account?
2. What is his average balance? (You won't get a specific dollar amount; the bank will reply, low, medium, or high four figures; low, medium, or high five figures; low, medium, or high six figures; and so on.)
3. Does he have a loan outstanding? If so, how much is it?
4. Is the loan secured, or unsecured? If secured, by what? Inventory, receivables, etc.?
5. When is the loan to be repaid? Has he had other loans in the past? What lines of accommodation would the bank allow him?
6. How does the bank regard your customer as a credit risk?

Banks generally are forthright in their replies, but your last question may elicit an evasive response. If the bank and your customer are located in a small town, the bank personnel may not want to jeopardize the business dealings of someone they probably know on a personal basis, so the answer may well be:

"Mr. Y is highly regarded, and retires his obligations in a satisfactory manner."

Or even more obtusely, ". . . and retires his obligations in a manner commensurate with his standing in the community."

Which tells you exactly nothing.

But the rest of it can tell you a great deal. For example, your customer's average balance may give you a good idea of his paying potential. Let's assume it's in the high four figures ($8,000 to $9,000) or low five (perhaps $13,000 to

$14,000); if you received a $2,000 or $3,000 order from this customer, you would be justified in worrying about it, especially if his annual volume should indicate a far better cash position.

If you'd rather not approach your customer's bank yourself, you can ask your own bank to give them the name of your customer's bank (if you don't have it, your bank can probably find out for you, but it would save them much time and effort if you did have the name). Allow a couple of weeks for the information to get back to you.

You can also use your bank for ordinary credit checking. Many banks have their own credit departments, which will supply information upon your request or even take the time to develop it for you. They'll only do this, however, if your company is a customer of the bank and if your account representative approves your request.

He'll do his best to help you. Competition among lending institutions is just as keen as competition among manufacturers and wholesalers. The bank where your company customarily deposits and/or borrows its money will do everything it can to retain your good will, since it is earning money from your firm.

If the credit department at your bank can't furnish the information you need, perhaps your account representative can. Sometimes, through his own sources, which may include other financial and lending institutions, he may be able to give you a different picture of your customer than will your credit agency.

Your salesman

Historically, the salesman was considered a prime source of credit information, for it was he who visited the customer, and it was he who established a personal relationship with the account. He was in a position to report on his customer's external conditions—the premises, the inventory, and so on. Also, by talking to local people and to other salesmen, he was able to develop a suitable profile for his credit department.

With the growth of the credit reporting agency, this historical role of the salesman was curtailed, so that no longer is he expected to provide information as a normal part of his activity. But the credit manager should not hesitate to call upon his salesman for his impressions and review of his customer's potential. The salesman today is still the one who is most familiar with the account, and he is just as interested in developing that account as is the company.

But many salesmen refuse to act as middlemen for their credit managers. Their function, they believe, is to sell, not to accumulate facts for the credit department. A salesman's approach to the customer for financial information, for example, may jeopardize his standing with that customer.

There's no reason, however, why your salesman cannot at least give you his observations—what kind of inventory does the customer normally carry; what does his place of business look like—is it neat, orderly, well organized; what do other salesmen think of this account; are the principals experienced; are they industrious, or dilatory?

Even if your salesman answers only one or two of these questions, his effort and yours would be well worth it. Don't expect him to furnish an all-inclusive report, but one fact not available elsewhere, or one impression sincerely stated, may be the piece that completes the picture for you.

References

References can be misleading; a credit manager who places too much reliance upon them can fall into a trap. Credit seekers have been known to provide *selected* lists of references—suppliers who have been paid on time only because their merchandise was desperately needed, or suppliers who have been paid on time simply to establish a presumptive history of prompt payments. Even relatives have been given as references.

What the credit seeker does not reveal is that for every supplier he lists as having been promptly paid, he may have dozens of others he pays slowly.

Still, references can be productive, and often are. A new account who needs your merchandise is not going to jeopardize his relationship with your company by sending you disputable references; he wants them to withstand your possible suspicions, so the list he supplies will be truly representative. If your potential customer has no one he's paying promptly, he probably won't send you any references at all.

If you do decide to follow through on a reference, you can either use a standardized form (most stores carrying office supplies have them) to send to the vendor suggested by your customer, or a letter embodying the same requests.

The form lists the name and address of your customer, the reason for your inquiry (a first order for X dollars), and it then asks the respondent to answer the following:
1. How long sold?
2. On what terms?
3. High credit?
4. Is anything owing; if so, how long?
5. Manner of payment?

Some forms even ask the respondent for his observations on the account; is it a satisfactory risk, or a poor risk, etc.

It may be too much to expect certain credit managers to give an opinion that can possibly backfire. So don't be too disappointed or surprised if they don't answer this last part of your form.

An individually typed letter will sometimes do a better job for you—especially if you suggest that your questions can be answered right on your own letter; in that way, the respondent doesn't have to take the time and personnel to answer your letter with one of his own. (Make sure to enclose a stamped, self-addressed envelope.) And you can also ask him to list other suppliers that he knows are selling the account.

If he does list other suppliers, then your use of references will indeed have been effective, and you'll have additional and valuable sources to help build a truer picture of your potential customer.

Your customer

For some organizations—where the credit department has a staff adequate for extensive search and investigation—accountants, lawyers, and the customer himself can well be fruitful sources of information. In smaller companies, it is far more difficult, and far less productive, to compile a list of friendly accountants and lawyers who may prove to be cooperative in the assembly of credit data. But the customer can, on certain occasions, be helpful.

During the course of your investigation, you request and receive from your customer his latest figures, the name of his bank, and a list of references. But you're still not satisfied; nor can your other channels completely fill in the picture for you. Under those circumstances, you may, as a final resort, appeal once more to the customer himself.

It would be wise to avoid this step, if possible; some credit seekers may think of it as harassment, and others, readily acquiescing, may be overoptimistic in discussing both their plans and their prospects. Bear in mind at all times that your customer is motivated by self-interest. He may be the most sincere person in the world, but sincerity doesn't pay bills; you need facts supported by figures, not unsubstantiated expectations.

Still, there are times when some kind of additional contact with your customer can be useful. He may have new plans he hopes will turn his business around—a loan, for example, from the Small Business Administration, or a partner with fresh capital—and he may be willing to discuss these plans with you. Or you may find that he has an insufficient grasp of the conditions affecting his business, and it may be that he is indeed, as all other evidence would seem to indicate, a poor credit risk.

Perhaps the person you reach is a corporate officer; he may have certain details his company is not ready to divulge to a credit agency or to any other commercial organization. He will, however, tell you enough to convince you that his company is deserving of credit.

These are some possibilities that may result from a contact with your customer. Once you've exhausted all other sources, and you still feel the account is worth developing, you at least ought to try your customer one last time.

But be realistic and don't expect earth-shaking revelations; your customer may tell you something about himself or his company that you don't already know, but the chances are far greater he won't.

Negative credit information

Some credit managers go beyond the traditional seven areas of credit information. They subscribe to legal digests and/or lists compiled by collection agencies. The legal digests show the suits that have been filed in a given jurisdiction on a given day. This information, of course, is negative; it will help you only if you have doubts about a certain account and you want to research every possible avenue in an effort either to refute or reinforce these doubts.

The same applies to lists compiled by some collection agencies. For a set fee (fairly expensive for this kind of service, as will be the cost of the legal digests), an agency will mail you at regular intervals, probably once a month, a listing of all the accounts that have been turned over to it for collection during that period. Here, too, the information is negative. But negative information, in certain marginal cases, can be important to you.

Legal digests and collection agency lists can help you in another way. They can alert you to impending trouble, or trouble already in the making, on active accounts, or on accounts you may have worked with in the past, and expect to see again.

How much to ship

The line of credit you establish will depend upon factors in your own organization as well as in your customer's. A supplier in direct competition with you may have a higher line for a specific account than you, or perhaps lower. He may have differing yardsticks for the establishment of that line, but that doesn't mean your own yardsticks are incorrect; they are right for you. Remember that you and your company are the only ones who can decide how much you can safely ship to a given account, or how much you want to risk.

A similar differential applies to requirements accounts. You would probably never question the size of an order received from any of your requirements accounts—unless one of them, whose aggregate orders in the past may never have gone above $50,000 or so, suddenly starts sending in orders that total $500,000. This is an extreme example, because it is almost beyond possibility for anything like that to happen. A customer who historically required only $50,000 from you, and like amounts from your colleagues, will not overnight ask ten times that much. If he's expanding and needs a greater inventory, his placements would be far more gradual.

The point is that not all requirements accounts are equally wealthy or have the same needs. One requirements account may have a net worth of $50,000,000 with annual sales of $200,000,000, while another may have a net worth of $5,000,000 with annual sales of $20,000,000. Obviously, the second company will not require, or ask for, as high a line of credit as will the first, yet both can fall into the requirements category.

So it is with credit grantors, particularly those in the same industry. One supplier, a competitor down the street, may be perfectly willing and able to ship a given customer $10,000, while you can only give him $2,500.

Each line of credit you establish, therefore, will be influenced by your organization's history, policies, needs, demands, rate of expansion (or lack of it), and production facilities. And of course, how it is affected by external conditions, such as the economy and competition.

But just as important is what you know about your customer. In order to establish a line of credit proper both for your company and for him, you must, first of all, be familiar with his financial condition and with the various factors that will affect his relationship with you. This means analyzing his balance sheet, the subject of the chapter that follows.

5
The Financial Statement

Methods for establishing a line of credit
The percentage method
    Using net worth
    Using working capital
Financial components of a customer's business
Validity of the financial statement
The four elements of the balance sheet
Assets
    Definition repeated
    Current assets
    Fixed assets
Liabilities
    Definition repeated
    Current liabilities
    Long term liabilities
Net worth, or equity
    Its place on the balance sheet
    Definition repeated

Working capital
    Definition repeated
The profit and loss statement
    Its importance emphasized
    Its seven basic ingredients
    A profit and loss statement illustrated
Important ratios
    Their significance
    The nine ratios
        Current and liquid
        Sales to inventory
        Sales to net worth
        Debt to net worth
        Inventory to working capital
        Fixed assets to net worth
        Net profit to sales
        Net profit to net worth
        Sales to receivables
Other ratios
Trend of the customer's business
Nonfinancial information

The credit manager who relies primarily upon his agency for the setting of credit limits simplifies his task, although not always with positive results. He may accept a line that, for his company, may be unrealistically low. But perhaps he uses the *percentage method*; here, too, he depends upon his agency, but in a different way.

If he subscribes to an agency that provides ratings, as do Dun & Bradstreet and Lyon, he has merely to verify his customer's net worth by glancing at the rating charts; then, with the use of ordinary arithmetic, he divides the net worth by an established percentage, and there he has a suggested line of credit.

He would use the percentage rate customarily utilized

by the rest of his industry, although it may not be the formula recommended by his agency. For example, some agencies suggest either 10% of the net worth or 20% of the working capital.

These ratios don't work equally for all credit managers. In some industries, 5% of the net worth has traditionally been the base. This is especially true in apparel; it is not unusual for a ready to wear retailer to have many suppliers in the apparel industries. If each of them used either a 10% or a 20% base, the retailer would be drowning in merchandise or, alternatively, he'd have to get rid of half or more of his vendors and thereby limit his variety of merchandise, which is often his chief selling point.

In some industries, perhaps yours, there are far fewer suppliers; each of them would necessarily have a proportionately larger share of one customer's business, so higher percentages would be used as a base.

Calculating your line of credit on *10% of the net worth* (total of all assets less total of all liabilities), an account that is rated by Dun & Bradstreet as DD ($35,000 to $49,999—see Table 1, Chapter 4) would then be allotted a range between $3,500 and $5,000. If he's in column 1 (High), you would allow him the higher figure of $5,000; in column 2 (Good), perhaps you would reduce that a bit; in column 3 (Fair), you would limit him to the lower figure of $3,500, or less, or perhaps not ship at all; and in column 4 (Limited), you would either stay away altogether or do a good deal of soul searching and figure studying before releasing any amount.

Using *20% of the working capital* (current assets less current liabilities), this same account conceivably could have a working capital much less than his net worth, say $10,000. His line of credit would then be only $2,000.

Both of these methods, while simplified and time-saving, are mechanical. Still, if a credit manager has been successfully using the percentage system, there's no reason for him to switch to something more complicated.

But no matter how you arrive at a line of credit for a given account, you at least ought to have certain elementary information about him:

1. Can you estimate, fairly accurately, how many other suppliers he has? Suppliers competitive to you, that is.

2. Do you know how much inventory he normally carries? During his slow season, and during his peak periods?

3. What are his average bank balances, and how much cash does he usually have on hand to meet his trade obligations?

4. What volume does your customer project for the coming year, or if you can't learn that, what were his sales for the previous year?

5. What kind of a paying record does he have? Do you know what the trend of his business is?

6. How about his assets? How much is centered in inventory, in cash, in accounts receivable?

7. What about his liabilities? Are they too great in relation to his assets?

There are other things you ought to know (these are explored later on in this chapter), but for the moment, let's discuss the points just mentioned.

Regarding *suppliers*—if your customer has a hundred or more, as in apparel, he would buy, and require, much less from you. On the other hand, you may be one of his major resources, as in paper goods or groceries. In this latter instance, the agency percentages would not work at all, for they would be too low.

If you know the usual amount of *inventory* he carries, and if you know how many vendors he has, it's a simple matter to calculate whether the amount he is purchasing from you is too much or too little.

As for his *bank balances* and his *cash on hand,* you can

estimate your chances of being paid on time once you know how many other suppliers he must pay, and about how much.

His *projected volume* or *sales for the previous year,* again can tell you whether your share of his business is in line or out of line.

Regarding his *paying record* and his *trend,* you can reasonably predict what his future payments will be like.

And finally, his *assets* and his *liabilities* provide some of the key ratios that lie at the heart of financial statement analysis.

We now move to the examination of your customer's balance sheet, and a study of the more important ratios.

There are four elements in the balance sheet that are of primary concern to you:

1. Assets
2. Liabilities
3. Net worth, or equity
4. Working capital

Validity of the financial statement

To be truly valid, a financial statement should be certified, preferably by the accountant who has audited the figures. If your customer prepares the statement himself, without the benefit of an accountant, he at least ought to have it certified by a notary public, so that you can be fairly certain he isn't offering fraudulent figures. And he ought to sign the statement.

If your customer sends his figures to you without signing them, suspicion would be in order, especially if the figures look very good. A statement definitely on the plus side should be willingly signed, although it's conceivable that your customer simply overlooked his signature or was too busy to double-check.

Another thing you ought to verify is whether the accountant has made a physical audit of your customer's assets, or whether he's simply accepting his client's book figures. Also, are the figures precise, or estimated? Estimated or rounded whole figures should be regarded with skepticism.

Your failure to question an unsigned or uncertified balance sheet would indicate that you have accepted your customer's word that his figures are valid. On the face of it, such failure could reflect laxity or negligence on your part. But numerous unsupported statements have been used with no harm to the supplier. Surveys of credit managers in various industries consistently reveal that many of them will accept unaudited and uncertified statements. The thinking, apparently, is that the credit seeker will not use the mails for the transmission of false or misleading information, since there are severe penalties involved.

In this connection, it should be noted that you may now encounter unfamiliar language in some of the financial statements being submitted to you. In the past, you undoubtedly received financial statements with this type of disclaimer from the accountant preparing that statement:

"The accompanying balance sheet as of December 31, and the related statements of income and retained earnings and changes in financial position for the fiscal period then ended were not audited by me (or us), and accordingly, I (we) do not express an opinion on them."

All that meant was that the accountant did not audit your customer's figures, nor did he take any kind of physical inventory. But if you were willing to accept your customer's uncertified statement, you most likely did not bother to question the fact that the statement was unaudited as well.

That language has been changed. As of July 1, 1979,

the American Institute of Certified Public Accountants now requires that an accountant conduct either a "compilation" or a "review" of your customer's financial statement.

If a compilation only has been conducted, the accountant's disclaimer will then read something like this:

"The financial statements were compiled by me (us), but because I (we) did not audit or review them, no opinion is expressed."

In a review, the accountant will still express no opinion as to the validity of his customer's figures, although he is required to perform a limited set of inquiry and analytical procedures that go beyond a mere "compilation."

In either case, whether it's a compilation or a review the accountant has performed, the result, for your purposes, will be the same as it's always been—you have been given an unaudited statement.

But again, the new language should make little difference to you if you have been successfully utilizing unaudited statements, as many of your colleagues have, and will continue to do.

Assets

Repeating our defintion from the checklist at the end of Chapter 2, assets are

> A company's resources, what it owns. Will be in the form of cash, both on hand and in the bank, inventory (merchandise), accounts receivable, equipment, fixtures, real estate, etc. Assets can be either current or fixed: current assets are those readily convertible and available at once to pay debts. . . . Fixed assets are those invested in property, equipment, and fixtures.

Assets traditionally appear on the left hand half of a balance sheet; the liabilities and net worth are listed on the right hand half. The total of one side equals the total of the other, hence *balance sheet*.

Now let's review the basic assets:

Current assets consist of cash on hand and in the bank; securities and bonds that are immediately convertible; accounts receivable, money due from those who purchased on credit (if your customer is a distributor, or jobber, his accounts receivable are from retailers; if he himself is a retailer, the accounts receivable are monies owing by consumers who purchased on the installment plan or on a charge account), and inventory.

There are a few other types of current assets, such as revenue stamps, trade acceptances, which are a special form of sight draft, and promissory notes. But these are much too special, and you may never encounter any of them, so for the purposes of our discussion, they have been omitted.

Of all current assets, you would be most interested in *cash on hand and in the bank*, for this is what your customer uses to pay his bills. If the total cash position is very light—as an example, $3,500 out of combined current assets of $75,000—then obviously your customer is operating with an unbalanced condition, with most of his current assets centered in inventory and/or accounts receivable.

But an unbalanced condition of that kind does not necessarily have to spell serious trouble, for you have to remember that your customer, as an actively operating organization, will be constantly generating new cash to meet his obligations; he may run late, and probably will, but a light cash position taken out of context doesn't have to mean disaster.

A recent statement, submitted to one of the agencies, reported cash of $12,805, accounts receivable $87,320, and merchandise $429,389—a distinctly unbalanced condition with light cash. Yet of ten suppliers reporting ledger experience, eight indicated prompt payments, the ninth showed prompt to 15 slow, and the tenth showed prompt to 30 slow.

A heavy cash position—as much or almost as much as total current liabilities—is generally a sign of a healthy condition, and most desirable. Occasionally, however, too much cash can be the result of overly conservative buying policies and might be indicative of a management behind the times.

Another note of caution must be sounded. There can be times when cash is not really cash; your customer may have loans outstanding, probably at the same bank where he makes his deposits. If so, the bank may have the right to offset the loans against the deposits, so that in effect the amount of the loans must be deducted from the cash, and only the balance, if any, is available for trade creditors. If a bank loan is listed on the statement, it would be wise to bear in mind the bank's right to offset.

Securities and bonds of a short term nature can be considered by the credit manager to be the same as cash, although he should watch for a possible variation in their stated value. The customer may list them at the current market rate, which may be higher than the price he paid for them. The actual cost would be of more interest to the credit manager.

Accounts receivable consist of three major categories:

1. Customer accounts receivable
2. Monies owed by affiliated companies
3. Monies owed by lessors of leased departments

If any part of this asset is centered in *customer* accounts receivable, a certain percentage should be set aside as a reserve for bad debts, and this in turn decreases the total current assets by a like amount—$100,000 in customer receivables, less $5,000 bad debt reserve, or a customer receivable asset of $95,000.

What about your customer's average collection period? If a number of his customers always run slow, then the chances are he'll run slow with you. He may not tell you the aging of his receivables, but it would be helpful if you knew, or even if you could estimate, how much of his receivables will be collected on time, and how slow the balance will be.

Accounts receivable from *affiliated companies* should be carefully examined, especially if they seem large in relation to the rest of the assets. Who is the affiliate, what is its financial condition, and can it pay the other affiliate everything it owes?

The third category, monies owed by *lessors of leased departments*, applies only to retailers who operate individual departments in someone else's store. It can be a jewelry department, stamps, women's wear, children's wear, shoes, toys, hardware, etc. If your customer is running such a department, he is the *lessee* (or tenant) and the owner of the store is the *lessor* (or landlord). Under normal arrangements, the lessor processes all income from sales, whether made on charge accounts or for cash, and credits this income to the lessee.

Occasionally, a lessor will experience financial difficulty and will not be able to pay his lessee everything he owes him; if that happens, it can hamper your customer's ability to meet his own obligations, even though, under normal conditions, he would have had no trouble at all.

One more point regarding your customer's accounts receivable. Are they pledged as security against a loan? If so, they are not available to trade creditors in the event of liquidation, but go, rather, as repayment to the institution making the loan.

Merchandise inventory has the same limitation. If your customer uses his inventory as security for a loan, such a pledge should be indicated by a footnote on the statement; as with accounts receivable, a pledged inventory is reduced in value by the amount of the loan.

Unlike cash, inventory can have differing valuations, depending upon the formula used. Your customer can inflate the value by appraising it at the current market price, which might be higher than what it had originally cost him—creditors would appraise his merchandise at the cost price, what he actually paid for it. This method of appraisal is known as *lower of cost or market*.

In addition, how is his merchandise moving? Does he have old goods on hand that he will have to mark down in order to sell? How much of his inventory will realistically return in sales an amount based upon its original selling price?

Accountants use formulas they refer to as *first in, first out,* or *last in, first out,* in computing the possible obsolescence of merchandise. Inasmuch as it's most unlikely that you will have enough information about your customer's inventory to use either of these calculations, the simplest approach for you would be to assume that, under a forced liquidation, your customer's merchandise would be worth a good deal less than his statement shows it to be. But given normal conditions in a normally operating business, the stated value should be fairly accurate.

Fixed assets are those invested in property, equipment, and fixtures, and are always shown on the balance sheet below the line, or under the current assets, and are therefore not to be considered available for the discharge of current obligations.

In certain industries, the fixed assets constitute a major share of the net worth; paint, glass and wallpaper stores can run up to 65.8%, while some service stations report a whopping 82.1% of their net worth invested in fixed assets. Obviously, anyone supplying these accounts would have to take into consideration these necessarily large investments in fixed assets, and would establish credit lines accordingly.

There are other *slow assets,* which can be lumped together with fixed assets, as far as their immediate availability is concerned; to name a few—officers' loans, pension funds, prepaid insurance premiums, advances to salesmen, and so on. Don't look to any of these for help in paying your bills.

And finally, there are the *intangible assets,* such as good will and brand names, which may be valuable to the debtor, but not to the creditor.

In essence, for the average credit manager, only *current assets* are meaningful, and of these, only the unencumbered and realistically valued have true significance.

Liabilities

Our Chapter 2 checklist gave the following definition of liabilities:

> What a company owes, its debts. Will be in the form of obligations for merchandise purchased (trade debts), taxes, loans, etc. Liabilities are either current or long term: current liabilities are normally the trade obligations, taxes, accrued salaries, interest on loans, and any current portion of a loan; long term liabilities are deferred loans, mortgages, etc., anything that is payable after a year.

The principal *current liabilities* are accounts payable, money owed to creditors for merchandise purchased and for services performed; notes payable to banks and to others for loans; and accruals, including payroll, taxes, commissions, interest, etc.

The credit manager immediately examines the first two, accounts payable and notes payable. Are the accounts payable in line with cash and with the inventory? If they are too close in total value, trouble may be looming. A statement that shows $10,000 cash, $100,000 in merchandise, and $100,000 accounts payable is evidence of serious problems, particularly if your customer is saddled with a slow moving inventory. And if the accounts payable exceed the cash and merchandise combined (assuming there are no accounts receivable), your customer is not only in trouble, he's on the verge of bankruptcy.

A light accounts payable position, in relation to the current assets, would, like heavy cash, be generally desirable. But again, might it also indicate too much conservatism in buying? How does it compare to the accounts payable position of a year before, or two years before? And what is its relationship to merchandise on hand, and to total sales? (These are discussed under *Important Ratios*.)

What about outstanding loans? Who carries the paper? Banks, insurance companies, factors, relatives, officers? And how much is currently owed, or is to be repaid within a twelve month period?

If the loan has been made by officers of the company, it is possible that they have subordinated their claim. This means they have agreed to wait for repayment of the loan, in the event of financial difficulty, until all general creditors have been paid. While this in itself does not guarantee solvency, it does reduce the risk by the full amount of the loan. There is an exception, however—the subordination may be limited in time or limited to one creditor—a bank. Your credit agency should know if such subordination does exist, whether there is a limitation, and its expiration date.

The principal *long term liability* is that part of your customer's loan or mortgage that falls due after his fiscal twelve month period. It does not affect his ability to meet current obligations, but affects his net worth, for it's still a liability, even though a large share of it doesn't have to be paid for some time.

Net worth, or equity

This section of the balance sheet can be mystifying and frustrating, for here you find listed, on the liability side, the net worth, or equity, and capital stock and retained earnings.

If net worth is equity, doesn't it belong to someone, and shouldn't it be listed as an asset?

The same for capital stock. Since it's owned by someone, shouldn't it therefore be an asset? And don't earnings imply profit, and shouldn't profit be an asset too?

Actually, the net worth is the owner's share of the business and exists as a liability because the business *owes* him that much. To illustrate:

Mr. Y is the proprietor of the ABC Hardware Store, which has assets of $40,000 and liabilities of $30,000. He decides to retire, and he pays all his creditors to the full amount of $30,000, leaving himself $10,000. On his balance sheet, therefore, the $10,000, which was his net worth, or equity, would have been shown as a liability, for, in liquidation, the store owed him that much.

The same is true of capital stock and retained earnings (which apply only to corporations).

XYZ Dynometrics, Inc. has total assets of $1,000,000, total liabilities of $600,000, capital stock of $250,000 (the shareholders' investment in the company), and retained or surplus earnings of $150,000. With the collapse of public interest in dynometrics, XYZ's directors vote to liquidate. Out of their assets of $1,000,000, they pay the $600,000 they owe, and are left with a total of $400,000 ($250,000 in capital stock and $150,000 in retained earnings) which they now distribute to the stockholders. Hence, the $400,000 was listed as a liability, for it was money owed to the stockholders.

This, of course, is a simplification, for the net worth section of the balance sheet, when applied to corporations, can begin to get involved, with common stock, preferred stock, par value, no par value, treasury stock, capital surplus, offsetting entries, and so on.

You can make it easier for yourself by remembering this formula:

Capital equals assets less liabilities.

(Net worth, equity, and capital all mean the same thing.)

In a proprietorship, which has a single owner (Mr. Y of

Table 4. Balance Sheet of ABC Hardware Store

Assets		Liabilities	
Current:		Current:	
Cash	$20,000	Accounts payable	$20,000
Accounts receivable	4,000	Note payable—bank (current portion)	2,000
Inventory	6,000		
Total current assets	$30,000	Total current liabilities	$22,000
Fixed:		Long term:	
Equipment	10,000	Note payable—bank (less current portion shown above)	8,000
		Net worth	10,000
TOTAL ASSETS	$40,000	TOTAL	$40,000

the ABC Hardware Store), or a partnership, which would have dual or multiple owners, the formula is simplicity itself, as per our own definition from the Chapter 2 checklist:

> *Net worth.* The owner's share in the assets of the business. Calculated by subtracting the total of all liabilities, both current and long term, from the total of all assets, both current and fixed. What is left is the net worth of the business.

Thus, in a proprietorship or partnership, you have three components in the equation—assets, liabilities, and net worth.

Table 5. Balance Sheet of XYZ Dynometrics, Inc.

Assets		Liabilities	
Current:		Current:	
Cash	$200,000	Accounts payable	$300,000
Accounts receivable	100,000	Note payable—bank (current portion)	50,000
Inventory	400,000	Accruals (taxes, etc.)	100,000
Total current assets	$700,000	Total current liabilities	$450,000
Fixed:		Long term:	
Equipment	100,000	Note payable—bank (less current portion shown above)	150,000
Property	200,000		
		Total liabilities	$600,000
		Stockholders' Equity	
		Capital stock	250,000
		Retained earnings	150,000
TOTAL ASSETS	$1,000,000	TOTAL	$1,000,000

In a corporation, you have the same three components, except that the third, net worth, can also be stated as a sum of capital stock plus retained earnings:

Subtracting XYZ's total liabilities from total assets, you have a balance of $400,000, which is the net worth, or equity; or adding the capital stock to the retained earnings, you also arrive at $400,000. Thus, for a corporation, the net worth is always the sum of the capital stock plus retained earnings.

Aside from knowing what makes a balance sheet balance, the net worth section of your customer's statement has no immediate significance for you in terms of his current obligations; it is important, however, in relation to the rest of the statement, and as a barometer of your customer's present condition and his trend, as you will find in the section dealing with key ratios.

Working capital

Not to be confused with net worth. Calculated by subtracting the total of current liabilities only from the total of current assets only. What is left is the working capital of the business.

In line with this definition from our Chapter 2 checklist, the credit manager who is analyzing his customer's statement will look, first of all, to the current assets as opposed to the current liabilities, and he will then calculate the working capital position.

Subtracting the current liabilities from the current assets of the ABC Hardware Store in Table 4, note that Mr. Y is left with a *working capital* of $8,000 to operate his business at this moment.

Now let's change the scenario a bit. Mr. Y decides to

Table 6. Revised Balance Sheet of ABC Hardware Store

Assets		Liabilities	
Current:		Current:	
Cash	$14,000	Accounts payable	$20,000
Accounts receivable	4,000	Note payable—bank (current portion)	2,000
Inventory	6,000		
Total current assets	$24,000	Total current liabilities	$22,000
Fixed:		Long term:	
Equipment	16,000	Note payable—bank (less current portion shown above)	8,000
		Net worth	10,000
TOTAL ASSETS	$40,000	TOTAL	$40,000

modernize his store, and he therefore buys new counters and shelving, which cost him $6,000; he pays for his new equipment in cash. His revised statement appears in Table 6.

You will see that Mr. Y's cash position has been reduced to $14,000, and his total current assets to $24,000 (from a previous total of $30,000), while his current liabilities still come to $22,000. Now his working capital is only $2,000, opposed to the $8,000 he had before.

His net worth, in the meantime, has remained the same—$10,000. The total of all his assets is still $40,000, while the total of all his liabilities is still $30,000. However, his *fixed assets* (in this case his store furnishings) have increased from $10,000 to $16,000, while his *current assets* have decreased by $6,000.

With this move, Mr. Y has considerably worsened his working capital position and undoubtedly caused grave concern to his creditors.

In a situation of this kind, the credit manager would have to consider other factors, such as depreciation. Even though Mr. Y paid $6,000 for his new counters and shelving, they would never bring that much at a forced sale.

The credit manager, above all, is interested in immediate protection. The possibility of a forced sale is something he lives with constantly, especially with his marginal accounts; he thinks of Mr. Y's $6,000 outlay primarily as depletion of current assets and working capital, and only secondarily as a depreciating fixed asset.

The working capital position, therefore, affects your customer's ability to continue meeting his current obligations and to operate his business profitably. Profit, after all, is the name of the game. Without it, businesses would have no reason for existence.

The profit and loss statement

Proper accounting procedure would consider the profit and loss statement, which is sometimes called the income statement, or operating statement, a necessary corollary to the balance sheet. In practice, many balance sheets are submitted without the profit and loss statement, and credit managers, as do agencies, assign lines of credit based solely upon the balance sheets and the annual sales figure. To a large body of credit managers, the balance sheet alone is the financial statement, and they often refer to it in that sense.

Although the average credit manager can certainly make do without profit and loss statements, he ought to try, wherever possible, to have them submitted along with balance sheets, for they will help him to assess his customers' progress or lack of it.

A profit and loss or operating statement has seven basic ingredients:

1. Sales
2. Cost of goods sold
3. Gross profit
4. Operating expenses
5. Operating income or earnings (including shipments)
6. Net income before taxes
7. Net income after taxes, or final net profits

As an illustration, we have a profit and loss statement from the Triple A Department Store of Idaho (a fictitious name). The figures reproduced have been taken from an actual statement, but they have been rounded for simplification.

With a statement of this kind, plus the balance sheet, the credit manager can now compute key ratios. As many as two dozen or so ratios are considered by various authorities to be important. However, no more than eight or nine are involved in the average credit manager's analysis. We will concentrate on these, while giving only a brief mention to some of the others.

Important ratios

Ratios are used to determine the *probable ability* of a business to meet its debts promptly and to operate profitably; they are calculated by balancing one element of the financial statement against another. The results are expressed in percentages, which are then weighed against the average percentages in each industry. It would be impossible, in the limited space available to us, to list every industry or every possible variation in percentages; we will

Table 7. Profit & Loss Statement of Triple A Department Store

Sales		$1,287,000
Cost of goods sold:		
Inventory, *beginning* of year	$ 240,000	
Cost of goods purchased *during* the year	803,000	
	$1,043,000	
Less inventory, *end* of the year	191,000	
		852,000
Gross profit		$ 435,000
Operating expenses (including payroll, rent, etc.)		385,000
Operating income		$ 50,000
Adjustments:		
Other income, earned discounts, etc.		33,000
		83,000
Less other expenses, bank interest, bad debts, etc.		11,000
Net income before taxes		$ 72,000
Less federal taxes		24,000
Final net profit		$ 48,000

therefore compare samples from the statement of the Triple A Department Store to the average percentages among other department stores, as compiled by a major agency. The agency percentage is shown in parentheses at the end of each ratio illustrated.

In every case, one element of the financial statement is divided by another; we will list first the *numerator*—the element to be divided—and second, the *denominator*—the element that does the dividing.

We have selected nine ratios that we believe the average credit manager would be most interested in; you may find that only three or four of these are important to you, or perhaps others we have omitted. In any event, these nine are basic and should be studied.

The nine ratios

1. *Current assets to current liabilities* measures the customer's liquidity and the extent of protection short term creditors have from current assets. Theoretically, the current ratio should be at least 2 to 1, or twice as many

Table 8. Balance Sheet of Triple A Department Store
(Sales—$1,287,000; net profit—$48,000)

Assets		Liabilities	
Current:		Current:	
Cash	$ 53,000	Accounts payable	$ 54,000
Accounts receivable	150,000	Accruals	
Inventory	191,000	(taxes, etc.)	51,000
		Note payable—bank	
		(current portion)	10,000
Total current assets	$394,000	Total current liabilities	$115,000
Fixed:		Long term:	
Real estate and		Note payable—bank	
fixtures	295,000	(less current	
Less depreciation		portion shown	
reserve	122,000	above)	91,000
	$173,000	Total liabilities	$206,000
		Stockholders' Equity	
		Capital stock	149,000
		Retained earnings,	
		beginning of year	164,000
		Surplus, end of year	48,000
TOTAL ASSETS	$567,000	TOTAL	$567,000

current assets as current liabilities. To determine the ratio, divide the current assets by the current liabilities.

$$\frac{\text{Current assets}}{\text{Current liabilities}} \quad \frac{\$394{,}000}{\$115{,}000} = 3.42 \quad (3.06)$$

In this case, the industry average shows a ratio of 3 to 1, ample protection for the short term creditor; compared to the industry average, Triple A's ratio of 3.42 indicates an even stronger position.

A variation that most credit managers use is the *liquid or quick* ratio, which involves only those portions of current assets that can be used immediately without dilution in value; the inventory, therefore, is removed, and only the cash and accounts receivable are utilized. Triple A's inventory is $191,900, leaving $203,000 in cash and accounts receivable, which is divided by the current liabilities.

$$\frac{\text{Liquid assets}}{\text{Current liabilities}} \quad \frac{\$203{,}000}{\$115{,}000} = 1.76$$

A quick ratio of 1 to 1 is the least a credit manager would look for; for every dollar owed, the customer has a matching dollar he can convert at once. Triple A has a much stronger liquid ratio, closer to 2 to 1—again more than ample protection for the short term creditor.

2. *Sales to inventory* determines the number of times the account turns his inventory in one year. If it's less than the industry average, it could mean obsolete merchandise,

poor buying or conservative buying. More than the industry average might indicate overtrading—using the suppliers' money to buy and sell merchandise; in other words, being undercapitalized for the amount of business being done. (Whenever possible, the average inventory should be used—the opening and closing inventories are added together and then divided by two. Triple A's beginning inventory is $240,000; its closing inventory is $191,000; for a total of $431,000. Divide this amount by two, and Triple A's average inventory is $215,500). Divide the sales, $1,287,000, by the average inventory to determine the ratio.

$$\frac{\text{Sales}}{\text{Average inventory}} = \frac{\$1,287,000}{\$215,500} = 5.9 \text{ times} \quad (5.5)$$

In the course of a year, Triple A turns its inventory 5.9 times, slightly better than other department stores, which average 5.5 times a year.

If you want to calculate the average number of days each turnover takes, divide 360 (the base that accountants normally use in this calculation—365 is too unwieldy) by the number of times arrived at in your earlier calculation.

$$\frac{360 \text{ days}}{5.9 \text{ times}} = 61 \text{ days}$$

You may not have both opening and closing inventory figures; your customer may have supplied only his closing inventory. If that's all you have, you can of course use that, but there might be a variation in your results, as the following computation shows, using Triple A's closing figures only.

$$\frac{\text{Sales}}{\text{Closing inventory}} \quad \frac{\$1,287,000}{\$\ 191,000} = 6.7 \text{ times}$$

$$\frac{360 \text{ days}}{6.7 \text{ times}} = 54 \text{ days}$$

3. *Sales to net worth* helps you to determine your customer's relative turnover of his invested capital. Putting it another way, does his net worth support his sales volume? If his ratio is too high, that might be another indication of overtrading—using more of your funds to buy his merchandise rather than his own. If the ratio is too low, you might then have undertrading—your customer is either not buying properly, or he has inadequate sales to support his business.

In short, this ratio tells you whether your customer is turning over his capital too rapidly or too slowly. Too rapidly, you have an excessive buildup of liabilities; too slowly, his funds become stagnant and his profitability suffers.

To see how well Triple A does in this category, divide its sales of $1,287,000 by its net worth of $361,000.

$$\frac{\text{Sales}}{\text{Net worth}} \quad \frac{\$1,287,000}{\$361,000} = 3.57 \text{ times (4.03 times)}$$

As you can see, Triple A's capital turnover is almost exactly the same as its industry average. Based upon the performance of other department stores, Triple A's performance in this category is more than adequate, especially when compared to a high of 6.01 times reported by some department stores (a definite sign of overtrading) and a low of 2.65 times reported by others (undertrading).

4. *Debt to net worth* measures the proportion of the owner's investment in the business compared to the creditors'. If the total debt exceeds the net worth, that means the suppliers have invested more than the customer. In other words, the customer owes more money to his suppliers than his business is worth. It might also be still one more indication of overtrading.

This ratio can be calculated in two ways—(a) current liabilities to net worth, and (b) total liabilities to net worth. In both computations, the liabilities are divided by the net worth.

$$\text{(a)} \quad \frac{\text{Current liabilities} \quad \$115,000}{\text{Net worth} \quad \$361,000} = 31.8\% \quad (45.0\%)$$

$$\text{(b)} \quad \frac{\text{Total liabilities} \quad \$206,000}{\text{Net worth} \quad \$361,000} = 57\% \quad (96.7\%)$$

In the first calculation, Triple A shows that its current liabilities are less than one-third of its net worth, almost 15% better than its industry average of 45.0%; in the second, the total liabilities are slightly more than half of the net worth. And this time, Triple A does far better than its fellow department stores, which show an average of almost 97%.

Normally, if one of your customers starts heading beyond 80% under (a), or beyond 100% under (b), you can anticipate trouble. You will note that the industry average of 96.7% for (b) appears to be excessive, but many department stores in the lower quartile (or less than the average) reported a ratio of 49.2%, which is even better than Triple A's healthy 57%. Your own department store accounts may fall into this range.

5. *Inventory to working capital* provides information on your customer's ability to finance the purchase of his merchandise. Under normal circumstances, this ratio should not exceed 80%, meaning that your customer's inventory should total no more than four-fifths of his working capital.

$$\frac{\text{Inventory}}{\text{Working capital}} \quad \frac{\$191,000}{\$279,000} = 68.4\% \quad (77.8\%)$$

As you can see, the industry average of (77.8%) is close to the suggested limit of 80%. Triple A's 68.4% is much lower and indicates, accordingly, that the business has more than enough capital to buy its merchandise.

6. *Fixed assets to net worth* tells you what percentage of the customer's net worth is invested in fixed assets. This ratio will work for you only if you know the average in your own industry. Comparing the percentage of an account in your industry to that in another industry would be meaningless. Among furniture stores the average percentage of fixed assets to net worth is only 12.7%, while among grocery stores it leaps to 76.5%.

$$\frac{\text{Fixed assets}}{\text{Net worth}} \quad \frac{\$173,000}{\$361,000} = 47.0\% \quad (27.3\%)$$

This is the first ratio in which Triple A exceeds the average in its own industry. The significance of this fact must be weighed in concert with the sum total of all the evidence; by itself, it might seem disturbing, but when judged by the remainder of the financial statement, it means far less.

7. *Net profit to sales* is an important yardstick for measuring the profitability of your customer's business. Too small a profit margin may indicate ineffective management or other internal problems. (This ratio is particularly effective when computed together with the one that follows—net profit to net worth.)

$$\frac{\text{Net profit}}{\text{Sales}} \quad \frac{\$\ 48,000}{\$1,287,000} = 3.73\% \quad (2.12\%)$$

The management of Triple A, on the basis of this ratio, cannot be faulted, for their profit margin is well above their industry standard. Putting it another way, on the basis of a 3.73% return, Triple A earned $3.73 for every $100.00 of sales, while other department stores averaged only 2.12%, or slightly more than $2.00. (A word of caution—profits may sometimes be taken out in salaries.)

8. *Net profit to net worth* measures the return on invested capital, and gauges the possibilities for future growth. Not too long ago, a 10% return, or $10.00 for each $100.00 of net worth, was considered a desirable objective, but in an inflationary period you would probably look for a 12% return, or $12.00 for each $100.00 of net worth. Divide Triple A's profit of $48,000 by its net worth of $361,000.

$$\frac{\text{Net profit}}{\text{Net worth}} \quad \frac{\$\ 48,000}{\$361,000} = 13.29\% \quad (8.18\%)$$

Triple A is obviously doing a good job in this area, for its return is $13.29 in profits for every $100.00 of net worth, while others are averaging only $8.18.

9. *Sales to receivables* is one of the more significant ratios; it can be helpful in analyzing the quality of your

customer's receivables. If this ratio reveals that his charge accounts are paying him much too slowly, then he'll have to run slowly with you. The best way to judge this ratio would be by a precise aging of each of your customer's receivables. But it would be most improbable that he would supply such information to you. You can do almost as well by computing this ratio yourself, based upon the figures you do have—divide Triple A's sales, $1,287,000, by its receivables of $150,000 to determine how many times its average receivables are turned over in a year.

$$\frac{\text{Sales}}{\text{Receivables}} = \frac{\$1,287,000}{\$\ 150,000} = 8.6 \text{ times}$$

To calculate the average collection period in days for all receivables, divide 360 (the same base as for inventory) by the number of times.

$$\frac{360 \text{ days}}{8.6 \text{ times}} = 41 \text{ days}$$

If you assume that most charge sales are made on terms of 30 days, then an average collection period of 41 days is very good, for anything that's paid within 10 to 15 days after the normal selling terms can be considered current. (Statistics are not listed for this ratio among department stores.)

A few additional ratios that may interest you have been compiled by investigative and service organizations. They are listed here for your further possible exploration:

1. Net profit to working capital
2. Sales to working capital
3. Total liabilities to inventory
4. Sales to fixed assets
5. Long term liabilities to working capital
6. Receivables to working capital

Trend of your customer's business

While key ratios can give you a good picture of your customer's business at this moment, they may not give you the entire picture, for there may have been a downward trend developing, which sometimes comes to light only through a comparison of the current balance sheet with those of two or three years before. You may have a situation where the net worth has increased, but the working capital has not.

A perfect example can be found in the three year figures of RST Superior (a fictitious name); while the figures have been taken from an actual report, they have been rounded for simplification.

Currently, RST shows a net worth of $292,000, an increase of $30,000 over the previous year, and $115,000 over the year before that. Its total current liabilities are $120,000. Measuring total debt to net worth (see Ratio 3), RST has a ratio of 47.9%, very good when you consider that anything coming close to 100%, or exceeding it, means little protection for the short term creditor. RST's net worth is more than twice its total debt, and that should be healthy.

But let's look a little closer. Two years ago, RST had a working capital of $65,000, last year it was $32,000, and this year it is only $3,700; their current ratio, at the same time, dropped from 2.97 two years ago, to 1.03 at the present, which means no quick protection for the creditor.

What happened? How can a business, which now shows itself to be worth twice as much as it owes, have such a tight working capital position?

The answer is expansion, without adequate funding. Inventory almost doubled in two years, from $58,000 to $107,000. As a result, the latest trade clearance showed six suppliers responding, with all of them reporting slowness ranging from 60 days to 150, and one supplier placing the account for collection.

Management was forced to admit that its slowness was "caused by excessive inventory in relation to sales volume."

Here then is a classic case where capital (the net worth) appeared to be more than adequate, but in fact it was not. Anyone watching the trend of this account should have suspected trouble, for while the net worth went up, the working capital went down much faster.

Previous financial statements may not always be available to you, as it was in the case of RST. Most reports you receive from your credit agency will list only the current statement. If you do have a report that shows the statements of the two previous years, use them, and compare them. The comparison could just as easily indicate an upward trend, and you would want to know that, too.

Nonfinancial information

Among other steps you can take to determine whether an account deserves credit is an evaluation of the customer's background and history of his operation. For the most part, an agency report supplies almost everything you need to know.

A typical report tells you when a business started, when the present owners took over, and where and when it was incorporated. It also gives you a thumbnail biography of the principals.

By reading such a report you will learn, for example, that Company A started twenty years ago, came under its present control a year later, and was incorporated under the laws of Delaware five years after that. Mr. Z, the president of the corporation, is 57, and married. Until he became active in Company A, he was involved in two or three other enterprises, all of which dissolved, paying debts in full.

Mr. X, treasurer of the corporation, is 55; he, too, is married. He graduated from a state university with a degree in business administration. He worked for Company A as its controller until his election as a corporate officer two years ago.

If there were any derogatory information about either of these gentlemen, or other principals of the firm, such as convictions for fraud, that would be included. Also, any bankruptcy in the past would be listed in the report. Thus, in a few short sentences, you have an elementary portrait of the owners, enough to tell you whether they are trustworthy, and whether they are experienced. Mr. Z obviously is, for he has been successfully operating Company A for nineteen years.

There are other things the report tells you—the location and physical appearance of the business (is it orderly, or slipshod?); its legal composition (is it a proprietorship, partnership, or corporation?); its method of operation and its principal merchandise; and its subsidiaries, divisions, and/or affiliates, if any.

Where a subsidiary or affiliate appears, you would look to your report for further information, for an order sent in directly by either one should be closely scrutinized.

Assuming a subsidiary has a poor credit rating, does the parent company accept accounting responsibility for its subsidiary—meaning does the parent guarantee payment of all the bills, or is that the concern solely of the subsidiary? (It should be pointed out that a guarantee from a parent company does not automatically guarantee payment. We saw that very point demonstrated in late 1978 when Food Fair filed a Chapter XI petition for reorganization. Food Fair for years had issued a guarantee on behalf of its subsidiary, J. M. Fields, Inc. Yet Food Fair had to file a petition in Chapter XI at the same time as did J. M. Fields. The result—Food

Fair's guarantee was only as good as its ability to meet its obligations, which proved no more viable than that of its subsidiary.)

If the affiliate has a poor credit rating, will the other affiliate allow you to bill your merchandise in their name?

The agency report usually supplies answers to questions like these, but in the event it doesn't, it would pay for you to write directly to your customer for the information you need. His response, or lack of it, can be significant.

If your customer's business is a proprietorship, or partnership, it is possible that certain of the listed assets may have limitations upon them. In a proprietorship or partnership, most assets belonging to the owners, even those outside of the business, are supposed to be available to creditors should a failure come about.

But, realistically, that isn't so. A sole proprietor, for example, may show real estate as an asset below the line, or below his current assets. The real estate can consist of a house and lot; if he owns them jointly with his wife, the creditors would have extreme difficulty in establishing a claim to the property, for most states zealously guard the rights of married women. The house and lot belong to the wife as much as to the husband.

So a balance sheet may not always be what it seems to be. One part of it may look great, and the rest not too bad. But then, when you begin a closer and more detailed analysis, especially by using a few of the key ratios, you may be astonished to find that your customer seems to be adequately funded, but in point of fact he is not. Or his net worth is badly inflated, because he's included in his assets property that only partially belongs to him.

The financial statement, therefore, is a tool that can work for the credit manager once he learns how to interpret it. The statement exists to help him.

6
Selling Terms

Fine print for the careless credit manager
Definitions of Net and EOM
Net terms discussed
Discounts
    Definition repeated
    Trade discount
    Cash discount
    Industry variations
Allowances
    For a new store opening
    Spiraling buyer demands
    Extra dating for new stores
    Advertising allowance
    Built-in dilemma
    The Robinson-Patman Act
Extra dating
    The two kinds of extra dating
        30x, 60x, 90x, etc.
        As of the 25th
    ROG as extra dating
    Extra dating and marginal accounts

CIA, CBD, or COD
    Differences discussed
    Cash in advance
    Cash before delivery
    Their hazards
    Certified check as a substitute
    Or letter of credit preferred
    Cash on delivery
    Its possible hazard
    Sight draft as variation
More fine print
    Invoicing
    Confirmations
    Signatures
    As had terms
    Automatic cancellations
The franchise operation
A helpful hint

Fine print has trapped many an unwary credit manager. Sometimes the fine print is in large, bold letters, easy to read, but just as easy to overlook. There is a practice, that appears to be growing among several large credit seekers, of inserting new stipulations on their order forms without prior notice to the seller. The seller automatically approves the orders without a second glance because he had always treated such orders automatically.

What happens in a case like that? The customer quickly charges back for a violation of his instructions, and the credit manager can fume and fret all he wants to, but it won't do him any good. The customer is technically right.

There are two areas the credit manager must pay particular attention to—selling terms and shipping terms. We discuss selling terms in this chapter, and shipping terms in the chapter that follows.

Selling terms vary with almost every industry. They can even vary with the fluctuation of the economy. But there are terms that are basic in the granting of credit; at a minimum, the credit manager should recognize such terms when he sees them, even if his own industry doesn't use them.

Two commonly used terms are *Net* and *EOM*. Our checklist gave the following definition of Net:

> The full amount your customer must pay. There will be instances where he will request and receive certain allowances, such as a percentage of the invoice total for a new store opening, or a set amount for advertising. In spite of such allowances, the terms will still read Net.

The definition for EOM spoke of it as:

> A term frequently employed in the payment of bills—End of the Month. If payment is to be made in the month following shipment, terms of sale will read, for example, Net 10 EOM, so that a shipment made in December will be paid for January 10th, the tenth day after the end of the calendar month.

Net terms

On the face of it, Net seems like a simple enough stipulation—no discounts permitted—but the term is often not observed. If you sell on Net terms only, make certain your customer understands that.

Orders will occasionally come to you bearing a discount—2/10 or 8/10, etc. It's not that the customer is deliberately trying to outsmart you in hopes you will overlook the discount; it's more probable that his accounting procedure is set up for some kind of a discount, whatever the rate may be.

If you do receive an order showing a discount, you can do one of two things:

1. Ask your customer, in writing, to change the terms to Net, and make sure he changes his own copies, especially those that go to the accounts payable department—and wait for his confirmation of the Net terms, again in writing, before you release the order.

You may not have to wait, or want to. It's possible that you have enough faith in your customer's integrity to release his order anyway, so you would simply ask him to send his confirmation of the correct terms for your records.

You can use either procedure with a form letter that would have appropriate boxes:

☐ We are holding your order awaiting your acceptance of the correct terms.

☐ We have processed your order without awaiting your confirmation, but ask that you forward it for our files.

2. You can jack up your price the amount of the requested discount, so that when payment is made, your customer deducts his 2%, or 8%, and satisfies his own records, and you still end up with a Net payment. But here, too, the price change upwards must be confirmed in writing, and you ought to go through your sales department for any price revision.

If there are federal, state, or local laws regulating your price structure, you have to be careful how your price is increased. It would be best to clear it with your company's attorney.

A form letter can also be used where the customer has indicated an incorrect price on his order. Just add other appropriate boxes advising him of the proper price. But you'll have to use a follow-up system of some kind for these form letters. Too many times, your letter finds its way to an inefficient clerk or to someone who buries it in a huge stack of others, so it ends up not being answered.

Remember, too, that many orders will have a cancellation date. If you do send a follow-up letter within a reasonable period, ask for an extension of the cancellation date.

There is one cardinal rule when examining an order: if a mistake has been made either in price or terms, don't take it for granted that your customer knows the correct price or the correct terms. Advise him every time, in writing, what the correct price should be, and the correct terms. And wait for his reply if you feel you have to. Once you process the order as he has written it, you're pretty much stuck with it as is.

Net is often used as the second half of a set of terms that allow a discount—for example, 2/10 EOM, Net 60. In other words, if the invoice is paid by the 10th of the following month, the customer is permitted to deduct 2%. Beyond that date, he must pay Net, or the full amount of the invoice, and he then has up to 60 days to make his payment.

There are many other terms that use Net without the EOM stipulation:

Net 10—to be paid in full within 10 days
Net 30—to be paid in full within 30 days
Net 60—to be paid in full within 60 days

If you sell on terms like these, or variations, you and your customer will have to agree on exactly what you mean—Net 10 is 10 days after the date of shipment, not 10 days after the end of the month, and so on.

Discounts

We now come to one of the stickier problems in credit checking—discounts. Let's review our Chapter 2 definition of Discount:

> The allowable percentage your customer is permitted to deduct from your invoice total (if freight charges are included, your customer must deduct those charges before computing his discount—discount is figured against merchandise costs only). There are two kinds of discount—trade and cash.

On a *trade discount*, your customer is allowed to deduct from the total of his invoice the amount of the discount agreed upon by you and him. Normally, these terms are the same as the rest of your industry permits—hence, *trade* discount.

On a *cash discount*, the customer must pay by the date agreed upon, or the discount is not allowed—hence, *time* discount. In a cash or time discount, the customer is rewarded for prompt payments, and is encouraged to do so by the discount. Note our previous mention of 2/10 EOM, Net 60. As long as the customer pays by or before the 10th day after the end of the calendar month, he can take off his 2%; beyond that date, there is no more discount allowed, and he then has 60 days before he will be considered past due on his net payment.

The true basis for a cash discount is to make it a premium, not for prompt payments by due date, but rather for payments ahead of due date. The principle, however, is more honored in the breach than in the observance. If you allow your customer 30 days in which to deduct 2%, it's not likely that he'll pay your bill any appreciable time before then. (He may even go beyond the 30 days and still take his discount. That can be a headache for you. See Chapter 8, "Deductions and Chargebacks.")

As for *trade discounts,* the term is almost a misnomer. Unlike the cash discount, a trade discount has no penalty for late payments. The customer is permitted to take his discount *anytime* he pays. So the vendor is not giving a premium—and he is fully aware that his buyers will all, without exception, deduct the full amount of the discount. To protect his own profit structure, the vendor therefore inflates his price to cover the discount. The same result would be achieved if the goods were sold and paid for on realistic net terms.

Beyond the continuing fallacy of the custom, trade discounts are sometimes misunderstood by the supplier, who creates trouble for himself by insisting that 2/10 EOM means exactly that—the customer must pay by the tenth day after the end of the month or there is no more discount allowed.

Actually the supplier is talking about a cash discount, not trade. Where it is the established custom in his industry to permit a certain discount rate, and he accepts orders on that basis, he cannot arbitrarily make his own rules and decide that for him alone it is to be a cash discount.

Although the 2% discount is the most widely used, there are variations extending from ⅓% in household appliances up to 9% in millinery. And most discounts are based on the date of sale, not the calendar month or payment month. 1/10 means that 1% is allowable up to ten days after date of shipment; 2/30 gives the customer exactly 30 days from date of shipment to deduct his 2%; and 4/60 allows him 60 days to take 4%.

Two variations are EOM and proximo, or prox., which means virtually the same thing as EOM; under proximo terms, payment is made in the month following shipment, but on a specific date, rather than on the 10th, as in EOM. If the proximo terms read 2/15 prox., Net 60, a shipment made in January permits the 2% discount to be deducted anytime up to and including the 15th of February.

Discount terms are sometimes stated without the qualifying Net, as in women's apparel, which customarily permits 8/10 EOM. This would then be construed to be a trade discount, and no penalty would accrue to the customer for late payments.

Your own industry may use a variety of terms; hardware, for *manufacturers and wholesalers both,* reports terms of 2/10, 2/10 prox., 2/10 Net 30, and 2/10 Net 60, while hardware *manufacturers* sometimes limit the customer to Net 30, or ½/10 Net 30. Terms offered by paper suppliers are more uniform—½/10 Net 30 the one most widely used, with 2/30 Net 31 close behind. This latter term indicates that paper suppliers prefer not to be lenient in the granting of cash discount, for even one day late requires a Net payment.

If you've just started working in a new industry, and you're not certain of the terms, try calling some of your colleagues in the industry for information; you'll find them to be most helpful. Credit managers, as a group, are extremely cooperative. They like to think of themselves as being part of a "credit fraternity," and they behave as if they are.

Allowances

You may be employed by a company that permits no allowances of any kind. If you are, consider yourself lucky. Allowances can get out of hand, for they seem to spread through an industry like a contagious disease. Once a large credit seeker requests a new kind of allowance, word gets around quickly, and others do the same.

Not too long ago, a major retailing chain devised an ingenious method for extracting additional discounts from its vendors—they called it *new store allowance*. Within a matter of months, dozens of other chains followed suit, and what began as an infrequent request mushroomed into an epidemic. And from the first reasonably modest 5% of the invoice for the new store's opening order, the requested allowance jumped to 10%, and now it has even reached 15%. Some chains prefer a flat dollar allowance, which in some instances can almost wipe out the new store's first invoice.

To put an extra bit of icing on their cake, most of these same chains ask for additional dating, as much as 90 days, so that not only do they stock their new stores with merchandise they bought at a bargain, they sell it out completely, and reorder before they have to pay for the original goods. (Most of the large retail chains turn over their inventory at least once every 60 to 70 days.)

Many suppliers look upon this practice with extreme disfavor, but because of their vulnerability in relation to competition, they have no alternative; they allow the extra terms or risk losing the account.

Nor is new store allowance the only imposition; another popular device is 1% for home office, or 1% for warehouse, or, as a major New England chain chooses to word it, "1% participating discount for central administration."

Finally, we have the cooperative advertising allowance, although sometimes it's none too cooperative. Under this arrangement, the supplier pays a portion of the customer's cost for a specific advertisement that includes the vendor's name and/or product. The customer may bill the supplier for his portion of the ad at a Net rate, while actually paying for it at a discount. Also, the vendor is not always advised exactly what the advertising rate for the particular publication is.

If you permit cooperative advertising, perhaps you ought to ask each customer who requests the allowance to furnish advertising rates and discounts.

A new store allowance can have a built-in dilemma, and few so far have found the way to resolve it. Should the additional discount be deducted after the original discount, or at the same time? To illustrate:

A new store invoice totals $1,000; your normal terms are 2/10 EOM, and on top of that, you allow your customers 10% for "new store opening." Deducting 2% from $1,000, you have a balance of $980; does your customer now deduct 10% of that, or 10% of the original $1,000? The difference in this case is only $2.00 (10% of $980, or $98.00, as against 10% of $1,000, or $100.00), but these small amounts can add up. Unfortunately, no precise policy anywhere seems to have been established, so the practice appears to vary, depending upon the industry and the strength of the supplier.

Allowances also relate to the federal Robinson-Patman Act, which was enacted during the late 1930's to prohibit discriminatory credit practices. Whatever discount, price, or allowance you give to one buyer must be given to all buyers in that same general class.

It is sometimes possible to use the Robinson-Patman Act as an excuse for not allowing additional discounts. You can advise your customer that under the provisions of Robinson-Patman you cannot permit the 1% for home office, or the 10% for a new store opening, since you don't allow anyone to have these discounts.

Your customer may agree with your reasoning, or he may tell you that your competitor down the street *is* giving these additional allowances. If you want the business badly enough, the chances are your firm will have to accede and thereby open the doors for everyone else to request the same.

Extra dating

Another custom that has become widespread in some industries is the practice of asking for extra dating. There are a number of ways in which extra dating can be given, although there actually are only two ways to word it:
1. 30 extra, 60 extra, or 90 extra, etc. (often written as 30x, 60x, 90x).
2. As of the 25th.

The first type is clear enough. The customer wants 30 extra days to pay your invoice, or 60 extra, or 90 extra, etc.

In some cases, the extra dating is established as a permanent part of the terms of sale for that particular customer, so that he always pays on that basis. In other cases, extra dating may be requested for a specific order: seasonal needs may be involved or your customer may want a stronger cash portion for his year-end figures.

Nor should you overlook the possibility that an account which has permanent extra dating may ask for even more additional time on given orders, as with a new store opening. It is conceivable that, where you have already allowed 30 extra and your customer requests an additional 90 days for a new store, payment will not be made for perhaps five months from date of shipment.

Extra dating can also be the second half of a set of terms, as in 2/10 Net 60. If the payment is not made within 10 days, the customer has 60 additional days before he is considered past due, although as stated before, once the initial 10 day period has expired, he must then pay Net.

The second form of dating—as of the 25th—is a bit more complicated, although fortunately for the average credit manager, it is limited to a few industries, notably apparel.

It is now the custom in these industries to consider that the shipping and billing month end on the 24th; anything shipped after that date, that is, beginning with the 25th of the month, is treated as a shipment in the following month and will therefore be paid on the 10th of the month following that—a shipment made on March 25th or later is treated as an April shipment and will be paid on May 10th.

In effect, when your customer requests dating as of the 25th, he is simply asking for 30 extra days to pay your invoice.

From a practical standpoint, however, there is a difference that can be important. As of the 25th is normally a one time request and must be repeated whenever the customer wants additional time, while 30 extra can begin as a one time request and end as a permanent part of the terms. Also, 30 extra can be joined to EOM or refer to the date of shipment, while as of the 25th is usually coupled to EOM only.

If the extra dating is based upon the date of shipment, you would then have terms that read, for example, 2/10, 30x—a shipment made on the 9th of the month is due on the 19th of the following month, 10 days after shipment plus 30 extra days.

If the terms read EOM as of the 25th, the same shipment is not due until the 10th day of the *second* month that follows. A shipment made on May 9th is dated as of May 25th, which is now treated as a June shipment, due under EOM terms on July 10th.

The same would be true of EOM, 30x; the May 9th shipment would normally be due June 10th. With 30 extra, the customer can now make payment on July 10th.

There is another way for your customer to have extra dating, although it won't be worded quite like that. He asks that the payment date begin from the time he receives your goods, not from the date when you ship them. His request reads ROG, or Receipt of Goods.

Depending upon his location, your merchandise may well be in transit two to three weeks, and even more. If you're in an industry that considers the billing month to end on the 24th, even a few days in transit can give your customer an additional month—you may ship on the 18th (which happens to fall on a Friday), the goods are moved by your trucker on the next Monday, which is now the 21st, and four days later the goods are delivered, on the 25th, just time enough for the new payment period to begin.

So pay close attention to the cutoff date; a number of major retailers are now insisting that their receiving month ends on the 20th, not the 24th, and their new payment period therefore begins on the 21st, not the 25th. Please note that we said receiving, not shipping. It doesn't matter when you ship the merchandise, due date for payment will be calculated ROG, receipt of goods. And in one most unusual instance, the cutoff date has been lowered to the 10th.

A supplier strong enough to resist can refuse to allow these terms, but the vendor who is vulnerable to competition will probably agree with reluctance. Much as you, the credit manager, may dislike it, you'll have to go along with your company's policy and do your best to juggle a proliferating variety of cutoff dates.

Two bits of advice about extra dating:
1. When you do allow extra dating, see to it that the information appears on your records, either on your ledger sheet or on the invoice. In that way, your customer won't be dunned for a past due after your normal terms have expired. Nothing irritates a touchy customer more than being improperly dunned for a past due.
2. Don't allow extra dating to a customer who is

traditionally slow. If you do, he'll probably take that much longer to pay. Advise both him and the salesman, in writing, why the extra dating is not being permitted, but word each letter differently.

You can be direct with your salesman and tell him the truth. Your customer never pays on time—he is always as much as 60 days late, so why give him 30 days on top of that?

To the customer, you again (as pointed out earlier in Chapter 3) put the onus on your company policy, not upon him. Advise him what your terms are, with everyone, and politely tell him you will look for his payment when normally due, without the requested extra dating.

CIA, CBD, or COD

For the customer who is a poor credit risk, you may have to employ terms most credit managers would rather avoid—prepayment, or payment in cash. A request for prepayment implies lack of confidence in the account, and that in turn implies no continuity. A profitable account is one who reorders. And since an important function of the credit department is to stimulate sales wherever possible, a one time customer has little allure. Still, a sale is a sale, even for cash, so why turn it down?

A cash transaction can be handled in one of three ways:

1. CIA, cash in advance
2. CBD, cash before delivery
3. COD, cash on delivery

The first two sound as if they mean the same thing, but there is a perceptible difference.

You request *cash in advance* before you will even

process an order; *cash before delivery* means that you will process the order and prepare it, but you won't release it for delivery until the money is in your hands. In both methods, you don't trust the customer's ability to meet his obligations, except that the first is a much harsher approach, and indicates a total lack of faith; in the second, you're willing to invest the amount of labor it will take to prepare your customer's order, but you won't commit yourself beyond that.

Either method can be hazardous. If you accept an ordinary check as payment, it would be wise to deposit it and let it clear before making shipment. Otherwise, you may find your customer stopping payment if your merchandise reaches his door soon enough. Or the check may bounce.

A *certified check* is one safeguard; so is a *letter of credit*.

When your customer sends you a certified check, he is sending you his bank's guarantee, or certification, that it has set aside from his account enough funds to cover the amount of that check. If he doesn't have enough money to cover the check, the bank of course won't certify it, and you will have saved yourself a bad debt. A *cashier's check* will do just as well—it's a check drawn on the bank itself and paid for by your customer.

A letter of credit involves more work and documentation, such as forwarding pro forma invoices, signed bills of lading, etc., and is used far more frequently for export purposes, rather than domestic. But it *has* been utilized, effectively, in domestic trade.

As with a certified check, a letter of credit is a guarantee by your customer's bank that you will be paid the amount specified, provided the transaction is completed by a specified date. Beyond that date, the letter of credit must be renegotiated. Also, make sure the letter of credit is irrevocable—meaning it can't be withdrawn or canceled.

Shipping under terms of COD has its own dangers. With *cash on delivery,* you take the risk of assuming all freight charges both to destination and back again if it turns out that your customer can't pay for your goods when they reach him.

But the risk may be worth it to you. Your customer may really want your merchandise, and even though he knows he'll have to pay for it immediately upon delivery, he'd rather have the use of his money while his goods are in transit instead of letting you have it during that period, as would be the case with CIA or CBD.

A variation of COD is the sight draft. The bill of lading, which controls title to the goods, or ownership, is forwarded to the customer's bank along with the draft. The bank does not release the bill of lading until the sight draft has been honored. But a sight draft offers no more guarantee of payment than does COD. If your customer doesn't have the funds, the draft will go unhonored. The merchandise of course will still belong to you, but it can deteriorate while in storage, and you'll have freight charges to contend with both ways.

More fine print

In addition to the terms of sale, there are a number of buyer stipulations that the credit manager, as the seller's representative, should constantly be alert for:

Invoicing. Does your customer require an invoice to be included with the shipment? Or a duplicate to the paying office? Or the original and/or duplicate to be sent to the paying office only, with a packing slip for its warehouse or branch store? Is the original invoice or duplicate to be mailed to a box number, and all other correspondence to the main office?

Violation of any of these instructions permits your customer to delay payment, and can leave you with skipped invoices that eventually will lead to requests for proof of delivery. Preparation of documents for proof of delivery can be time consuming, as will be explained in Chapter 8.

Confirmation. If the order is written on your own form, must you have a confirmation from the customer before shipping? Must it be signed? By whom? If you do not need a confirmation, are the terms that appear on your form understood and accepted by your customer? If your customer's normal terms differ from those on your form, will you accept payment on his terms rather than your own, even though your salesman neglected to include your customer's differing terms on his order? And what about an order number? Perhaps your customer telephoned his order in, and neglected to give you an order number. Can you still ship, even without an order number—or, in many cases, a department number?

Signature. Must all of your orders be signed by your customers? Some accounts insist that only signed, and countersigned orders are valid; others are not that formal. Be certain you know which of your orders must be signed and/or countersigned, generally by the buyer, the merchandising manager, or perhaps one of the principals. Unsigned orders can result in refused shipments and costly freight charges.

As had. Instead of specific terms, or prices, or instructions for packing or shipping, does the order simply read, "As had"? Is it clearly understood by both parties what "As had" specifies? Be particularly careful if your company has seasonal price increases, or if increases become necessary because of inflationary pressures. To your customer, "As had" may mean the previous prices, not the new ones.

Automatic cancellations. Does your customer prefer

complete shipments only and ask that you automatically cancel any balances due? Also, does he show an outside shipping date? Some of your accounts may accept partial shipments but charge you for the freight on a back order. Others don't want back orders shipped at all and will return them to you at your expense; the same for anything shipped after the automatic cancellation date, even if it's an entire order.

The franchise operation

Another possibility for error is the franchise operation, which has now spread into the retailing field. The credit manager who deals with franchised retailers must carefully watch their billing and shipping instructions.

Often a franchise headquarters will forward a general order for shipment to its entire chain, including branches owned by the main office and franchises owned by others. The instructions will probably indicate that the main office is not responsible for payments to be made by the franchised stores. If that's the case, then each franchise must be treated as an entity and as a separate account.

Investigate each franchise thoroughly, and don't be misled by the credit rating of the main office or franchiser. The franchiser itself can be a requirements account, but the franchise may not deserve credit of any kind.

Remember that you have the right to hold up shipment for any part of a general order that is not guaranteed by the franchiser. The same applies to individual orders.

Don't be lulled into shipping a poor credit risk simply because the order was sent to you by a top-rated franchiser.

A helpful hint

One thing you ought to do is to indicate in some fashion the date you receive an order. Sometimes a buyer or merchandising manager may hold an order, either deliberaely or inadvertently, and then mail it to you perhaps a few days or a week before the cancellation date that was originally placed on the order.

By then, it may be impossible for your company to prepare and ship the order on time, and the buyer may want to know why.

To protect yourself and your company, stamp the date of receipt on the back of the order. This may not mollify your customer, for he may still insist that he mailed his order in plenty of time. But you and your organization will know that he didn't, and your sales department will at least have a point of departure for discussing an extension of the cancellation date.

7
Shipping Terms

The movement of freight
Relationship of freight charges to ownership
    of the merchandise
The FOB point
    Definition of FOB
    FOB Shipping Point
    FOB Destination
    Possible misinterpretations of FOB point
    FOB consolidator
Ownership of the merchandise
    When terms read FOB shipping point
    Non-delivery
    Burden of proof upon the shipper
    Delivery to a consolidator
    Prepaid terms
Shipping routes
    Customer's instructions
    Cheapest way
    Shipment of back orders
    Transfer to a consolidator

Freight allowances
    1% for shipping charges
    Partially prepaid shipments
    Free area
    Possible double charges in free area
Refused shipments
Reasons for refusal
    Shipment after cancellation date
    Partial shipment
    Shipment ahead of time
    No invoice with shipment
    No packing slip with shipment
    Incorrect markings, or no markings
    Multiple store shipment violations
    Neutral gum tape
Redelivery and storage charges

The movement of freight seems like a simple enough process; the shipper forwards goods to a point designated by his customer, who then signs for and accepts the merchandise. But involved in this procedure are two significant factors that are frequently misinterpreted and misapplied, despite their apparent simplicity:

1. Who pays the freight charges and at what point does responsibility for these charges begin?

2. At what point does title to the merchandise pass to the consignee?

In one sense, the second question can be linked with the first, for it should follow that ownership of the goods will be tied to the freight charges. At the point where the consignee accepts responsibility for the shipping charges, he also accepts ownership of the merchandise.

That's how it should be, but speaking practically, it often happens otherwise. In many instances, where final delivery has not been consummated, the burden of proving delivery or bearing the cost of possible loss falls upon the shipper even though title to the goods had previously passed to the consignee. Too frequently a customer will refuse to pay for merchandise that has not been delivered, in spite of legal requirements and terms of sale.

Shipping terms may be clear enough in principle, but enforcement of them can be trying.

Much of the material in this chapter would seem to fall into the province of the traffic department, which normally handles many of the problems we are now discussing. But most of the smaller companies do not have either a traffic department or traffic manager. Like other chores around the office, refused shipments, proofs of delivery, and filing claims for loss or pilferage often devolve upon the credit manager. And even where a traffic department does exist, it is still the credit manager who has the task of enforcing collection for unpaid shipments and for unauthorized freight chargebacks.

The FOB point

In itself, the term FOB should be easy enough to understand, as demonstrated by our checklist definition in Chapter 2:

> FOB. *F*ree *o*n *B*oard. The most commonly used term for the shipment of goods. And the most frequently misunderstood. It does not mean *freight* on board, as so many people believe. Simply put, it means the point at which responsibility for the freight charges begins and title passes. If the terms read FOB Destination, the supplier is responsible for all shipping charges to the customer and he

still owns the merchandise until it reaches its designated destination. If the terms read FOB Shipping Point, or FOB Factory, or FOB Mill, the customer pays all shipping costs, and title to the goods passes to him at that point.

Under terms of FOB Shipping Point, the supplier pays the preliminary loading charges. If a carrier comes to your factory or warehouse to pick up the merchandise destined for your customer, the cost of loading the goods aboard that carrier is yours, not the consignee's. The same applies to parcel post shipments—you pay the cost of getting the merchandise to the post office.

Once the *free on board* requirements have been satisfied, all charges from that point on become the sole responsibility of the consignee. For the most part, there will be a single through rate from shipping point to destination, no matter how many times the merchandise is transferred from one trucker to another; the various carriers are paid on a pro rata basis. Actually, your customer pays only the delivering carrier, and he in turn distributes the prorated shares of the revenue to the other truckers.

Occasionally, when delivery must be made to an isolated community, the through rate does not apply, and charges will be correspondingly higher. Your customer should be aware of this and should not complain about excessive shipping costs.

Under terms of FOB Destination, the shipper pays all charges for movement of his merchandise to the point of delivery. If these are the terms you have permitted, choice of carrier should be left to you, not to your customer. Inasmuch as you are bearing the full burden of all freight charges, the option of delivery method should be yours.

All of the foregoing should be clear enough. And yet misinterpretations do arise.

Let's assume you ship from Industrial City, Illinois,

and your customer has his place of business in Urban Area, South Carolina. Undoubtedly, for that distance, you would ship Collect, and your terms would therefore read FOB Factory. Or you might word it FOB Industrial City.

But supposing your customer indicates on his order FOB Illinois, without specifying Industrial City? And supposing further that he requests you transfer his merchandise to a trucker in Chicago, which may be 200 miles from Industrial City? You do ship his goods to Chicago, as per his instructions, only to find that he charges you for the cost of moving his merchandise from Industrial City to Chicago.

Can you dispute this chargeback?

Perhaps not successfully. His order did read FOB Illinois, which you assumed meant your factory, but your customer assumed no such thing. He meant for it to be Chicago.

This is only one example of how the FOB point can be misunderstood. If you intend to pay no part of any freight charges, you must make that clear to your customer. FOB Factory should mean exactly that and nothing else.

One other possibility for error exists. Does your company have more than one division, and does it ship from factories that might be in different states? Sometimes your customer, either through carelessness or an oversight, will send in an order for Division A, but will show Division B's shipping point.

Unless you advise him of his mistake before making shipment, you leave yourself open to a possible chargeback for violation of instructions.

Your customer may request that you transfer his goods to a consolidator. If the consolidator is in an area some distance from your shipping point, who pays the charges?

Your customer does—unless he specifies FOB Consolidator and you agree.

What about an order that reads Ship Prepaid and your terms are Collect only? Don't accept it until the customer changes it to Collect, unless you know from past experience that he'll pay you for the shipping charges. But once again, don't take anything for granted. Your customer may have appointed a new traffic manager, who decides, in his zeal, to justify both his position and his salary; he therefore takes advantage of every shipping violation on your part. The previous traffic manager may have been far more lenient and looked the other way, especially if you could prove, to his satisfaction, that his stated terms did not agree with yours. The new manager may not be that liberal. So make it a rule to process prepaid terms only if prepaid costs are to be added to the invoice and only if the order so specifies.

In some industries, shipments frequently will be forwarded under Prepaid terms, but the customer absorbs the cost, or at least a large part of it, by accepting a parallel increase in price.

There may be occasions when you will *have* to prepay shipping charges, especially with small shipments that can go only via parcel post or United Parcel Service. You can't ship Collect with either of them, so you'll have to prepay the charges and add them to your invoice as a separate item.

An exception is the COD shipment, which both the Postal Service and UPS will accept. They'll add a collection fee, which the customer will have to pay, along with all COD charges and all shipping costs.

Ownership of merchandise

Technically, your customer assumes title to the goods at the moment shipping charges become his responsibility.

With terms of FOB Shipping Point, you own the merchandise until you load it upon a carrier that is to begin the process of delivering it to your customer; title to the goods passes to the customer along with the bill of lading, which you hand over to the driver or his agent. The same is true of parcel post; once you bring your customer's package to the post office, the goods inside that package no longer belong to you—they become the exclusive property of the consignee.

That's what is formally supposed to happen, but it frequently does not. No matter what the law may state, if a customer advises you that he did not receive a certain shipment and refuses to pay for it, proof of *shipment* will budge him not at all. He wants proof of *delivery*, and even though he supposedly owns the merchandise from the moment you release it to a common carrier, the burden of supplying that proof of delivery will be upon you, not upon him.

If you have been instructed to deliver to a consolidator, your customer should not require you to prove delivery beyond that point. Under his specifications, his consolidator is his agent, and conveyance to the consolidator, therefore, is the same as making delivery directly to the customer. Responsibility for any loss that occurs between the consolidator and final destination cannot be your responsibility, in the same way that you cannot be held responsible for pilferage of your merchandise from the consignee's premises after you have completed delivery.

The use of Prepaid terms sometimes creates confusion regarding title to the goods. Shipping your merchandise Prepaid does not mean that you have accepted responsibility for the goods until they reach the consignee. You can ship Prepaid and specify FOB Shipping Point at the same time. What you're doing is accommodating your customer by paying the freight charges for him and adding them to your invoice or to your price. As long as you specify FOB

Shipping Point, he owns the merchandise even though you've temporarily paid the shipping charges on his behalf.

Shipping routes

When your customer requests transfer to a specific carrier in a specific city, it will then be up to your shipping department to comply. These instructions do not depend upon the FOB point; your customer may want a certain carrier because he finds it more convenient or more cooperative than others in the same area.

If such a connection is impossible, advise your customer and wait for alternate instructions, provided there's enough time before the cancellation date. But you may not have enough time; ship the best way you can, and straighten it out later. It's far more important to retain your customer's good will by moving his goods out when he wants them. In such a case, ask your sales department to advise the buyer or purchasing agent of your deviation from instructions. There may be a sizeable penalty involved for such a violation, even though you have only the best interests of your customer in mind. Such penalties, frequently as much as 5% of the invoice, plus all shipping charges, are becoming commonplace, and are clearly spelled out in your customer's terms, or in his traffic and/or shipping guides.

If your customer does not specify a carrier or route, your shipping department may choose any method, as long as it's the cheapest. Frequently, your customer may not be sure of transfer points and connecting freight lines, so he will indicate "cheapest way" on his order. When he does, let your traffic or shipping department beware; cheapest way does not mean easiest. Your customer may not be too sure of connecting freight lines, but he most certainly will know approximate shipping costs. Anything out of line will be quickly charged back to you.

Also, watch for the fine print instructions that involve back orders. These can be small balances that your customer will want shipped in an entirely different way from the bulk of his order.

Instructions to transfer to a consolidator can, on occasion, be mystifying; your customer's consolidator can be in a direction exactly opposite to the ultimate destination, and it may seem like a waste of time and money to send your goods away from where it's supposed to go and then double it back again.

Your customer has a good reason for these instructions. As our definition in Chapter 2 explains, a consolidator will hold various smaller shipments for his client until he has accumulated one large bulk shipment that can then be forwarded as a single lot.

This method can result in a considerable saving for your customer; the rates and total cost for one large bulk shipment will be far less than the collective charges for many small individual shipments.

You can sometimes violate your customer's instructions to ship FOB Consolidator. If you have a small order, or a small back order, the cost of forwarding it directly to its final destination may be the same as, or less than, sending it to the consolidator. And since that part of the cost is yours, it may be a good idea to ship directly.

But have your shipping department make certain that your customer will accept merchandise not delivered by his consolidator; some receiving departments may be instructed to refuse.

Freight allowances

Does your customer's order form have boxes under Freight that say "We pay" or "Vendor pays"? If it does, give particular attention to these boxes; the wrong one can easily be checked.

Also, instead of the 1% for home office previously mentioned, your customer may request 1% for freight and shipping charges. However he words it, it will still come to the same thing—an additional discount—except in this instance you may have to look for it on a different part of the order.

What about Prepaid shipments to certain areas and not to others? For example, if you operate within or near a major urban area, it may be a long established practice in your industry to ship free of charge anywhere within a 50 mile radius of that urban location. Beyond that, the consignee must pay. A word of warning—keep an eye on your local geography; 50 miles has a habit of becoming 60 and 70, and so on.

This free area may sometimes involve what amounts to double shipping charges that the supplier must pay. The customer issues instructions to deliver merchandise for all his branches to a receiving station or consolidator within the 50 mile radius. As per the established custom, the vendor pays for delivery to that point.

But then the customer adds one more stipulation—free delivery to all *local* branches, those within the same 50 mile radius. So the vendor pays for shipment to the consolidator, and again from the consolidator to the local branches. It may have been cheaper for him to skip the consolidator and ship directly to the branches themselves, but the customer's procedure won't permit that. Only the consolidator can make final delivery. The result is a double charge, which the customer insists the supplier must absorb.

Where you and your industry operate in a free shipping zone, it would be prudent for you to examine carefully shipping instructions from any of your customers who have both a consolidator or receiving station, and branches within that local area. Watch particularly for the double charge.

Refused shipments

Another frequent source of vexation can be the refused or the undelivered shipment. At times, merchandise is refused for what may seem like capricious reasons, but closer examination will reveal that the consignee's receiving department did indeed have the right to refuse.

Refused shipments are of course not actually a part of shipping terms, but they can result from violations of these terms; they must therefore necessarily be included in any discussion of freight movement.

Of the many possibilities for the refusal of shipments, the following is a representative listing, although complete by no means:

1. *Shipment was made after cancellation date.* There may be a technicality involved here, for sometimes the instructions are vague—does the outside date shown on the order mean the outside shipping date or receiving date? "Ship by such and such a date," does not mean the same as "Ship to arrive by such and such a date," and can make a difference of days, and perhaps weeks. There can also be occasions when the cancellation date is not actually stated on the order but is implied, as in the instructions "Ship by March 20"—the words *or cancel* are not included, and yet that's what the customer means. To avoid possible prob-

lems, try to learn which of your customers mean "or cancel" when they don't specifically state it.

2. A *partial shipment*. The order may read "One shipment only," or "Complete shipment only." Where a back order has been necessitated, your shipping department may take it upon themselves to make a second shipment in hopes the customer will nevertheless accept it. Sometimes he will, but if he doesn't, you'll have no choice except to take your merchandise back and assume shipping charges both ways.

3. *Shipment is made ahead of time*. Your customer may have requested that you ship to arrive by a certain date, which he may have set up for a special occasion—such as an anniversary sale, or to count his inventory, or to avoid inventory tax in that period.

In some states, a tax is paid on a specified date for all inventory being carried at that time; by having his goods delivered after that date, your customer delays payment of his tax on your merchandise.

Or your customer's allocation of funds for your goods may not be available until the requested date of receipt—if you ship to arrive before then, the merchandise may have to be included in the wrong allocation period, which won't work for your customer at all, and he'll have to refuse.

4. *No invoice is included with the shipment*. If this is a requirement stated in your customer's instructions, your shipping department must comply. Your customer's method of operation is geared to receipt of the invoice at the same time as the merchandise; receiving it by mail won't do the job for him.

This stipulation can complicate matters for you if you customarily bill after shipment has been made. In a case like that, your shipping department may have to prepare a pro forma invoice, but make sure your billing department doesn't then mail its copy, too. And you'll have to develop some kind of numbering system for the pro forma to control your ledger posting.

5. *No packing slip accompanies the shipment.* This would only happen as an oversight in your shipping department, but it can happen. When it does, you may be able to save yourself shipping charges back to your factory by requesting the carrier to hold your goods long enough to get a copy of the packing slip to him.

You can do the same with an omitted invoice. There may, however, be storage charges that result if the trucker and your customer are located some distance away, and they have to wait until the necessary document reaches them. In most cases, the storage charges would be far less than the cost of returning the entire shipment.

Once you have determined that the fault is yours, advise the trucker that you will accept all additional charges, including redelivery, and suggest he bill that portion to you. He may not want to separate his charges in that way and may insist upon presenting the entire freight bill to the consignee. Under these curcumstances, advise your customer immediately that he can charge the excess portion back to you.

6. *Incorrect markings on the cartons, or no markings at all.* This kind of oversight or mistake can be a real headache. Your customer may have requested that department numbers or order numbers be clearly indicated on each and every carton. If there is more than one department involved, or more than one order number, the only practical way to resolve it is to return the entire shipment to your factory or warehouse and start over again. The carrier holding your shipment has no way of knowing which carton is to be marked with which department number or order number. And even if that could be determined, how many carriers would be cooperative enough to do that much extra work for you?

7. In a multiple store shipment, you did not prepare separate packing slips or separate invoices for each store. If your customer's terms clearly require individual packing slips or invoices for each of his stores, and each store is to be packed separately, your packing, shipping, and billing departments will have to do as asked. Your customer wants each store shipment properly segregrated and identified, for his convenience, not yours.

8. And finally we have the demand that *gum tape must not have printing of any kind*. In other words, the shipper's name and/or address must appear neither on the gum tape nor on the carton itself. While this request is relatively rare, it may one day receive wide circulation, as did new store allowances.

Your shipping department will have to comply, or else, as one recent form letter put it, "Failure to do so will be grounds for us to refuse delivery of the merchandise."

On occasion, your customer will refuse a shipment in error. If you can prove that, you shouldn't have any difficulty convincing him to accept redelivery—and he will probably even accept the resulting additional charges.

The important point to remember in all refused shipments is the time element. When you receive a notice of refusal from the carrier (which should tell you why the shipment was refused—Shipped too late, or No invoice, etc.), don't waste time, do whatever you have to do to get the goods reshipped or recalled, and do it without delay. Merchandise sitting in someone's terminal doesn't do anyone any good.

If a lapsed cancellation date is involved, ask your sales department (or the salesman himself, if he can be reached) to request an extension of the cancellation. Sometimes your customer will listen to reason, and if it's at all feasible, he'll accept the merchandise. Perhaps he won't, so an outright refusal means that the goods will have to come back to you, but it's worth the try.

As for redelivery and storage charges, don't argue about them, even if the fault lies with your customer. Get the goods delivered, and worry about responsibility for the charges later. Even with ever increasing freight rates, redelivery and storage charges should not be large enough to jeopardize the value of your merchandise; if you leave it sitting in the terminal too long, it can be the victim of twin vandalism—pilferage and deterioration (not to mention obsolescence, if seasonal goods are involved).

Pilferage, unfortunately, has become a part of the normal routine for the average credit manager. Until such time as a foolproof system can be devised, the problems of pilferage and lost shipments will face the credit manager constantly. He can't avoid them, so he has to know how to handle them. Both are more fully discussed in the following chapter.

8
Deductions and Chargebacks

Nine general areas of deductions and chargebacks
    Discounts
    Anticipation
    Allowances
    Violation of customer's instructions
    Freight chargebacks
    Shortage claims
    Pilferage or damage
    Non-delivery
    Returns
Discounts
    Cutoff date for cash discounts
    Unearned discounts
Anticipation
    Definition repeated and illustrated
    Time differentials
    Anticipation on extra dating
    Rate of anticipation
Allowances
    How to verify

Violation of customer's instructions
    Multiplicity of instructions
    List of violations
    High cost of violations
    Service charges
Freight chargebacks
    Violating customer's instructions
    List of possible violations
    Illustration of possible violation
    Responsibility for freight chargebacks
    Charging entire cost of shipping
        to the vendor
    Detention charges
Shortage claims
    Possible defense against shortage claims
    Verification of shortages
    Inspection system
Pilferage or damage
    Free and clear bill of lading
    Result of bill of lading incorrectly signed
    Burden of filing claim upon the shipper
Non-delivery
    Filing a claim
    Letter requesting proof of delivery
    The formal claim
    Parcel post losses
    Private transit insurance
Returns
    Authorized and unauthorized
    Responsibility for charges

After the credit manager has processed his orders, including those from his marginal and troublesome accounts and those he may have temporarily set aside for more information, he next turns his attention to the checks he has received. Perhaps, under the procedures his company is using, he doesn't actually see or handle the checks that have come in. But, by necessity, he must be interested in the invoices being paid and in possible deductions and chargebacks.

He must determine whether these chargebacks are legitimate or authorized and who should bear the responsibility for them. There are nine general areas he must give his attention to:

1. Discounts
2. Anticipation
3. Allowances
4. Violation of customer's instructions
5. Freight chargebacks
6. Shortage claims
7. Pilferage or damage
8. Non-delivery
9. Returns

Discounts

In this category, the first point to be decided is whether the discount is trade or cash. If it's customary within your industry to allow a certain percentage to be deducted from your invoice regardless of date paid, or days slow, this is presumed to be a trade discount. If, however, a time limitation has been placed upon the deductible percentage, we then come to one of the major headaches for a credit manager.

As an assumption, we will set your particular terms at 2/10 EOM, Net 60. You have therefore allowed your customer until the 10th day after the end of the calendar month to take his 2%. If he doesn't pay his bill by that date, he can still pay it within 60 days of the date of shipment before you will mark him past due, although he must now pay Net.

But here's one of the trouble spots—what is the exact cutoff for 2/10 EOM? Is it actually the 10th day of the calendar month? Or will you consider another day, or two days, or three, or a full week, or two weeks, as still falling within your specified EOM terms? Speaking realistically, most credit managers look upon a payment 10 to 15 days after the 10th as being current.

And what about your major customer who has everything on computers and insists that it is impossible, because of the necessity of feeding the right information into these computers, matching receiving records, and so forth, to process any payments by the 10th of each month?

In the first instance, if a customer is late a few days, do you penalize him by not allowing the discount? And do you also penalize your major account who *never* pays on time? Or do you look the other way in both cases?

The same thinking applies to all cash discounts, whether they be based upon EOM or date of shipment. If your terms are 2/10 Net 30, do you refuse to allow the 2% discount if your customer's check arrives, not on the 10th day after shipment, but upon the 12th or 13th?

There can also be times when your customer waits the full 30 or 60 days and still takes his discount. What then?

You can return the check and advise him politely but firmly of the correct terms. If he's a small account who needs your goods badly, he'll probably send you a corrected check, or an additional check along with his original. But you'll have to be careful. Taking an unearned discount is an old trick; your customer may feel fairly certain you'll send his check back, and that will give him another week, or two, or three, to hang on to his cash and to delay paying your bill. It's also possible he wants you to return his check because he simply doesn't have enough money to cover it.

Another trick you should be aware of is the unsigned check. The signature may not have been deliberately overlooked, but too often it is.

A larger customer can be more of a headache for the credit manager, because someone (most likely on a supervisory level) may have "forgotten" to program into the company computer your proper terms—the net half has been omitted. Checks come through from this account with the discount always deducted, no matter when the invoice is paid, or how late.

By the time you get everything straightened out and your customer's accounts payable department understands what your terms are, months may have gone by, and the unearned discounts keep piling up. And at this point, someone else "forgets" to authorize repayment.

In the meanwhile, do you ship or hold all orders?

Since this is probably a major account, you'll ship, unless your company decides it no longer needs a customer like that. When that happens, you may still have to carry the unearned discounts on your books, and end up threatening suit. Either way, you won't enjoy it.

The problem of handling unearned discounts will, in the end, be determined by the general course followed by the rest of your industry. A strict industry program of enforcing the cash discount to the day and not beyond it of course strengthens your own hand. But if there appears to be no definite approach to the problem within your own industry, the question will reduce itself to one single point—your company policy.

With a liberal policy, you may not mind at all that your customer's discount has been taken a few days late, or a week or so late. But don't let him think that he can use the entire Net period and still deduct his discount. Let him know, as often as is necessary, exactly what your terms are and why he cannot take his discount after the allowable period has passed.

If your company prefers to be more conservative, then begin to bear down upon offenders much more quickly. In all cases, make your point firmly, but tactfully, until your customers get the idea. If there is a major accounts payable department involved, write your letter to the supervisor. Try to get his name if you can, for a personally addressed letter will carry much more weight than one simply saying, Attention: Supervisor Accounts Payable.

You and your company alone must decide when the discount period must absolutely end. Whether you prefer to be conservative or liberal, never let unearned discounts get out of hand. A too liberal policy extended to one favored customer at the expense of others will inevitably lead to a similar extension to more and more of your customers—not to mention that, in the interim, you are probably violating the Robinson-Patman Act.

When unearned discounts have been taken, you can either return the check to your customer and request him to correct it, or you can deposit the check and charge him back. In some cases, it may be more advantageous actually to send an invoice for the unearned discount. An open and unpaid invoice cannot be ignored as readily as can a statement of unauthorized deductions or a letter.

All of the foregoing applies equally, of course, to Net terms, although your problem is simplified. There is no grace period to consider. If a discount has been taken, at any time, return the check at once. But you may have customers who will deliberately take a discount they know they're not entitled to, and then mail in their payment a month or two late, hoping you will either allow the discount simply because the payment *is* late, or deposit the check for the same reason. If you then bill them for the unauthorized discount, they may take their time in repaying it.

You may encounter another type of unearned discount that is beginning to surface. One of your customers has purchased $5,000 worth of your merchandise on terms of, let us say, 8/10 EOM. He therefore owes you $4,600–$5,000 less $400 eight percent discount. But he decides that he has to return a sizable part of your shipment. So he sends back $2,000 worth of your merchandise. (If you have a strict policy against returns, this problem may not apply to you, since your customer will have to prove, to your satisfaction, that his return is justified.)

But assume, for the sake of illustration, that you have agreed to accept this return. When you receive your customer's check, you find that not only is he taking his eight percent discount for the full $5,000, he is then charging you *net* for the returned merchandise; actually, he should have reversed the discount for the return, and only charged you $2,000 less eight percent discount of $160, or $1,840, not the full $2,000 he did take.

Was this an oversight on your customer's part? Also, did he deliberately overbuy so that he would have to return merchandise to you? Since you can't possibly answer either of these questions, the only course for you is to assume innocence on his part, and either return the check with a politely worded request for the proper amount, or deposit his check, and ask him to send you an additional check for the $160 improperly deducted.

However you handle it, this kind of unearned discount should be vigorously disputed, since it is so obviously exactly what it says—unearned.

Anticipation

Generally, anticipation will not be spelled out in the terms of sale. Some vendors do take the trouble to state, on their order form or their invoice, that no anticipation is permitted, but most vendors do not. If you do not so indicate, your customer will take it for granted that you will allow it.

In Chapter 2, we gave the following definition of anticipation:

> Like the cash discount, a reward for prompt payment, although in this case, ahead of due date. In other words, you are permitting your customer to anticipate the date his invoice is to be paid. Anticipation is based upon the annual interest rate paid for commercial loans and is allowed only for each day ahead of the due date that payment is made.

The above can be simply illustrated:

Your normal terms are Net 10 EOM. You ship on the 15th of July; payment is due on August 10th. Your customer decides to anticipate, and mails you a check dated July 21st. He takes anticipation of 19 days—10 days remaining in July and the first nine days of August.

But supposing you don't receive that check until July 28, only 12 days before the date it was due? Should you still permit the full 19 days? The amount may be small, perhaps only pennies, and even larger differences may not be worth your time and trouble to dispute.

Your circumstances alone should determine whether you will accept the check as written. Your company may need the money at that point and perhaps would rather not go to the bank, or it may have drawn to the limit of its line. So even though the rate of anticipation may be higher than the rate of interest your company would have to pay to borrow a similar amount, it may be more beneficial at that particular moment to allow the excess anticipation.

Also, keep in mind the time involved for your customer to process the payment and mail it to you. This could well make a difference of a few days and would

Deductions and Chargebacks

therefore have to enter into your decision. But remember too that once you establish a liberal policy towards anticipation you may have trouble changing it in the future.

There is one area of anticipation, though, where you ought to say no at all times. If your customer requests extra dating and then anticipates that extra dating, don't hesitate—send his check back at once.

You have given him extra dating as an accommodation only, not as a device to make an unearned discount (which is what that kind of anticipation is). Do not, under any circumstances, permit anticipation on extensions beyond your normal terms.

Another possibility for misunderstanding, and difficulty for you, can involve the *rate* of anticipation. For years, when commercial interest was stabilized at 6% per annum, anticipation was pegged at the same rate (it came to ½% per month). But once the economy fluctuates so do the rates of interest, and anticipation not only follows suit, it sometimes goes beyond, even reaching an astronomical high of 20% in the spring of 1980. But unlike the commercial rates, anticipation is far slower in coming down.

Here, too, the decision on the allowable rate of anticipation must come from your company alone. Don't permit it to go beyond your control; base it as closely as you can on the commercial rate currently in use.

If you receive a check with too much anticipation taken, or if you don't permit anticipation at all, always return the check. The whole point of anticipation is to make money on money. Once you deposit your customer's funds, he no longer has the use of them. Charging him back for excess anticipation isn't good enough; he wants his money back so he can use it elsewhere.

When you return such a check, make your point clearly:

1. You do not permit anticipation at any time, from anyone; or

2. You do not permit anticipation at the rate deducted; or
3. You do not permit anticipation on extra dating

A customer on ROG terms may require special handling. If he insists on ROG, he should not anticipate, as he should not anticipate on extra dating.

Allowances

The only problem you should encounter with allowances may result from your own internal procedures, not your customer's. Every permissible allowance should be indicated somewhere on your records so that verification becomes a simple matter. The best place to show them would be on your ledger, posted against your customer's invoice, so that in each case, you can tell immediately whether he is correct in taking a particular allowance.

Your system may not allow that kind of posting. You would then have to check the deduction against your customer's order to see whether it's justified, and whether the amount is correct; don't take his word alone.

If his order doesn't show anything, go one step further and check it out with your sales department. An allowance may have been permitted after the order was processed, and the sales department may have neglected to advise you.

You should also devise a method whereby you can avoid allowances being taken twice. For example, where a new store allowance is involved, it should be taken only against the opening order for that store, or only in a specific amount, and then only once. But watch out for back orders, any balances left against the opening order still entitles your customer to his prorated portion of his entire allowance, even though other orders may have been processed and shipped before that back order has been completed.

Violating customer's instructions

Despite your vigilance and your constant monitoring of your customer's terms, inevitably you or your factory (or your shipping and/or billing department) will violate a customer's instructions. The result can be a sizable chargeback that is unsettling and palpably unfair, yet must be permitted because you had accepted the customer's order *and* his terms. The instruction itself may be impossible to satisfy—at least under your particular operation. But if you don't advise your customer that you cannot fulfill a certain instruction—and wait for his acknowledgement—the responsibility becomes yours, and your customer will undoubtedly charge you for violation of that instruction.

It may be that, as a matter of policy, your company objects to the entire principle of penalties for violations, and perhaps you're in a strong enough position to reject such penalties. Many suppliers, unfortunately, are not that strong, and must accept the customer's position, no matter how galling it may be.

Even more exasperating is the multiplicity of instructions many major retailers now force upon you. Here is a partial listing from a California company, which carefully points out that its deductions "will be made for but not *limited to* (author's emphasis) the following violations":

1. Failure to show department number, order number or number of cartons on every package label, invoice, duplicate invoice, packing slip and bill of lading.

2. Failure to indicate product description on invoice or to list styles by color and size on invoice.

3. Invoicing more than one department per invoice.

4. Showing more than one purchase order per invoice.

5. Shipping merchandise in excess of the quantity ordered.

6. Shipping merchandise prior to specified ship date.

7. Shipping merchandise subsequent to cancellation date.

8. Splitting shipments without buyer's approval.

And so on. There are more, many more requirements this customer imposes upon you (violations of freight instructions will be explained in the section that follows—"Freight chargebacks"). If you want to work with this account, you must conform with this long list of instructions or accept as much as 5% of the invoice total as a chargeback, with a minimum of $25.00 for each violation.

Is this customer trying to take advantage of you? Not according to them, as they explain in their "Chargeback Policy Purpose":

"The purpose of this chargeback policy is not to effect an increase from our sources, but rather to offset any actual and/or administrative expense caused by our shippers' failure to implement instructions outlined in this Guide. The major objective of this policy is to stimulate resource management's attention in correcting the violations outlined."

Maybe so. The net result, however, can be very profitable for this customer; 5% of your invoice total can add up to a large sum. And because there are so many instructions, inevitably one or more will be violated; but such instructions *can* be followed—once you and your packing, shipping, and billing departments realize these instructions are to be part of your normal, day-to-day procedures. In time they will seem routine, as previous instructions and customer requirements have become routine.

Freight chargebacks

In this area, it may sometimes seem to you that freight chargebacks are just as unfair as others, but you will find they aren't always unwarranted. Your shipping department may have violated your customer's instructions, contained either in a violation guide similar to the one described in the previous section or in a separate traffic guide. Or, in processing the order, you yourself may have inadvertently overlooked shipping terms that do not agree with yours.

Your California customer, for example, includes these as some of the freight violations you may incur:

1. Failure to observe consolidation instructions, namely failure to combine all orders for the same destination on one bill of lading.

2. Using carriers not authorized by the Routing Guide.

3. Failure to indicate department and order numbers in the body of the bill of lading.

4. Failure to show on the bill of lading released value or density (where required by carrier classification).

5. Failure to observe the "ship to" location indicated on the purchase order.

6. Deviating from Standard Routing Guide without prior approval from the Traffic Department.

With this lengthy list of "don't's" facing you, plus many more that other customers force upon you, you can take nothing for granted. A situation may arise that you may be unprepared for, simply because you've never had problems with this account before. Suddenly, you do have a problem, as in the following example:

Your customer has hired a new and ambitious traffic manager who wants to justify his salary and his position; he issues a revised Routing Guide, containing all the violations we have just listed. They are, of course, far more restrictive than the regulations your shipping department has been using for this customer. Their new traffic manager later insists that a copy of his revised guide was sent to your factory or warehouse.

But your shipping department never did receive this new guide. What happens then?

Supposing all your orders from this customer (who happens to be one of your major accounts) now bear a notation, in fine print, added after the new traffic manager assumed his job, that shipments must conform to the specifications spelled out in his revised guide. Your company has been dealing with this customer for years and has never experienced trouble before. As for the fine print, you never bothered to read it; there was no need to.

This time there was. If the customer now charges back for a violation of its instructions, can you refuse to honor it?

You can try of course; perhaps you can even appeal to your customer's buyer or merchandising manager. If you've been dealing with them long enough, they may be sympathetic and try to help. Or they may not, with the excuse that traffic problems are out of their hands, as they may at that point very well be. It's probable that the change of traffic managers was prompted by a change of corporate policy; rigidity at all levels is now the byword.

In that case, what do you do?

You have three choices:

1. Leave the chargeback open on your books and continue to press for payment, with the knowledge that in the end you'll have to wipe it out.

2. Disallow the chargeback and advise the customer you will no longer ship until he repays. If this is the course you choose, you and your company would be allowing spite to stand in the way of good business sense.

3. Allow the chargeback and vow to be more vigilant in the future.

If you make the third choice, you are demonstrating prudence and a sound credit practice. Emotion and anger may serve as a safety valve for your growing frustration, but they won't sell merchandise, and the function of the credit department is to facilitate the sale and movement of your company's product.

Freight chargebacks, therefore, must be analyzed for responsibility and adherence to terms. You must determine, first of all, if you or your shipping department violated your customer's instructions, whether contained in a traffic guide or on a specific order. If the fault is demonstrably not yours, do not accept the chargeback, no matter how small. One unjustified chargeback can lead to others, and probably will. Some of your accounts may require constant reminders of your terms.

On the other hand, even an inadvertent acceptance of terms entirely contrary to yours will often make it difficult, if not impossible, to reverse a chargeback that you may consider thoroughly unjustified. Examine all the circumstances and try to decide, from your previous experience with a particular account, whether it pays for you to dispute a freight chargeback that originally resulted from your own carelessness. It may not pay at all, but at the least it will alert you to be more watchful in the future.

A new device gaining wide momentum is the *service charge* for failure to follow instructions. The excuse here is that such failure to follow instructions results in additional expense to your customer because of the excessive cost of processing extra documentation.

This is a debatable point. And even more questionable are the amounts being charged. In one recent instance, a supplier was charged $50.00 for failure to include a packing slip with the shipment. The credit manager successfully fought this service charge, but only after many letters between him and his customer.

One of the more common reasons now being cited for the issuance of a service charge is shipping Collect when the order or traffic guide specifies Prepaid. Or shipping directly to the ultimate consignee rather than to a consolidator or central warehousing point. This one, in particular, can be galling, for the direct shipment may have been cheaper.

Nor is the service charge the only questionable freight chargeback; there is another device, which consists of billing the shipper, under Collect terms, for the *entire cost* of a shipment if instructions are violated.

Here is an example. A shipment moving out of New York to California should have been transferred, under the customer's instructions, to XYZ Transportation Company. Instead, your shipping department routed the merchandise to ABC Motor Transit. Your customer claims that shipment via XYZ would have meant a saving to him of 20%. If that is so, then he should only bill you for that 20% and accept the 80% it would normally have cost him. But he doesn't. He bills you for the entire 100%, and ends up moving his merchandise across the country for free.

If it's possible, don't accept the entire cost. The violation should be prorated, and only that portion resulting in excess costs to the consignee should be charged back to the shipper. However, there may be a problem here. You may have received, and signed for, a traffic guide very much like the one described earlier. This traffic guide undoubtedly warns that you will be charged the entire cost of moving the customer's freight in the event of violation. If that's the case, you will have no choice but to accept all of the chargebacks, and probably an additional service or handling charge.

As if the service charge were not bad enough, we now have a "detention charge." This too may gain wide circulation, but in this instance, the charge is initiated by your carrier, not by your customer. But your customer nevertheless passes the charges on to you, even though you have absolutely nothing to do with the violation.

What is happening is that too much freight is being brought in to some receiving departments, which are not properly equipped to handle the vast amount of merchandise truckers and other carriers offer for delivery. One result can be lengthy waiting time for some of the drivers. This can happen even when the carrier has been given an appointment as required by the receiving department. With labor costs constantly rising to keep pace with inflation, common carriers no longer are willing to absorb this expensive waiting time. They therefore charge the consignee "detention charges," and the consignee, your customer, passes the charges on to you.

And how much can these detention charges amount to? Quite a lot. In one example, the carrier's driver waited a total of 8-3/4 quarter hours—despite an appointment. The carrier permitted a waiting time of two and a quarter hours without charge, but billed the balance of 6½ hours at a rate of $7.33 for every 15 minutes, for a total of $190.58. To add insult to injury, the customer tacked on its own service charge of $40.

Both the detention and service charges were ultimately voided by the customer, after a process that involved much discussion and correspondence among the supplier's credit manager, the supplier's salesman, the customer's buyer, merchandising manager, accounts payable department, traffic department, and receiving department.

Obviously, in this instance, the customer's system was at fault, not the supplier's. But because of the vastness of the customer's organization, reversal of an admittedly unfair chargeback wasted much valuable time for the credit manager. And, needless to say, the credit manager could not send his own service charge to his customer, much as he would have liked to. The customer was far too important, and would have ignored the service charge in any event.

So here is one more chargeback you may encounter, and one more chargeback to reject, and to reject forcefully.

Shortage claims

If your company has not established a double check and provable procedure for guarding against undershipping, shortage claims can be hard to deny. A debit for a hidden shortage may not, in your view, be justified, but unless you can absolutely prove that all merchandise was shipped as billed, you may find yourself pursuing a fruitless course if you press for a reversal of the charge.

One defense is the shipping weight. Your bill of lading or manifest will indicate the total weight of your shipment; you can determine the weight of each unit, multiply by the total units shipped, add the necessary poundage for the shipping containers, and if your total weight matches that shown on the bill of lading, you have grounds for disputing a claimed shortage.

But make certain your shipping department doesn't just estimate the weight of each shipment, rather than actually weighing it. Very few truckers reweigh each individual shipment; they accept the vendor's version, for they know he may be over on some shipments and under on others, so that in the end their revenue is balanced.

A few shortage claims will bear the notation that they have been verified by two people (perhaps the second one is the manager himself). Claims like these are particularly hard to dispute, for your customer has made certain in advance that his chargebacks cannot be disproven and must therefore be honored.

If most of your shortage claims are minor, it may not be worthwhile for your organization to establish an expensive method of double checking each shipment. Over a long period, the cost of allowing small claims may be far less than the expenditure of setting up and maintaining an inspection system.

But watch out for repeaters. Too frequent shortage claims from the same customer should be thoroughly investigated.

Pilferage or damage

Where pilferage is being claimed, or damage to your merchandise while it was in transit, your customer has to make certain that the claimed pilfering is obviously the fault of the carrier and not a hidden shortage. The same is true for damage to your goods. Your customer's receiving department will have to indicate on the carrier's delivery receipt that certain cartons were received in a damaged or tampered condition. It is also a good idea for him to segregate these cartons until the carrier's representative has a chance to examine the contents and verify the extent of the pilferage or impairment to your merchandise.

A delivery receipt signed free and clear, without exception, absolves the carrier completely, even though the entire shipment has been glaringly rifled. Once the consignee accepts the shipment without protest, the burden of loss is placed squarely upon the shipper or the consignee, no matter how obvious it may be that the carrier was responsible.

In a recent incident, a New York manufacturer shipped some $5,000 worth of merchandise to one of his customers in the Midwest. The receiving clerk, as it happened, was new on the job, and no one had thought to advise him on the possibility of receiving merchandise in tampered cartons. Some of the cartons had indeed been tampered with, but because of his inexperience, he signed a free and clear delivery receipt. Actually, all he did was to sign for the shipment without noting any exceptions; in effect, he was admitting that the shipment had arrived in perfect condition.

It was shortly discovered that about $450 in merchandise had been pilfered while the merchandise was en route. The customer promptly charged the supplier for the loss, and the supplier just as promptly rejected it. He was sympathetic, but when he learned that no exception had been noted on the delivery receipt by the novice receiving clerk, he realized his hands were tied and no provable claim against the responsible carrier was possible.

The customer was outraged by the supplier's refusal to accept a loss that was manifestly the consignee's responsibility. The customer immediately canceled all remaining orders and has not since then reordered.

At this moment it would appear as if the supplier has lost this account for good. Was it worth it? Should the supplier, solely in the interest of good will, have absorbed the $450 loss?

He did not think so. He was prepared to lose a customer rather than sacrifice two basic principles: *(a)* the shipper was not responsible for the loss in any measure at all; and *(b)* under his terms of FOB Shipping Point, even if a claim against the trucker had been possible, the burden for filing that claim should have been the consignee's.

While an incident of this type is rare, it points up the need for exercising the greatest care in the reporting of lost, damaged, or pilfered merchandise. If this sort of thing happens to a customer of yours, only you and your organization can decide how to handle his claim. You cannot rely upon custom, for it doesn't take place often enough to establish a tradition.

But pilferage itself does happen frequently, or damage to your merchandise, either from rough handling or from the weather. And in most cases, delivery receipts are so noted. If your customer then leaves it to you to seek restitution, you'll have little choice except to file the claim. At least, with the exception properly indicated on the delivery receipt, you'll have proof on your side.

Where the pilferage or damage is clearly the fault of a particular carrier, you will eventually be reimbursed for the loss, but the entire process can be time consuming and can, coincidentally, tie up your money. This is especially true when the carrier is self-insured—some carriers have had so many thefts they cannot get insurance, or else the premiums are prohibitive. A self-insured trucker won't be in a hurry to pay you for a pilfered or damaged shipment, and you may have to keep after him.

Passing the buck to the consignee, since, as we have already demonstrated, the merchandise really belonged to him, won't do any good at all once he refuses to pay you. You can try suing him, and maybe you'll win your suit, but you'll most certainly lose the customer.

Non-delivery

Many of these same points apply equally in instances of partial non-delivery, that is, when a portion of the shipment is offered for delivery, with the balance lost or stolen en route. As long as the consignee signs only for what he actually receives, claim can then be filed against the responsible carrier for the missing part. But if, as in the example of the novice receiving clerk described in the previous section, the entire shipment is signed for without exception, then no claim can be made against the carrier.

When one of your customers reports a non-delivery, either in part or in whole, he will unquestionably ask you to provide proof of delivery. Many consignees will not take it upon themselves to file a claim against the carrier but expect their shippers to do the job for them.

Sometimes a partial non-delivery is not a non-delivery at all. A portion of your shipment may have been misplaced by the carrier, which delivers to your customer the part it does have. The rest of the shipment may appear to have been lost, and your customer signs only for the merchandise it receives at the initial delivery. Your customer then charges you for the merchandise it did not receive. But this missing merchandise is later found by the carrier and delivered to your customer on a free and astray—a delivery receipt that says exactly what it sounds like—some merchandise has gone astray but is ultimately delivered to the consignee without charge.

Should you therefore wait before filing a claim for a partial non-delivery?

No, do not wait. The missing merchandise may actually be lost (sometimes it's been stolen, either from the carrier's truck, or from his warehouse). If the merchandise *is* ultimately delivered, you'll be so advised by the carrier, which will send you a copy of its signed free and astray to prove final delivery. By this time your customer is probably aware that all of your shipment has been received, but neglects to let you know, and neglects to reverse its original chargeback. Perhaps the neglect is deliberate, perhaps an oversight. In any event, with the signed free and astray you can now ask for payment in full.

When requesting proof of delivery from a carrier for a complete non-delivery, you can use one of two methods:

1. Ask him to supply proof of delivery without actually filing a claim against him for the loss.

2. Skip this first step and *file* the claim.

Your choice of method will be dictated by certain factors, notably the time lapse, and the attitude of the carriers involved. Under the tariff regulations established by the Interstate Commerce Commission, you have exactly nine months from the date of shipment, and not one day beyond that, to file a claim against the carrier. If the shipment moved via parcel post, you have twelve months to file a claim for *insured* parcel post, and no time limit for *ordinary* or uninsured parcel post.

Don't bother with step number one if you have a partial non-delivery. Even though you may eventually be supplied with final delivery by way of your carrier's free and astray, you have no way of knowing that your merchandise has only been misplaced, not irrevocably lost. What you do have is a notice from your customer that he did not receive part of your shipment, and he's charging that part back to you, which means he will pay only for the merchandise he did receive.

Give your customer the benefit of the doubt. Accept his word of partial loss; do not assume that final delivery will eventually be made on a free and astray. But be careful that your customer is correctly reporting his loss. Has he in fact received the same number of cartons you shipped? If so, it's not a partial non-delivery, but a hidden shortage—or a miscount by your customer's receiving department.

Another point to bear in mind is a growing tendency among carriers to levy their own form of service charge for each proof of delivery they are asked to supply. Deplorably, too many accounts make a habit of asking for proof of delivery for all skipped invoices, no matter how many there may be. This is especially true of the large retail chains; their accounts payable departments are either swamped with paperwork or are staffed with inefficient personnel who find it easier to place the burden upon the shipper rather than making their own attempt to match up records that have been misfiled or improperly processed. It's much easier to say to the vendor, "We have no record of receiving the merchandise on invoice so and so. Please send proof of delivery."

But some carriers are beginning to balk. Such promiscuous requests for proof of delivery place an ever-increasing load upon their own staffs, for in almost every instance the merchandise was indeed delivered and properly signed for. If a service charge for each such request becomes commonplace, perhaps the larger offenders will learn to improve their own paperwork.

Some of these same carriers, however, do not object to the simpler request indicated above, asking for proof of delivery without filing a claim. If they don't have to process a full claim, which goes through many more steps, they don't seem to mind as much.

In this simpler method, you can use a form letter that can be run through your copying machine from a master. Inasmuch as you won't know where the loss of your merchandise occurred if more than one trucker has been used, you will have to send your letter to the first carrier, and let him forward it to anyone else responsible.

Your form letter should be addressed to the Tracing Department. List your invoice number for your own control, and then say something like the following:

[Date]

Please furnish proof of delivery for the following shipment:

Consigned to:

Date shipped:
No. of cartons:
B/L# [or B/L date]:
Weight:

A copy of the original bill of lading is enclosed.

Deductions and Chargebacks

If we do not receive the requested proof of delivery within three weeks from the date of this letter [or whatever time limit you choose to impose], we will assume that you are unable to prove delivery, and we will, therefore, file a formal claim for the full amount of the loss.

The final paragraph is most important; your notice of intent to file your claim stays the nine month statute of limitations, so that if for some reason you fail to file within the required period, your claim will still be valid after the nine months have elapsed. It won't matter that you don't file within three weeks of the date you mailed your form letter. Actually what you're saying is that the carrier is to prove delivery within three weeks, or you will then file your claim. You have stated your *intent to file claim*, not the date you expect to file it.

(A note of caution: be sure to include the dollar amount in this notice. You can do that by inserting, at the head of your form, an invoice number—or claim number—followed by the dollar amount. Some courts have refused to recognize a simple intent to file a claim without such dollar amount. If you're not sure how the courts in your jurisdiction will act, it may be best to check with your attorney.)

This form letter is particularly useful for those carriers who have given you prompt replies in the past. There is very little information for you to fill in, since you're using a form that already has most of your message, and you can make a copy for your files on your copying machine. Your cooperative carriers can attach their proof of delivery to your letter without writing one of their own and return everything to you. (You can add a line to your form letter advising the carrier to answer that way if he likes.)

But don't use this simplified method with carriers who take much too long to answer, or if your customer's notice of non-receipt is more than four or five months from the date of the original shipment. Some of your accounts may have procedures that take far too long for them to decide that your merchandise has not been received.

If your letter is not answered, or if you decide to file a claim right away, there is a standard form you can use for filing your claims (see Figure 4).

With a standard form of this kind, many carriers do not require original documents, but they do want a certified copy of your invoice and the bill of lading. The certification is simply a line typed across a copy of your document.

"I certify this invoice [or bill of lading] to be true and correct." Below that will appear your title and signature. You needn't have them witnessed, or signed by a notary public.

You also need some evidence that the customer has requested proof of delivery, such as his advice of non-receipt, or a chargeback for the missing merchandise, usually accompanied by a debit memo (a copy of that can be included with your claim).

Some carriers want a document of indemnification to protect them against a possible duplicate claim; the consignee may decide that he ought to file a claim as well and may present the original paid freight bill to support his own claim. (Under Collect shipping terms, the consignee has the freight bill, so that's one document you will not be able to produce.) This indemnity agreement is also a standard form and can be ordered along with the one illustrated.

For a parcel post loss, there are two other forms you have to use, both of which the Postal Service supplies free of charge.

For *ordinary, or uninsured,* parcel post, use Form 1510, which requests the Postal Service to institute a trace on the missing merchandise. The form is forwarded to the consignee, who then indicates whether he has received the shipment. Since ordinary parcel post does not require a

General Order No. 41   P. DF. D.G. D.G.

STANDARD FORM FOR PRESENTATION OF LOSS OR DAMAGE CLAIMS

Approved by
THE INTERSTATE COMMERCE COMMISSION
THE NATIONAL INDUSTRIAL TRAFFIC LEAGUE
THE FREIGHT CLAIM ASSOCIATION

....
(Address of Claimant)

....
(Date)

Claimant's Number §

....
(Name of person to whom claim is presented)
(Name of carrier) ....

(Carrier's Number)

(Address) ....

This claim for $............ is made against the carrier named above by (Name of claimant) ....

.... for (Loss or damage) .... in connection with the following described shipment:

Description of shipment..
Name and address of consignor (shipper)................................
Shipped from (City, town or station)............., To (City, town or station)..............
Final destination (City, town or station)............ Routed via................
Bill of Lading issued by..................................Co.; Date of Bill of Lading............
Paid Freight Bill (Pro) Number.................. Original Car number and Initial............
Name and address of consignee (to whom shipped)................................
If shipment reconsigned enroute, state particulars:................

DETAILED STATEMENT SHOWING HOW AMOUNT CLAIMED IS DETERMINED
(Number and description of articles, nature and extent of loss or damage, invoice price of articles, amount of claim, etc.)

Total Amount Claimed

**IN ADDITION TO THE INFORMATION GIVEN ABOVE, THE FOLLOWING DOCUMENTS
ARE SUBMITTED IN SUPPORT OF THIS CLAIM.***

( ) 1. Original bill of lading, if not previously surrendered to carrier.
( ) 2. Original paid freight ("Expense") bill.
( ) 3. Original invoice or certified copy.
   4. Other particulars obtainable in proof of loss or damage claimed.
....
....

Remarks:..
....
....

The foregoing statement of facts is hereby certified to as correct.

....
(Signature of claimant)

§ Claimant should assign to each claim a number, inserting same in the space provided at the upper right hand corner of this form. Reference should be made thereto in all correspondence pertaining to this claim.
* Claimant will please check (x) before such of the documents mentioned as have been attached, and explain under "Remarks" the absence of any of the documents called for in connection with this claim. When for any reason it is impossible for claimant to produce original bill of lading, if required, or paid freight bill, claimant should indemnify† carrier or carriers against duplicate claim supported by original documents.

† Indemnity agreement for lost bill of lading. Form 71, Unz & Co.

Figure 4

signature for delivery, you will have only the consignee's word that he did not receive your merchandise. The Postal Service bears no responsibility; the burden of the loss is the shipper's or the consignee's.

For *insured* parcel post, use Form 3812, which combines a request to institute a trace together with a formal claim against the Postal Service for the amount insured (because of the excessive cost of private insurance, your parcel post shipments should be insured for their full amount). Insured parcel post requires a signature from the consignee or his agent; this method, therefore, protects both the shipper and the Postal Service against fraudulent claims of non-delivery. If the Postal Service cannot prove delivery by way of the consignee's signature, it will make restitution for the loss, usually within a matter of weeks.

For parcel shipments out of the country, use form 542, which is an inclusive form covering several types of mail—registered article, insured parcel, or ordinary parcel. You have the same time limitation as with domestic insured parcel post, twelve months from date of shipment, to make a claim for a foreign shipment.

As for private transit insurance, it will provide almost no coverage at all for your smaller shipments; the deductible portion is prohibitively large—in other words, the shipper must bear the cost of the first $100, or $200, or $500, and so on. If you make many small shipments in these ranges, this type of insurance can do nothing for you; full parcel post insurance, or declaring the total value of your UPS shipments (which necessitates paying a little more for this protection) offers much better coverage. The cost of the insurance can be added to your invoice; most of your customers will pay it without protest. A few may not, but the total annual expense to you will be minimal, even when you have to pay some of it yourself.

In one sense, private transit insurance should not be necessary for the shipper who moves all his merchandise on Collect terms. Once he loads his goods Free on Board a common carrier, the carrier is then responsible. Any loss or damage that occurs in transit will have to be paid by the carrier or his insurance company.

Transit insurance for the shipper does have one benefit that may be attractive to you. When the shipments are large enough, you can file a simultaneous claim with your insurance company; if, for some reason, the carrier or his insurance company won't make restitution, your insurance company will; it will then look to the other people for repayment. In this way, you are always certain of getting your money within a reasonable time, although the premium for this service is rather high.

If you move all or only part of your goods FOB Destination (or FOB a point removed from your factory or warehouse), you will *have* to carry private insurance, no matter how expensive, unless your annual incidence of loss has always been lower than the cost of the insurance. Or unless, like some common carriers, you can't get private coverage at all because of excessive losses.

In most cases, however, you will not need private coverage. Under an Interstate Commerce Commission regulation established in 1972, every common carrier must resolve your claim within 120 days of the date he acknowledged that claim. (Such date of acknowledgement must fall within a reasonable time. If he takes too long to acknowledge your claim, get after him, and if he still won't send you his acknowledgement despite your prodding, ask your regional ICC office for help or advice.)

This ICC regulation, 49 CFR 1005, changes the rules in favor of the claimant, although it does have one loophole that can favor the carrier, as will shortly be explained.

In prior years, a carrier could delay making restitution for a lost, damaged, or pilfered shipment for as long as he could get away with it; about the only recourse you had, if he refused to pay, or if he would not even answer your letters—which happened all too frequently—was to turn the matter over to a collection agency, or to file suit against him.

Now, under the specifications of 49 CFR 1005, the carrier has four options, any one of which he must utilize within 120 days:

(1) He can pay your claim.

(2) He can decline your claim, with appropriate reason—the claim was not filed in time, it is not his responsibility, and so on.

(3) He can offer you a settlement.

(4) Or he can explain, by the 120th day, why he is not resolving your claim, or why he cannot.

Unfortunately for the claimant—meaning you—this fourth option (the loophole previously mentioned) gives the unscrupulous carrier an opportunity to delay payment indefinitely, as under the previous system. All he has to do, once he exercises this fourth option, is to keep reporting to you every 60 days thereafter the status of your claim. If he wants to, he can simply send you a brief note, or even a form letter, advising you that he is still working on your claim, and he will let you know what he finds out, although he does not have to spell out either what he's doing about your claim, or when he expects it to be resolved.

Happily, very few carriers take advantage of this loophole. By far the vast majority use only the first three options. But if you should encounter a carrier who abuses this 60 day loophole by using it too often, get in touch with your regional ICC office. They are not legally empowered to collect your money for you, but they will do all they can to force the delinquent carrier to resolve your claim.

Returns

The problem of returns revolves, generally, around two points:

1. Will you accept a return of any kind, whether part of a shipment or the entire shipment, without prior notice, or do you insist upon authorized returns only? (Authority for the return can be a letter, a sticker, or some other form signifying your approval.)

2. Why is the return being made? Was it shipped after cancellation date? Is it a back order that your customer specifically requested you not ship? Is it defective merchandise? Or substituted merchandise? Or merchandise that does not, in the customer's opinion, measure up to the sample he was shown?

If you have a rigid policy against any unauthorized return (perhaps paralleling the course usually followed by the rest of your industry), your old customers will know about it, and your new customers can be quickly educated.

With any return, whether authorized or not, a proper assessment of responsibility must be made by the credit manager, for sometimes rather considerable shipping charges are involved, as well as service charges.

Did the customer, under the terms of his order, have the right either to refuse a shipment or to send it back? If he did, accept the return and all shipping charges as well. Ask your personnel to be more careful, and you yourself give this particular account a little extra attention. Advise your packing and shipping departments that this customer will not accept substituted merchandise, late shipments, back orders, or whatever.

If the return is neither authorized nor justified, you may have a problem on your hands. You have the right to reject the return, but this can create more trouble than it's worth.

For his part, the consignee may refuse to take it, and you will have a confused and frustrated carrier trying to give your merchandise to *someone*. In the end, there will be storage charges piling up, redelivery charges, and rapidly deteriorating merchandise.

In a case like this, what should you do? It is probably wiser to accept the return and argue about responsibility and authorization later, before the merchandise isn't worth anything to anybody.

Occasionally, returns of defective merchandise are made. Here, too, if the fault is yours, accept the return without protest. But watch out for excessive service charges.

If a single unit is being returned, the service charge frequently can be more than the unit is worth, and much more than any possible expense your customer might incur in processing the return.

By all means voice your objection to such excessive charges. Your customer has no right to establish an arbitrary fee of that kind in the same way that you would have no right to raise your prices without proper notice and acceptance.

If business is to be conducted to the mutual advantage and benefit of seller and buyer, reason and trust must be evidenced by both parties. This principle is true of all your dealings with all of your customers.

But add your own common sense to the formula. Sometimes, even if your customer is wrong, you may be better off taking the blame yourself and absorbing the cost, whatever it may be.

Prudence, like good service, never lost a customer.

9
Past Dues

The collection procedure
How to handle a new order from a delinquent account
The twelve categories of past dues
The collection intervals
    Polite reminder
    Formal appeal
    Firm demand
Using a standard printed reminder form
The statement as a past due reminder
    Possible messages on the statement
The form collection letters
    Three characteristics of the successful letter
    The six letter series
    Time spread of a series
The final notice
    Other alternatives
    The salesman
    A certified letter
    A mailgram
    A sight draft

    Telephoning the customer
    Writing to the president of a corporation
    Mailing the final notice
The last resort
    Using a collection agency
    Responsibility for collection costs
    The judgment clause
    A collection agency's free demand period
    The agency's additional steps
    Referral to an attorney
    The debtor's general denial
Interest
    Possibility of charging interest
    Debtor's failure to pay
Proof of delivery
    Relationship to past dues
    When to request a proof of delivery
    As an aid for your collection agency
Days sales outstanding (DSO)

The process of collecting past dues cannot be scientifically plotted or calculated. Too many variables come into play, variables the credit manager can never determine with any degree of accuracy. The best he can do is estimate.

He must, first of all, try to know his individual customer, and then consider this customer's pattern in relation to the economy, his previous history, his trend, and his current degree of solvency. Nor can the credit manager overlook his own competition, for frequently the fellow down the street is paid before he is. And vice versa.

Yet some kind of definite program for collections must be established and followed. Bearing in mind his company policy, the credit manager must decide exactly when an invoice becomes past due, and he must then decide on the appropriate method for effecting collection. In line with this, he will probably set up a series of letters or reminders, all of which will be mailed to the delinquent customer at predetermined intervals.

No matter what your particular procedure may be—how soon you mail your first reminder, whether it be days or even weeks after due date, or when you mail your final notice—you will never be 100% effective. You will always have those customers who consistently ignore all reminders and pay only when they're ready. And you'll have those customers who may want to pay, but don't have the cash flow to take care of you on time. And, finally, you'll have those accounts who always skip invoices, whether by intent or as a result of inefficiency.

Expect a certain percentage of frustrating disappointments in your collection campaigns. Even the most carefully designed system will have its failures, and that's just as true for the giant corporations as it is for the small vendor.

But your collection procedure should be meticulously maintained, as close as possible to a regular timetable, whether it's only 90% effective, or 80%, or less. You may not have the time to go after your continuing delinquents as you would like; perhaps if you did, some of them might improve their paying patterns. But at least let them know you are aware of their delinquency. Develop a schedule and try to stick to it as closely as you can.

Constant survey of your past dues is just as necessary for the processing of new orders as for collection purposes. In Chapter 3, we discussed the various steps you might take when confronted with a reorder from a delinquent account. To review briefly:

With a requirements or automatic account, continue to ship even though a number of invoices have not been paid. A high rated customer normally doesn't have a money problem. If he does, you'll hear about it soon enough, either through an industry group, from your credit agency, or in your trade paper. In line with this, try to make time each day to glance at a trade publication or the financial page of your newspaper.

With your average accounts, one past due invoice shouldn't be enough to hold up new orders, especially if you've been dealing with a customer for years and he's always been prompt in the past. But if a customer who has habitually ordered only once a year reorders with an invoice still open, you may want to find out why he is now past due. Unfavorable information should be enough reason to withhold his order until he sends his check.

It's possible that a well-rated account may fall into this category, that is, placing an order only once in a long period. Don't hold his reorders; payment of your invoice may have been delayed for causes not readily apparent to you.

Where a marginal account owes you money, don't ship until he pays everything that's past due. And try not to allow him terms that go beyond your normal payment periods. Sometimes, when he's been given extra dating, he'll reorder before his delayed maturity date, and you will then have to decide whether to add the amount of his new order to the total already owing but not yet due.

As a part of your daily routine, after you've checked your orders, and new payments have been applied, you may want to examine your delinquent accounts to determine the collection procedure for each. Past dues will fall into one of the following groups (you may not classify them in this way, but as you work on your own, you'll find yourself mentally segregating them in some fashion):

1. The requirements or automatic account who skips invoices.

2. The well-rated account who may have honestly overlooked your invoice.

3. The average account who may have overlooked an invoice.

4. The formerly well-rated customer who is beginning to experience difficulty.

5. The average account who is now experiencing difficulty.

6. The chronic slow payer who makes promises he never keeps.

7. The chronic slow payer who makes no promises because he never answers your letters.

8. The marginal account you've been carefully watching.

9. The marginal account you've sold for the first time.

10. The complainer who refuses to pay for any reason that he can think of.

11. The dissembler who insists he's already mailed you a check that's still sitting on his desk.

12. And any others that you yourself have encountered.

Each of these must be handled in its own way, for although every one of the dozen classifications must be included among your past dues, they are by no means similar. Nor would you employ similar collection techniques for the entire range.

You would not go after 2 and 3 in the same way that you would 6, 7, 8, and 9. And 1 would be treated much differently than 4 or 5.

Your collection program, therefore, must be flexible. It must be designed to cover all your past dues, while conforming to your company policy. First of all, does your organization expect that your customers will be reasonably prompt, or will a certain amount of leniency be extended? When is the proper time for you to begin pressing for payment? One day after an invoice becomes past due—a week—a month?

This part of your program will necessarily be affected by your terms; usually the longer the paying period, the longer the credit manager will delay his dunning process. The credit manager whose terms require payment 10 days after shipment will send his first reminder much more quickly than will the credit manager whose terms are Net 60.

If you're new in your particular industry and not yet certain of your collection intervals, discuss the question with management. Let them tell you what turnover they hope to achieve with their receivables, or what their average collection period should be. Once you've established a reasonable goal, experiment for a few months. You'll find out soon enough whether you're being too hasty or too slow.

Asking other credit managers in your industry about their collection procedures will be only partially helpful, for each credit department tends to set its own schedule. You can get a general idea, in the same way that key business ratios express high, low, and middle averages. For example, among manufacturers of toys, amusement and sporting goods, the upper group reported an average collection period of *42 days*, while the lower group reported 93 *days*, with those in between averaging *60 days*. That makes quite a gap—42 days and 93.

Now what about your collection letters? Should you have a definite sequence—perhaps a series of four or five or six, each one becoming progressively sterner? Can they be form letters, or must they be individually typed?

Form letters can certainly be used—but then so should letters that are individually typed. Each delinquent account must be approached purely on its own; what may work for one customer will not work at all for someone else, as can be seen from the twelve classifications previously described.

As for the content of the letters, try to avoid the gimmicky or the cute. Sending a piece of string as a reminder may have had merit not too many years ago, but communication in the business world has become far more sophisticated.

And keep in mind who the addressee is. If your past due reminder is going to a clerk in a huge accounts payable department, he couldn't care less how it's worded. In that case, you'd do as well by sending an ordinary statement stamped PAST DUE and nothing more.

The collection intervals

Some authorities suggest three stages in the collection procedure:

1. The polite reminder
2. The formal appeal
3. The firm demand

Each stage, according to these same authorities, should take place at *30 day intervals*. Following this timetable, you can either use three letters, each of them going out once a month, or as many as six letters to be mailed at *two week intervals*. Of these six, each set of two should be fairly similar in tone, so that in every stage, the debtor would be doubly reminded of his delinquency.

But you may prefer to compress the procedure and begin it far earlier, perhaps with a *polite reminder* only a few days or a week after maturity date of an invoice, with a second letter or statement (the *formal appeal*) following within ten days or so, and the *firm demand* going out ten days or so after that. Your procedure, in other words, may cover only 30 or 40 days, not 90.

Whatever your timetable, you must also determine the kind of collection procedure you will employ. For most of your delinquencies, you can use a standard printed form, or a statement, or a series of collection letters.

The standard printed form

Many stationery suppliers feature a simple four part preprinted collection form to fit into a window envelope. Your company name can be imprinted on each of the four parts, all of which have different colors for easy identification. The form can be ordered with carbon between the parts, or without it if you prefer.

The advantage of this form is its simplicity. The debtor's name and address, and delinquency information, including the invoices, amount owing, and due date, are typed in only once. Your carbon does the rest.

The first part of the form is the polite reminder:

Just a friendly reminder that your account is past due. Your payment by return mail will be appreciated.

Part two is the formal appeal:

Is there any reason why payment of this past due account has been withheld? If so, please tell us; if not, may we expect your check at this time?

Part three is the firm demand:

FINAL NOTICE! Repeated requests for settlement of your past due account have apparently been ignored. Unless payment is received by————————immediate action will be taken.

The fourth part is your own copy.

For the understaffed credit manager, a form of this kind has a definite appeal, but perhaps a statement will serve your purposes as well.

The statement

Using a statement as your past due reminder can frequently be an effective element in your collection procedure. You can run the original statement through a copying machine and stamp the copies with a simple message—one or more of the following:

Please remit
This account is now past due
Second Notice
Third Notice
Final Notice

All of the above are available in inexpensive self-stampers that are good for 10,000 impressions. Or you can create your own messages. Those mentioned above constitute a series of reminders, with each carrying its individual implications.

For those customers who may need just a gentle nudge, use the first one alone—*Please remit*. If you combine that with the next one—*This account is now past due, Please remit*—you have a perfect first reminder. And adding any of the others tells your customer exactly how you feel and what you expect of him. For a computerized statement, your data processing service or your own data processing department can add any message of your choice to the body of the statement.

With your larger customers, a stamped or computerized statement of this kind will do as good a job for you in the early stages as a form letter. And some of your smaller customers won't mind them, either. Remember it's the message that counts, and what your statement is saying is that certain invoices are past due. That's enough for an overworked business man, or for a clerk in an impersonal accounts payable department.

But don't rely solely upon statements. For many of your customers, a form letter will do a better job, and for others, only the individually typed letter will be persuasive.

The form letter

Many books have been written on the proper way to write business letters, including the collection series. Whether you follow the advice of the authorities or prefer to develop your own approach, remember that a collection letter must, above all, be:

1. Firm
2. Courteous
3. Succinct and to the point

Don't shilly-shally or sound as if you're pleading. It's your money you're trying to collect. But don't insult your customer; he may be past due, but his business is still valuable to your organization.

And come to the point as quickly as you can. Your customer isn't interested in flowery and rambling openings, or in pretentious closings. Say what you have to say in a minimum of words.

If the recipient of your letter is the owner himself, he'll know your objective immediately; he's probably as busy as you are, and he'd rather not bother with a windy letter that will tell him, in the end, the same thing as two or three concise sentences. If your letter reaches a clerk or bookkeeper, neither one will be impressed by the literary quality or the length.

The National Association of Credit Management has compiled some representative letters used by credit managers in various industries, ranging from the larger corporations to the smaller companies. Many of these letters are remarkably similar in tone, and, according to their creators, have consistently produced results. All of them, without exception, embody the three basic elements outlined above: they are firm, courteous, and to the point.

Perhaps your own letters employ a similar technique; perhaps not. In any event, it would be helpful to make a comparison.

Most of the *collection letters* are in series of five or six. The following group, based upon those compiled by The National Association of Credit Management in its book *Credit and Collection Letters*, illustrates the general approach taken by the various authors (letters are not quoted verbatim, but the simulation represents both style and content):

Letter 1

> Reviewing our last due invoices, we find yours as follows:
> [List invoices, dates, and amounts.]
> We would appreciate your payment for the above.

Variation of letter 1, with a statement enclosed

For your convenience, we enclose a statement showing the past due invoices on your account.
We would appreciate your check.

Letter 2

We don't find a reply to our recent reminder that your account is past due. We show ———— due us. Won't you please send us your payment?

Your cooperation will be appreciated.

Variation of letter 2, with a statement enclosed

Your account continues to show the overdue amount indicated on the enclosed statement.

Won't you please send us your payment or let us know the reason for your delay?

We will appreciate your cooperation.

Letter 3

Once again it is necessary to call your attention to the past due balances on your account as shown by the following:

[List invoices, dates, and amounts.]

In the absence of your reply to our recent reminders, we assume there is no question concerning the amount indicated. Since it is now so long past due, we must ask that payment be sent without further delay.

Variation of letter 3, with a statement enclosed

Once again it is necessary to call your attention to the past due balance on your account as shown by the enclosed statement.

In the absence of your reply to our recent reminders, we assume there is no question concerning the amount indicated. Since it is now so long past due, we must ask that payment be sent without further delay.

Letter 4

Regretfully we must once again refer to the long past due condition of your account which shows an outstanding balance of ─────────

Three previous letters appear to have been ignored.

We hope you understand that there is a limit to the length of time an account can remain past due. We must therefore insist upon payment in full by return mail.

Variation of letter 4, with a statement enclosed

Regretfully we must once again refer to the long past due condition of your account, as shown on the enclosed statement.

Three previous letters appear to have been ignored.

We hope you understand that there is a limit to the length of time an account can remain past due. We must therefore insist upon payment in full by return mail.

Note that for the first time in the series, the letter writer has assumed a more rigorous posture; he now uses the word *insist*. In letter no. 5, which follows, some of the writers make their final demand, while others appeal one more time to the customer's sense of fair play. As a possible way out for both parties, many credit managers suggest a partial payment.

Letter 5, suggesting a partial payment

We have advised you a number of times that your account is long past due our normal terms, and we have now reached the point where further delay is unacceptable. But perhaps you have a problem. In that case, send us a substantial enough payment so that we can work with you toward settlement of the total balance.

Variation, a tougher letter, setting a date for response

We have still not received payment of your long overdue balance despite a number of recent reminders. We have now reached the point where further delay is unacceptable.

But perhaps you have a problem. In that case, send us a substantial enough payment so that we can work with you toward a settlement of the total balance. However, we must ask you to respond by————. We can't help you if you won't help us.

Letter 6, the final notice

We have received no response to our previous letters requesting payment of your account, nor have you sent us your acknowledgment.

You must certainly realize that we have been fair and patient, but your continued silence leaves us at a loss, and gives us no alternative except to refer your account to our collection agency. This is a step we would sincerely regret.

We hope that you will respond to this final appeal for cooperation, so that you can avoid a procedure that can only mean inconvenience and additional expense to you. Unless we hear from you by return mail [or give the debtor a specific date], we will have to transfer your account to our collection agency.

Some letter writers speak of legal action and mention an attorney, rather than a collection agency. Also, many of the writers show a balance due above the body of each letter, so that the amount does not have to be mentioned or listed in the letter itself.

In this series of letters, the earlier ones are mild in tone, and it is not until the fourth that any hint of threatening action can be perceived. And it is only the sixth that places the burden squarely upon the debtor, for not until then does the credit manager set a definite date, *or else*.

Because the time spread may be far too long for you in a series of this kind, it is possible that you may not want to use six letters. For your purposes, three may be better, or four.

The final notice

Try to avoid the final notice as long as you can. Use every method available to you before taking a step that is difficult to revoke. You do have some alternatives.

Number one is your salesman. Even though he consistently balks at finding credit information for you, he should be interested in saving his accounts. He may be able to visit his customer personally and see firsthand why he hasn't paid, or if there's a chance for you to collect. Often a solicitous call from a salesman may be more fruitful than all of your previous efforts.

At the least, ask your salesman to learn, if he can, the circumstances regarding his customer's delinquency. There may be a sound reason (of which you are not aware) for the past dues, and for your customer's silence as well. If your salesman is willing to cooperate, and there's no logical reason why he shouldn't, use him whenever necessary.

As your second alternative, after you've exhausted your normal procedure, whether it be form letters or statements (and perhaps even an individually typed letter), send a *certified* letter, requiring a signature from the addressee alone, who should be one of the principals or the financial officer. A certified letter always has more urgency than does ordinary mail, and you'll know from the signature that your addressee at least received your letter.

Or try a *mailgram*. Like a certified letter, a mailgram attracts attention and is rarely ignored. Make the message seem final, without actually committing yourself.

"We must have your payment for balance due within 48 hours."

You haven't said what you would do if you do not receive payment within the time specified, but a mailgram of that kind does imply action will be taken.

You might also try drawing a *sight draft* on your customer's bank. (His previous checks will give you the name of his bank, or perhaps your credit agency can supply it.)

A sight draft, to be honored within five days or whatever period you select (don't make it too long), can be embarrassing to your customer, especially if it's presented to his own bank. He won't want to jeopardize his standing with them; he may have a loan outstanding or he may be getting ready to ask for one. Under those circumstances, he'll do his best to settle with you quickly, and he'll have to come up with some plausible answers for his loan officer.

But don't use the sight draft ploy unless you fully intend to go ahead with a collection agency or a lawyer as a last resort. It's not too good an idea to embarrass a customer you'd like to keep for a long time.

Another suggestion—telephone your customer personally; if he's the sole proprietor or owner, talk to *him*. Speaking directly to him should clarify the situation for you. You can pretty much tell from his attitude and from what he says whether he intends to pay you, and how soon. But don't be put off by vague promises. If he agrees to make a payment, insist upon a definite date. Don't accept "Sometime in the next week or so." Tell him that you *must* have his check by whatever date you think is reasonable for both of you. And always make a record of your conversation—the name of the party you spoke to, the date you spoke to him, and the promises he made.

If the delinquent account is one of your major customers, try to get the name of the company treasurer or financial officer (sometimes he's a vice president); you can get this information from your credit agency, from one of your colleagues, or from the company itself. Even in the largest organizations, it is often possible to communicate directly with a corporate officer. Just remember to be patient; don't lose your temper. If you discuss the matter reasonably with someone on a corporate level, you may be surprised by the results.

Or *write* to the *president* of the corporation. Apologize for taking up his time, and then tell him the reason for your letter. His company owes you X amount of dollars; you've sent a number of letters and statements, without response of any kind. You would be grateful for his help.

Where there is no money problem, the corporate president won't be too happy receiving a letter like that, even though it may have been his own policy that precipitated the past due situation; he probably won't bother answering you himself, but someone else will, most likely with a check.

On the other hand, if your customer, whether large or small, is in serious financial difficulty, not all the letters in the world, no matter how deftly phrased or to whom they've been addressed, will get your past due invoices paid. Nor will it help to threaten legal action, or sometimes, even to take legal action.

Nevertheless, once you've reached this stage in your

collection procedure, you must make every additional effort to settle the account, even though you suspect it's hopeless.

Inasmuch as you've tried everything else, you now have only the *final notice* left. Mail it (certified will tell your addressee that this time you mean business); set a definite date for response, not too far ahead, and stick with that date. Be prepared to use either a collection agency or a lawyer, and don't expect miracles. The account, by then, may be uncollectable, as it may well have been from the moment you made shipment.

The last resort

A letter from a lawyer or collection agency may provide the final stimulus that provokes your customer into action. There is something disturbing about such a letter. It's the one psychological edge you have, and it sometimes speeds a check to you.

But if your customer is hopelessly in debt and/or on the verge of insolvency, a letter from your lawyer or papers filing suit against him will have no effect at all, unless he has personally guaranteed his debts to you. If he hasn't, he'll simply add your letter to his pile, for undoubtedly others besides you are after him.

Still, collection agencies do manage to collect a good percentage of delinquent accounts. Part of it, of course, is due to their own techniques and approach, and part of it stems from the inherent dread most businessmen have of such agencies. So collection agencies can be useful; in some cases, they will fail, as you had failed, for there simply won't be enough money in your customer's till to satisfy creditors. And where the agencies succeed, it can be expensive for you.

Take a moment to go back to Letter 6 in the collection series. Note the third paragraph, in particular the line that reads: ". . . so that you can avoid a procedure that can only mean inconvenience and additional expense to you."

Don't be misled by the four words *additional expense to you* (meaning the debtor). Only in certain circumstances can the debtor be charged the collection fees and/or costs of filing suit. Some jurisdictions permit the collection agency or lawyer to add their commission or fee to the total owed, but in many jurisdictions it isn't permissible at all, and the shipper therefore pays that portion of his collection costs, although he can recoup some of his other expenses such as accrued interest and the cost of filing suit.

There is, however, one method that does permit you to add reasonable costs to the total owed, even in those jurisdictions where this practice is forbidden. You can insert, in your original sales contract, a judgment clause that allows you to charge such reasonable collection costs to your customer. If he accepts this clause, so will the courts.

From a practical standpoint, what are your chances of collecting once you've taken this final step—referring your account to a collection agency or lawyer?

As with the entire procedure of collecting past dues, beginning with your first reminder, there are too many variables involved to make an exact computation. Your agency or lawyer will be successful with some, and not with others. No one will guarantee you a 100% return. And your debtor, if he wants to use them, has available to him delaying tactics that can forestall payments for months, or until he decides to call a meeting of his creditors (see Chapter 10, "Bankruptcies and Bad Debts").

All collection agencies allow what they call a free demand period. This is a period, not to extend beyond ten days, in which no charge is made to you if the customer pays within that time. Some agencies ask you to mail out the free demand forms yourself (a copy goes to the agency for follow-up after the free demand period has expired), while other agencies send out the free demand upon receipt of your claim. You must, however, specify free demand, and bear in mind that you cannot ask the agency for free demand only. You have to use the rest of their procedure as well.

After the free demand, the agency then goes through various stages, beginning perhaps with a letter or a phone call to the debtor on up to personal visits from an agency representative (if the agency is large enough to have branches all over the country). A small local agency will probably have to skip this last stage of personal visits for out of town claims unless it has reciprocal agreements with similar small agencies elsewhere.

If the agency fails to achieve collection through its own efforts, it will then turn the case over to an attorney in the same community or general locality where the debtor has his place of business, assuming you have given prior approval for this step. If you haven't, the claim will be returned to you as uncollectable.

Collection agencies prefer to collect your claim without referring it to an attorney, for once they do that, their share of the fee is reduced. But most collection agencies are reputable; they'll devote reasonable time and efforts to your claim. When they realize they can go no further with it, they *will* refer it to an attorney even though it means a reduction of their commission.

There are many worthwhile collection agencies operating on a countrywide basis; some of them may have branch offices within your particular area. All of them offer similar services for an established fee—commission rates are uniform and are set by law. There is one system of collection bureaus, however, that should have a special appeal for the credit manager.

The National Association of Credit Management operates approximately 58 individual collection bureaus nationwide. Since each bureau is owned and administered by its members, primary consideration is given to their interests rather than to profits, as would be the case with a commercial collection agency. The linkage of these 58 bureaus across the country gives each claimant, no matter where he may file his claim and no matter where his debtor may be, a thorough and comprehensive coverage. These activities are coordinated and supervised by the National Collection Service, a division of NACM in New York. For more complete information, get in touch with your nearest NACM branch or national headquarters at 475 Park Avenue South, New York, New York 10016.

On some claims, it may be wiser for you to go directly to a lawyer specializing in collections. He won't give you a free demand period, and his fee will be higher than those you might have paid to an agency in the earlier stages. But an experienced attorney can get to the debtor immediately; even if your customer is in a precarious situation, your lawyer can sometimes get enough of a payment to have made his services and his fee worthwhile. (He may not accept a small claim; a collection agency will, but the cost to you will be high—as much as 50% of the total.)

But lawyers cannot produce water out of stone, nor can they force money out of those who have none. And like you, they can be completely helpless in the face of legal procedure.

As you have a right to bring suit, the debtor has a right to deny your charges. Once he becomes a defendant in a suit, your debtor can file a general denial; he doesn't have to be specific or prove anything. He simply denies the validity of the charges against him, even though it is apparent to everyone, perhaps even to the court itself, that he is absolutely wrong on all counts. Your case is then entered on the court's calendar and put off for a hearing at a future date.

In the meantime, while your suit awaits its turn on a crowded docket, the debtor finally decides he's had enough and he files for help under the Bankruptcy Code. You then become one of the general creditors and stand in line with everyone else. You can console yourself with the thought that you had referred the account to a collection agency months before, and you had later decided, with your attorney, to file suit in plenty of time—or so it had seemed.

But you were defeated by the long process a collection procedure can be and by the protection the law affords your customer.

Could you have done otherwise? Probably not. Once this particular customer reached the point of financial difficulty that impelled you to start the entire tedious process in the first place, it is likely he could not have paid no matter what steps you may have taken, nor how quickly you moved.

Interest

If you suspect that one of your major accounts is deliberately withholding money from you by not paying on time, why can't you charge him interest, especially when you know that he's saving bank costs by using your money instead?

You can. Interest can be added to your past due invoices, but collecting it is another matter. If your customer disregards your additional charges once he finally does remit for his past dues, how do you force him to pay, aside from bringing suit against him?

Also, how will interest charges affect your good will? In a recent poll of credit managers conducted by a credit publication, it was found that charging interest to delinquent customers had mixed results.

Since 1969, one manufacturer of awning and tent hardware has been adding a monthly interest charge to accounts more than 60 days past due. No orders are shipped to customers who have not paid these charges. Resistance, initially, was high, but since then this manufacturer has encountered no problems in collecting the interest.

On the other hand, a credit manager for a Philadelphia steel service center has a different story. His firm employed a similar concept—adding a 1% per month charge on all amounts over 60 days in age. At the end of two years, it was found that this supplier had lost approximately 10% in sales, and the interest charge was abandoned.

Your own policy, in the end, will probably be determined by your own industry. If your competitors are doing it, and doing it successfully, then it may be worth a try for you. But only if your position as a supplier is strong enough.

In a suit, of course, interest *can* be added; once you win your case, your customer will then have to pay the interest as well as other costs. But is it worth it to you to gain the few dollars such interest charges represent and perhaps lose one of your larger customers in the process?

Proof of delivery

Be careful of the customer who chronically skips invoices. When he does at last answer your statements or letters, he may blandly advise you that he needs a proof of delivery for every unpaid invoice.

Whenever you can, beat him to the punch. As soon as one of his invoices has reached a third month of delinquency with no response from him, request a proof of delivery on your own. Have it ready, so that when he asks for it, you can send it to him by return mail. Or send it as soon as you get it, so that he will have no further excuse to delay payment.

Proofs of delivery are also helpful when you have a claim with a collection agency. A favorite delaying tactic for some debtors is to insist they never received your merchandise. You can forestall them by requesting your proofs of delivery beforehand in case your collection agency needs them.

Days sales outstanding (DSO)

An important adjunct to the collection procedure should be the credit manager's analysis of his days sales outstanding, or the average turnover rate of his receivables. If he has averages of other manufacturers for comparison, he can also determine whether his organization is ahead of or behind its competitors.

The Credit Research Foundation of Lake Success, New York, compiles quarterly figures from approximately 600 companies comprising manufacturers and wholesalers in all principal lines of business. The data received from these companies is summarized to determine an average DSO on a national basis.

Some firms compute their receivables turnover annually. Such annual computation will give a correct picture for the entire year, but the twelve month time lag can be a disadvantage. A quarterly percentage furnishes much more current information, so that the credit manager and his company can stay on top of the situation and take corrective measures if necessary.

The following is the formula for determining quarterly days sales outstanding:

Over a three month period, take the average balance of your month end trade receivables (sales for which payment has not yet been received), multiply by 90 (representing the number of days in the quarter) and divide by the total of sales made on credit in the same three months.

As an example, at the end of January you showed a trade receivable balance (unpaid) of $400,000; at the end of February, the balance was $380,000; and, at the end of March, the unpaid balance was $420,000. Your average balance, therefore, was $400,000. In the meantime, your credit sales in those same three months totaled $800,000.

Your DSO is thus computed by the following calculation:

$$\frac{\$400{,}000 \times 90}{\$800{,}000} = 45.0 \text{ or } 45 \text{ days}$$

Assuming selling terms of one month, it is taking you roughly an average of 15 days more than your normal terms to collect your receivables.

In its most recent survey, Credit Research Foundation reported the average turnover rate for manufacturers was 43.9 days and for wholesalers 40.5.

But the receivables turnover rate must be considered in context. Selling terms vary from one industry to another and will thus have a parallel effect upon the collection period. Meat packers show an average of 14.6 days while the median rate for manufacturers of small electric appliances zooms up to 78.4.

Even within a specific industry the DSO will vary because of differing marketing practices and customer characteristics. A competing company with many marginal accounts may show perhaps 50 or more days sales outstanding; someone else, concentrating on a more stable type of business, will report that his receivables are collected within 37 days, while your own rate of 45 days is more than one full day behind the rate reported by manufacturers in general.

For you, the DSO measurement spotlights the efficiency of your collection procedures as well as the trend of your turnover rate. But here, too, other factors must be examined. Your sales and the quality of those sales will affect your DSO.

Remember that your DSO reflects the amount of money your company has tied up in its trade receivables. If your DSO increases and your sales remain the same, that means even more money invested in receivables, and less funds available for other company uses; you may have to be more diligent in pursuit of your past dues.

10
Bankruptcies and Bad Debts

Credit department goals
    To help increase sales
    Keep bad debts at a minimum
The bad debt ratio
    For all industrial groups
    For wholesalers and manufacturers
    The extraordinary situation
    Minimal losses
Bankruptcies and debtor rehabilitation
    History of the bankruptcy statutes
    Principal causes of business failures
    Four possibilities for the customer in financial difficulty
An out of court settlement
    Advantages and disadvantages
    The first meeting
    The creditor's committee
    The creditor's role

> Attempted settlement without a meeting
> Assignment for the benefit of creditors
> > When settlement attempt fails
> > Hazards for the debtor
> > Assignment as the first step
> Chapter 11 of the Bankruptcy Code
> > Differences from Chapters X and XI
> > New features of Chapter 11
> > The debtor's role
> > The first meeting
> > The creditor's committee
> > The debtor's plan
> > The creditors' plan
> > Question of credit in Chapter 11
> Voluntary bankruptcy
> > Under Chapter 7
> > As the debtor's first or last step
> > The creditor's role
> > Filing of claims
> Involuntary bankruptcy
> > Creditors' right to file
> > Two new grounds as opposed to six old
> > Possible pitfalls for filing creditors
> > Use either of Chapter 7 or Chapter 11
> Chapter 13
> > Who can file
> > Possible effect upon creditors
> Summary
> > When to file claims
> > Attendance at creditors' meetings
> > Completing a proof of claim
> > Power of attorney
> > Proofs of delivery

Every credit manager worries about his bad debts. He'd rather not have any, but he must learn to expect his share.

Inevitably, unless ultraconservatism is preferred by management, a certain percentage of bad debts will be accumulated.

But how many? What percentage of bad debts is acceptable to you and your organization?

Like many other segments of credit checking, the answer to that depends upon your company policy and upon other factors both internal and external.

One of your competitors may aggressively and intentionally go after the risky account, while another competitor may shy away completely. And your company may be like neither, but rather fall in between.

Each of the three organizations may have policies that are influenced by differing profit margins and production philosophies as well as by the economy and competition. Conservative Competitor B would rather have a smaller volume with a lower risk potential, while aggressive Competitor A pursues increasing sales even though this can mean a higher ratio of bad debts.

In both cases, the organizational approach is a product of the diverse elements that determine the individual policy. As a result, your aggressive competitor may have more bad debts than you have, and the other fellow may have less. In one given industry, therefore, you can find a wide variance in the percentage of bad debt losses.

Similarly, as with fixed assets, there can be a substantial difference in the bad debt ratio from one industry to another. A steel processor whose principal customers are General Motors and Ford will have a much lower percentage of bad debts than will a manufacturer of beauty and barber equipment. The latter will have a far different customer mix.

The credit manager must consider all of this in the analysis of his own losses. At the same time, he must keep twin goals constantly before him:

1. Help increase sales
2. Hold bad debts to a minimum

The bad debt ratio

Speaking in actual figures, exactly what is a desirable percentage of bad debts for you?

While there is no way to advise you in precise amounts, a general picture can be described, so that you can make your own assessment for your specific requirements and policies.

The Credit Research Foundation conducts periodic surveys to determine the annual rate of bad debt losses among manufacturers and wholesalers. This percentage is based upon total sales made on credit within a calendar year; all payments received within that twelve month period against any bad debt, whether incurred in that year or in prior years, are to be deducted, so that the final rate of loss is a net percentage.

In its most recent survey, the Credit Research Foundation reported the median percent of net bad debt loss for wholesalers was .0900% (on a scale of 100.00%); for manufacturers, the percentage was .0475%.

Within these median ranges, there were extensive variations; among manufacturers of electronic products, for example, the average loss was only .0152%, while the average loss for manufacturers of printing and publishing supplies jumped to .2884%; for wholesalers the average percentages ranged from a low of .0552% to a high of .1975%.

Broken down into dollar figures, these percentages would read as follows, on a total of $1,000,000:

.2884%	=	$2,884
.1975%	=	$1,975
.0900%	=	$ 900
.0552%	=	$ 552
.0475%	=	$ 475
.0152%	=	$ 152

If you're a wholesaler, your net bad debt losses should range from above five hundred dollars to $2,000 for each $1,000,000 of sales; for a manufacturer, the spread would be larger—from a low of a hundred and fifty dollars to not quite $3,000 for each $1,000,000 of sales.

Credit insurance companies expect your "normal" loss to approximate two-tenths of one percent of sales, or $2,000 for each million dollars. You will note that this figure is roughly a thousand dollars less than the manufacturers' high of .2884%, and almost the same as the wholesalers' high of .1975%.

What about an extraordinary loss that goes way beyond any of these figures? It *can* happen, particularly if you're dealing with marginal accounts.

In the first place, where there is a very large amount involved and a possibility of financial loss exists, responsibility for shipping to a shaky major customer should not be yours alone. Management may look to you for credit decisions on a normal basis, but an extraordinary situation calls for extraordinary procedures.

Your principal task will be to compile all the available facts on your shaky customer and report them to management. Undoubtedly, your principals will ask for your own assessment.

If you're still new at your job, they will respect your hesitation. And even if you have years of experience behind you, the entire decision should not be up to you, but rather should be a joint one with management.

Discuss the entire question with your principals—the nature of the risk, the possibility of loss, and the dollar amount your company is willing to invest and can safely absorb.

If the customer under discussion is an old one, and you've done a large volume with him over the years, it's difficult to cut him out entirely. For the sake of your continuing relationship (assuming he pulls through, perhaps with the help of the Bankruptcy Code), your company may decide to ship reduced amounts on an order to order basis.

With a new customer, be doubly careful. Perhaps his previous suppliers have either cut down drastically on their shipments to him or refuse to ship altogether. The amount of business he offers may be tempting, but may not make sense in terms of sound credit practice. Again, as with your old customer, ask management to reach a decision with you, especially where the credit requested far exceeds your routine approvals.

As for minimal losses, they may not be desirable, either. It's a credit truism that something is very much wrong if you have no bad debts of any kind. You may be turning away valuable business and needed profits for the sake of zeros in the bad debt column. It would be constructive to repeat, at this juncture, a paragraph from Chapter 3:

> It is true that marginal businesses constitute the largest percentage of bankruptcies; but it is just as true that *not all marginal businesses fail*. Most of them continue, perhaps struggling, but they manage to survive, honorably, with the trust and cooperation of their suppliers.

Don't be afraid of bad debts; almost everyone has them.

Bankruptcies and debtor rehabilitation

When the American colonists cut their ties with their English cousins in 1776, one of the European traditions they retained was the treatment of debtors. Bankruptcy was still considered a disgrace by the Americans, despite their tolerance in other areas. Debtors were thrown into prison until rescued by family or friends, or perhaps not rescued at all, but allowed to languish in jail for indefinite periods.

Perhaps the most poignant of the early bankruptcies concerned the man who had been largely responsible for raising much of the finances to fight the American Revolution. Robert Morris of Philadelphia has been recognized as the financial wizard of the revolution, but heavy personal speculations after the war, particularly in land, did not pay off, and his financial wizardry failed to save him from the ultimate disgrace—debtors' prison. Rather than honor the man who had done so much to stabilize its economy, the young republic demanded its pound of flesh, and Robert Morris entered a Philadelphia debtors' prison on February 15, 1798. His debts totalled $2,948,711.11.

Friends, however, did at last come to his aid. As a result of their agitation, Congress passed the first Bankruptcy Act. Under the provisions of this act, two-thirds of Morris' creditors agreed to his discharge from prison, and he was released in October of 1801. He was sixty-six, and penniless.

Unlike our forefathers of the late eighteenth century, we now look upon bankruptcy not as a disgrace, but as an unfortunate condition that requires understanding and help, although the understanding did not come easily. Since the time of Robert Morris' imprisonment, we have had four other bankruptcy statutes, the first three resulting from economic crises and business panics, and the fourth, the one now in use, enacted from a recognition that modifications and refinements in the existing bankruptcy laws had become necessary.

The first bankruptcy statute, which helped Robert Morris secure his freedom, was enacted by the Federalists in 1800; it was repealed three years later by the Jeffersonians, who believed that the statute favored the mercantile class to the detriment of the farmers.

The second statute was passed in 1841 during the administration of John Tyler. It lasted even a shorter time than the first, for it was repealed in 1843, partly because of a commonly held view that "debtor relief was immoral."

The economic crisis following the Civil War produced the third bankruptcy statute, which was enacted in 1867 and repealed eleven years later; its death was due, in large measure, to the refusal of creditors to extend additional benefits to their debtors.

A fourth statute was passed in 1898. Major changes were made over the following decades, culminating in the Amendatory Act of 1938. There were additional amendments over the next thirty years, including two that were passed in 1966 as a result of ten years' effort on the part of the National Association of Credit Management.

Popularly referred to as the Chandler Act, the changes of 1938 became effective on September 22nd of that year and included comprehensive provisions for debtors' relief. It was this fourth statute that most credit managers had become familiar with, for it was under that law that we had the well-known and widely utilized Chapter XI.

We now have a fifth bankruptcy act, H. R. 8200, or the Bankruptcy Code. This Code was necessitated by the many changes in the business world in recent decades. For example, 10,000 bankruptcy cases were filed in 1946; for the year ending June 30, 1979, 226,500 cases were filed. Of these, 87 percent, or 197,000, involved individuals; the remaining 29,500 were business actions. This number is considerably higher than the business failures of 1946. In addition, the nature of commercial dealings had been substantially altered by the adoption of the Uniform Commercial Code by virtually every state in the early 1960s.

The resultant passage of H. R. 8200, or the Bankruptcy Code, forced credit managers to concern themselves with new—and in some instances more restrictive—provisions regarding their rights and procedures in bankruptcies and matters of insolvency.

Under the former bankruptcy act, any credit manager involved in a bankruptcy—and that must include practically everyone—was primarily interested in Chapter XI, for it was that provision that permitted a debtor to reorganize his business. Now, under the Bankruptcy Code, credit managers must still concern themselves with chapter number eleven, but with some alterations. For one, the number has been changed from the Roman XI to the Arabic 11. (All chapters now use Arabic numerals instead of the Roman.) Also, the old chapters X and XII have been consolidated into the new Chapter 11. This and other changes that affect you as a credit manager will be explained later.

H. R. 8200 was the result of a legislative process that covered eight years, beginning in 1970 with the congressional establishment of a Commision on the Bankruptcy Acts of the United States. Many interested parties, including the National Association of Credit Management, presented their views and offered suggestions. The resulting report was submitted to Congress in July of 1973, but it was not until October of 1978 that the final version, the one now in use, was finally approved by both House and Senate and signed into law by President Carter; it became effective on October 1, 1979.

Some of the provisions in the Bankruptcy Code may appear to benefit debtors to the detriment of creditors.

While it is true that certain provisions make it more difficult for creditors, for the most part the new act attempts to be fair to all parties. But before discussing the rights and responsibilities of creditors under the Bankruptcy Code, it would be beneficial to examine the circumstances that lead a debtor to seek relief under the Bankruptcy Code.

What are the principal causes of business failures?

High on the list would have to be *overexpansion* and *undercapitalization*, but the knowledgeable credit manager watches out for the more subtle symptoms:

1. Incompetence
2. Lack of experience
3. Unbalanced experience

The above are *underlying causes*, evidencing an inability to avoid conditions that lead to these *apparent causes:*

1. Inadequate sales
2. Competitive weakness
3. Inventory difficulties

Neglect, fraud, and disaster take their place in the production of failures, but only to a minor degree. According to surveys, it is the major three that credit managers must guard against. During a recession or economic turndown, the credit manager must be especially vigilant, for any one of these apparent causes of business failure can be intensified by a troubled economy.

Can the credit manager predict when one or all three of these apparent causes might lead to real financial difficulty? Perhaps he can.

In Chapter 4, we cited the results of a survey conducted among 500 credit managers, whose annual sales totaled under $5,000,000 to as high as a billion and over. They were asked to classify and appraise the marginal account.

Quoting this survey, we said the following:

> More specifically, the basic characteristics and risk factors of a marginal account can be listed as:
> 1. Unsatisfactory finances
> 2. A poor payment record
> 3. Incompetent or inexperienced management
> 4. Insufficient credit information
> 5. Continuing losses from operations
> 6. Inadequate working capital
> 7. A deteriorating trend in financial condition

Comparing these both to the underlying and apparent causes of business failures, you have a marked similarity. To the perceptive credit manager, these can serve as danger signals and alert him to the potentiality of financial embarrassment.

But one of your customers may find himself in trouble through no fault of his own—illness, or dishonesty on the part of a trusted and key employee. There is no way to predict anything like that. You will simply have to suffer along with him, and help him, if you can, to retrieve something from the ruins.

When your customer experiences financial difficulty, he has four courses open to him, the last two governed by the provisions of the present Bankruptcy Code (much the same as in the past, with some variations):

1. An out of court settlement.
2. An assignment for benefit of creditors.
3. A petition in Chapter 11 of the Bankruptcy Code (formerly Chapter XI, and in some cases the old Chapter X, now consolidated into Chapter 11), or in Chapter 13.
4. Voluntary bankruptcy.

Actually, there are other possibilities. Your customer

can arrange for a bulk sale of his business without providing for payment of his debts. Or he can simply disappear. It will then be up to the creditors to proceed against him or his estate (the remains of his business) by filing an *involuntary* petition in bankruptcy against him. An involuntary petition can be filed against honest debtors as well, and you need not wait until they disappear. (More on that later.)

Out of court settlement

It is sometimes possible for a distressed debtor to consummate an out of court settlement with his creditors. There are some advantages to both parties in an adjustment of that kind. A settlement can be reached much more quickly, and heavy administrative expenses that often result from in-court negotiations can be avoided.

For the debtor, there are other benefits he must consider. An out of court workout, or settlement, averts the possibility of a trustee's being appointed in a Chapter 11 reorganization proceeding. A trustee might well usurp and interfere with the management of the debtor's business. Further, the debtor must bear in mind that now, under the Bankruptcy Code, creditors have the right to propose their own plan of arrangement, which would then force the debtor into court, with time-consuming appearances and additional expenses (see "Involuntary bankruptcy").

But there are disadvantages as well. A common law or out of court settlement requires the consent of almost all creditors, both large and small. Ideally, a one hundred percent creditor agreement should be the goal, since a non-consenting creditor has the right to obtain a judgement against the debtor even though everyone else has agreed to the terms arrived at. Where there are many creditors involved, however, unanimity may not always be possible, but it should be noted that cases are resolved without the participation of every single creditor.

On occasion, particularly when a creditor has a relatively small amount owing to him, he will leave it to the major and interested creditors to conduct the negotiations and to arrive at a settlement, and he will accept whatever the creditors' committee recommends. Perhaps only 85% or 90% of all the creditors will thus have been actively involved; because of the disinterest of the remaining 10% or 15%, the settlement is concluded as if by unanimous agreement.

It should also be pointed out that a creditor's actual presence at meetings is unnecessary. He can assign his power of attorney to the creditors' committee to negotiate and vote on his behalf. Such power of attorney does not necessarily extend to consent or acceptance of a plan. Even though you have given your proxy to the creditors' committee, you still retain the right to accept or reject a plan offered either by the debtor or by the debtor and committee together.

How is the first meeting of creditors called for an out of court settlement? Who calls it? And where is it to be convened?

Sometimes one or more of the major creditors may suggest to a financially embarrassed debtor that he meet with his creditors in an attempt to save the situation before it must be handed to the courts. Or the debtor himself, on the advice of counsel, may ask some of his larger creditors to help him arrange such a meeting.

It is also possible for some of the major creditors to meet informally with the debtor, without advising the general creditor body. These few creditors, who may represent a large share of the debtor's liabilities, may agree to a moratorium on their claims—that is, delay payment until a later date—so that the debtor can remain in business. Their hope is, with the removal of current pressure, the debtor can straighten out his affairs so that everyone, including the major creditors, will eventually be paid in full.

When a first meeting of the general creditor body has been called, it should take place in the offices of a trade association or a credit bureau specializing in adjustments for the industry or industries involved. (The National Association of Credit Management offers adjustments as one of its services.) If no such association or credit bureau is available, the offices of an attorney for the debtor is a suitable substitute.

As for the composition of the first meeting, which creditors are to be invited? All, or only the largest? If only the largest, why not some of the smallest so that their interests can be protected, too?

The interests of the larger creditors don't always coincide with those of the smaller. It is undeniably true that no arrangement is possible without the approval and fullest cooperation of the largest creditors, and since they have much more invested in the proceeding, their voices should therefore carry that much more weight. But it is just as true, in an out of court settlement, that the vote of the small creditor counts for exactly the same.

A plan should therefore be constructed to satisfy the small creditor so that he will not be moved to scuttle a settlement previously approved by the major creditors. A workable device, frequently employed, is to pay in full any creditor below a certain amount—say $200. As part of this proposal, any other creditor may elect to reduce his claim to that amount. For example, in a 35% settlement, a creditor who is owed $300 would do better by reducing his claim to $200 rather than taking the 35%, which would only come to $105.

Once the first meeting is convened, assuming both

large and small creditors are favorably represented, a committee of those creditors present will be constituted to work out the details of the settlement. Normally, the largest single creditor becomes the chairman, unless he defers to someone more experienced or capable in heading a committee.

If the meeting takes place at an adjustment bureau, that agency will probably be chosen as secretary to the creditors' group. The committee can then select, if it so desires, an attorney specializing in bankruptcy law to represent the creditors, and/or an accountant to review the debtor's books. The fees for attorney, accountant, and secretary to the committee are to be paid by the debtor, but practically speaking, they come out of the pockets of the creditors, for any fee will eventually affect the final settlement.

Because a debtor is still operating his business in his own name during negotiations for an out of court settlement, the creditors' committee should ask for controls to protect the interests of all creditors. It will also ask each creditor to mail a proof of claim signifying the amount owed.

Note that inasmuch as this is to be an out of court or common law settlement, there is no statute that insists your claim must be filed with the committee. Even if you don't file a claim, you will be paid your share of the settlement, provided your debtor's books carry you as a creditor. If they don't, burden of proof will then be upon you.

It is in the best interests both of debtor and his creditors to reach an agreement expeditiously. During the period of negotiations, the debtor will need new merchandise; the committee may permit purchases for cash only, and then reluctantly, for that would reduce the availability of funds for the final settlement, which can, and usually does, involve a substantial first payment in cash.

Sometimes a debtor will attempt an out of court

settlement without calling a meeting of his creditors. He will simply prepare a letter that he sends to all his creditors explaining why he cannot now pay them in full and offering them X percentage in settlement. He may also tell you that he's already received consents to his plan from many of his suppliers.

Beware of such a letter. Without an independent audit made by an outside accountant, how do you know whether your customer's claimed figures are correct? It's true that the dangers of mail fraud exists for him if he deliberately falsifies the figures he sends you along with his letter, but he may be perfectly willing to take that chance. Or the accounting procedures he has been using may be irregular if not exactly fraudulent.

If you do receive such a letter soliciting your consent to a plan unsupported by a creditors' committee, immediately send the letter to your credit or adjustment bureau, or to your company attorney to investigate on your behalf.

Don't agree to an out of court settlement unless and until you have all the facts.

Assignment for the benefit of creditors

As one of its safeguards, your creditors' committee will most likely ask that the debtor assign his assets for the benefit of creditors to be held in escrow by the committee. If no out of court settlement can be reached, the next step probably will be to liquidate the debtor's estate.

The debtor still has the right to file a petition in Chapter 11, but if an unofficial common law settlement cannot be consummated, there would be little point in his seeking the protection of the Bankruptcy Code.

But there are times when a Chapter 11 will have to be filed, to avoid attachment or diminution of assets by the actions of disgruntled creditors who refuse to accept the committee's proposals. In such a case, the Chapter 11 petition is filed with the knowledge and approval of the committee; judgments, attachments, or levies would then be automatically stayed.

Once all parties realize no out of court settlement is possible, the estate can be liquidated by filing the assignment that has previously been held in escrow. The income realized from the sale of the assets is then distributed on a pro rata share to each creditor, after payment of administration expenses.

From the debtor's standpoint, an assignment can be hazardous, for the debtor will still be liable for that portion of its debts that remain after distribution has been made. Because of this, rarely will an individual proprietor or a partnership make such an assignment unless assured that no creditor will later insist upon payment of the balance due him.

In the case of a corporation, an assignment poses no danger at all; once its assets have been turned over to a creditors' committee, all that will remain is an empty shell with no one to sue.

An assignment can be the first step instead of the last. A debtor may realize that he's so hopelessly insolvent no plan is possible, and he therefore hands over his assets to his creditors without requesting an out of court settlement or a Chapter 11 proceeding. By making such an assignment, he avoids bankruptcy; some may consider this to be desirable.

Unlike common law settlements, which do not have guidelines established by statute, assignments come under the jurisdiction of the courts and must therefore be governed by legal requirements. In the state of New York, for example, every assignment for the benefit of creditors is administered under the Debtor and Creditor Law.

Chapter 11 of the Bankruptcy Code

One of the major changes of the Bankruptcy Code is the consolidation of the old Chapters X, XI, and XII into the new Chapter 11. Under the old Bankruptcy Act, debtors frequently filed petitions in Chapter XI without attempting out of court settlements. Under the new Bankruptcy Code they can still utilize Chapter 11, with some major differences. But whatever the changes, debtors still have the right to ask for the protection of the courts; they may be forced to do so by the imminence of suits or judgements against them. Once such a petition has been filed, all liabilities, including taxes, are automatically frozen, and creditors are thereby enjoined from seeking individual preferences.

In some cases, petitions were filed under Chapter X, but this was used primarily in the case of public corporations, with many stockholders, where the public interest was at stake. Sometimes, the various parties, including the Securities and Exchange Commission (the S.E.C.), would engage in protracted debate as to whether a Chapter XI really belonged in Chapter X.

The result might well have been expensive and long-lasting litigation, which served to diminish the assets available for creditors. Another disadvantage of Chapter X for unsecured creditors was the displacement of management by an independent trustee. The creditors may well have been satisfied with an experienced debtor-in-possession, which they would have had under Chapter XI, but Chapter X left them no choice—they had to have an independent and possibly inexperienced trustee whether they liked it or not.

Chapter XII concerned real estate arrangements by

individuals and partnerships, and almost never affected the average unsecured creditor.

Chapter XI provided debtors—individuals, corporations, or partnerships—with an opportunity to restructure their debts, or rehabilitate themselves, by arriving at an arrangement with their creditors in an expeditious and inexpensive manner. Any plan worked out between debtor and creditors had to be in the "best interest" of the creditors; that is, the creditors had to receive at least as much as they would have realized if the debtor had been liquidated.

The protective features for public investors and public debt that we found in Chapter X are contained in the new consolidated Chapter 11, but it is now possible to retain a debtor-in-possession, if the creditor body so desires. As for an independent trustee, one will be appointed by the courts only upon request by a "party in interest," and only if it can be demonstrated that there may have been fraud, dishonesty, incompetence, or gross mismanagement by the debtor before or after commencement of the case.

Removing the inflexible requirement that an independent trustee had to be appointed, as in Chapter X, makes the new law more palatable for creditors who may be working with large, publicly held corporations. For the average trade creditor, however, Chapter 11 has other features of more immediate concern.

Previously, there were two important differences between an out of court settlement and a filing in Chapter XI:

1. In Chapter XI, the matter came under the jurisdiction of the courts and was protected by the judicial umbrella of the Bankruptcy Act, while a common law settlement was not.

2. In Chapter XI, it was necessary to have only 51% of

the creditors in number and amount to give their consents, not 100% as in an out of court settlement.

Under the new Chapter 11, the matter still comes under the jurisdiction of the courts and the debtor is still protected by the judicial umbrella of the Bankruptcy Code, as opposed to a common law settlement.

But, and this is a major change, an *involuntary* petition can be filed under Chapter 11, and the creditors can offer their own plan of arrangement to the courts without the participation of the debtor, or without waiting for the debtor to file his own petition, or without any attempt at an out of court settlement. Under Chapter XI, only the debtor had the right to submit a plan of arrangement; an involuntary petition could be filed only to liquidate the debtor's estate, not to preserve it for the debtor, as Chapter 11 now provides.

As for point number two, regarding the number and amount of consents required for the approval of a plan, this too has been modified, so that you, as a general unsecured trade creditor, will be affected. (You are an unsecured trade creditor if you sold goods to your customer on open terms.) Also, the size and composition of the creditors' committee is now strictly regulated by the new Bankruptcy Code. (Both of these items will be elaborated later in this section.)

For reasons apparent only to those drafting the codifications, the Bankruptcy Code has no even numbered chapters. We now have Chapters 1 through 15, skipping all even numbers in between. Of these eight new chapters, only 7, 11, and 13 should be of interest to you—the others deal with definitions and procedural matters.

A voluntary petition under Chapter 11 may be filed by any person, other than a stockbroker or commodity broker, a bank, or an insurance company. The Code defines "person" in the broadest sense, to include individuals, partnerships, and corporations.

Once a debtor decides he needs the protection of the

courts, he can file directly with the courts before meeting with his creditors, or he may request a meeting with his creditors before filing. Or the creditors themselves convene such a meeting, usually at the offices of their trade association or adjustment bureau. If it's a large enough case, a hotel room may be rented.

At this first meeting, the creditors select a committee, appoint a chairman, and choose its secretary, attorney, and accountant. As in a common law settlement, their fees will be paid by the debtor's estate.

Don't be confused by the term *first meeting*. There will be an official first meeting of debtor and creditors to be held after the judge has issued an "order for relief." Such order for relief is issued upon the filing of a petition by the debtor. (It is interesting to note that the word "adjudication" is no longer to be used. The Code now reads "order for relief." Adjudication, which was always part of the phrase "adjudication in bankruptcy," assumed from the start of a case that the debtor was probably bankrupt, even though he had the right to request rehabilitation. The Code now makes no such assumption.)

At this *official* first meeting, the creditors' committee, which had either been selected at the creditor body's *unofficial* first meeting or had been appointed by the judge, begins its work under the jurisdiction of the court. If the creditors meet, either by themselves, or with the debtor, prior to the debtor's filing a petition and prior to the order for relief, such meetings are unofficial.

So far, these steps do not vary all that much from the procedure previously employed under Chapter XI. But now we come to our first major change.

In the past, it was always the custom to choose as many creditors as feasible to serve on the committee. This frequently created much dissension, with shouting and wrangling from all sides, especially in a large case involving many millions in liabilities. In smaller cases, you sometimes had only a meager representation of creditors, so the size and composition of the committee were not problems.

It was the bigger cases that brought on discord and controversies at the first unofficial meeting. You may have had large trade creditors present who insisted upon being on the committee, and may even have preferred one of their own to be chairman. Then you had, on the other side, banks or insurance companies who were even larger creditors; they too, insisted they had as much or more right (since they had far more invested in the matter) to be either on the committee or to serve as chairman.

Beyond the size of the committee, groups of trade creditors may have wrangled among themselves as to which had the right to serve. The result often was a committee of unwieldy size, though perhaps of reasonable composition. And frequently, with a committee that huge, the referee in bankruptcy, at the first official meeting, promptly reduced it to what he considered a workable proportion.

All such dissension and wrangling have now been eliminated. The Code requires that the committee consist only of the seven largest claimants willing to serve, with the largest creditor to be the chairman, if he is willing and able so to function. Under certain conditions, the courts will permit a creditors' committee to be enlarged, if it can be demonstrated that the original composition of the committee did not fairly represent the creditor body. Or additional committees may be appointed by the court if it is found that such committees are needed to represent the various interests in a case.

It is also possible, under the Code, for an official first meeting to be called without an unofficial meeting between the debtor and his creditors. In such an event, the court appoints the committee, but again, the composition must be the seven largest creditors willing to serve.

The creditors' committee, whether the choice of the

general creditor body at the first unofficial meeting or the choice of the bankruptcy court, negotiates with the debtor and his attorney as they would for a common law settlement. The debtor in the meantime is designated Debtor-in-Possession. Previously, under the former Bankruptcy Act, a receiver was sometimes appointed to operate the business, usually with the help of the debtor. Under the Code, management is favored to remain in control.

Once an "order for relief" has been entered, the debtor has 120 days in which to present an acceptable plan. Unlike the procedure used in Chapter XI, the creditors' committee cannot now solicit acceptances from the creditor body unless such solicitation is accompanied by a copy of the plan and by a full disclosure statement approved by the court.

Practically speaking, what this means is that the creditors' committee, in one sense, loses some of the clout it once had. In the past, the creditors' committee was permitted to ask for your proof of claim and power of attorney before a plan was formulated. By sending in your proof of claim and power of attorney, both of which were usually part of a standard form, you gave your committee permission to negotiate for you by way of your power of attorney. If the committee had enough proxies from the creditors, its hand was considerably strengthened in dealing with the debtor.

Now, acceptances can be solicited only upon presentation of a plan approved by the court. No powers of attorney are therefore necessary. Also, you, as an unsecured general trade creditor, no longer have to file a claim to participate in the dividends. But since you have no way of knowing whether you are shown on the debtor's books as a creditor, or whether the amount he shows owing to you corresponds to yours, it would be wiser for you to file a proof of claim with the bankruptcy court as quickly as possible. And it's a good idea to have the bankruptcy judge indicate on a stamped, self-addressed postcard, or a copy of your letter to him, that he has received your claim, and the date of receipt.

As for approval of a plan, we encounter another major change. In the past, with a Chapter XI proceeding, a majority in both number and amount of claims filed and allowed was necessary to approve a plan. Now, the number of claims must still be at least 51%, but the amount (the money portion) must be two-thirds. In some instances, there will be exceptions to this requirement, but generally you will find 51% and two-thirds to be operable. More smaller creditors—perhaps you're one of them—will thus be represented in the final arrangement, unlike the previous 51% of amount, which permitted a few major creditors, notably banks and insurance companies, to control the money portion of a settlement.

The plan itself must be filed by the debtor within 120 days after filing his petition. The court may increase or reduce the 120 day period for cause. But again, as in other matters now subject to modification by the courts, we can assume that in most cases the 120 days will apply. If the debtor does not file a plan within that 120 day period, any creditor as well as the creditors' committee can then file its own plan, and seek solicitations for acceptance with the consent of the court.

Further, if the debtor does file a plan within the prescribed 120 days, but fails to obtain the required consents within 180 days, the creditors' committee or any creditor can file its own plan. Also, if a trustee has been appointed to operate the debtor's business, creditors can file their own plan.

These provisions, plus the requirements for committee composition and the increased money amount needed for approval of a plan, are the major significant revisions embodied in the new Chapter 11.

A question that frequently arises during Chapter 11

negotiations involves shipment of new merchandise to the debtor. How much merchandise is he to buy, and on what terms?

Normally, the creditors' committee recommends the terms, but both terms and amounts are a matter of negotiation between the debtor and the individual shipper. The court does not fix terms of sale, but under the provisions of the new Code, it will consider purchases on credit as administrative claims entitled to priority, even over other administrative claims if necessary. As a further encouragement for the extension of credit to the debtor, the court may even offer the creditor a lien—this time with top priority. Previous liabilities, those incurred before the filing, become secondary. In other words, the new purchases will be paid for first, before the old debts.

In itself, this is no guarantee of payment. If it develops that the debtor-in-possession is once again insolvent and is forced into bankruptcy, new claims will be paid only on a pro rata basis, except in those instances where liens have been granted. But it's possible that nothing will be left after the payment of fees and the expenses of liquidating the estate. In such an event, your new claim would be paid nothing at all. A decision to ship a debtor-in-possesion on open terms must be made with the full knowledge that no ironclad guarantee of payment is possible.

Any plan of arrangement must be in the best interests of the creditors. It may be that liquidation of the estate will realize more money than will the plan proposed by the debtor. The committee will therefore insist that the debtor offer at least as much as will be realized from liquidation. If he cannot, bankruptcy will be the next step.

Assuming that the creditors' best interests are being protected, tbe debtor will request the court to confirm his plan of arrangement once he has obtained the necessary consents and has deposited the necessary funds. If the plan is to be a single cash payment, the debtor is discharged and he is no longer liable for any balances that may still be due on his old debts, and he is no longer under the jurisdiction of the court. The money that he has deposited to cover the cash payment to his creditors will be distributed by a court-appointed disbursing agent.

If the plan of arrangement involves payment of notes, or deferred payments to cover a specified period of time, the debtor is discharged as debtor-in-possession, but he will, in most instances, still be under the jurisdiction of the court until the last note has been paid. In the event of a default on any note, the case can be reopened, and the creditors can petition the court to declare the debtor bankrupt.

During the deferred portion of the plan, again there is no guarantee of payment in full for shipments on open terms. Once the debtor is discharged, even though he remains technically under the jurisdiction of the court, new shipments to him must be treated as would any open account, with the responsibility resting entirely upon you. Should he then be declared bankrupt, as a result of default, your new shipments become claims against the new estate, as do the remaining portion of any notes still owing.

Voluntary bankruptcy

As the fourth course open to your debtor, he may choose voluntary bankruptcy under Chapter 7 of the Bankruptcy Code, which is the chapter covering liquidation. It might be the first step your debtor takes, or perhaps the last. He may be fully aware that he is too deeply in debt to to make an attempt at a settlement, either out of court or in Chapter 11; he may also, because of the possible hazards of an assignment, prefer bankruptcy so that he can be discharged, by specific order of the court, from all his liabilities.

A voluntary bankruptcy often results in no dividends at all to the general unsecured creditor, especially if it's the first step taken by the insolvent debtor. But assets of any kind must be protected; the judge, upon the filing of a voluntary petition, appoints a trustee to supervise the liquidation of the bankrupt estate. The judge also sets a date for the first meeting of creditors and so advises the general creditor body.

A creditor who cannot take the time to attend this first meeting or who may not want to because his claim is too small, may designate an attorney to act on his behalf, or assign his claim to an adjustment bureau. He may then have to pay a percentage of his realized dividend for their services.

Actually, in a voluntary bankruptcy proceeding, where there is no question of dishonesty, deceit, or fraud on the part of the debtor, there is little for the creditor to do except to file his claim and await final liquidation of the estate. Because a voluntary bankruptcy often means few or no assets, ultimate dividends can be nonexistent, or small at best.

But no matter how small your dividend, file your claim as soon as you can, as you should do in any proceeding under the Bankruptcy Code. Because of the complexity of the Code, and the various rules and regulations governing the responsibilities of the individual creditor, you would be wise to file your claim with the bankruptcy court without delay. You are no longer required to file, as in the past, to participate in a dividend in Chapter 11, but if you happen not to be shown on your debtor's books as a creditor (perhaps because of a clerk's inefficiency or oversight), or if your customer's figures are lower than yours, your failure to file, or filing too late, may affect your ultimate dividends in a plan of arrangement under Chapter 11. If the case has been resolved under Chapter 7, you *must* file your claim, or you lose out entirely.

Involuntary bankruptcy

In the past, if no plan of arrangement was possible or feasible under Chapter XI, creditors, on their own, had the right to file an *involuntary* petition in bankruptcy against the debtor, and to ask that he be adjudicated a bankrupt and his assets taken into custody for distribution to them. Where there were twelve or more creditors, and the debtor owed at least $1,000, three creditors were then required for an involuntary filing, and their claims had to aggregate a minimum of $500. Where the debtor had less than twelve creditors, only one creditor was required for filing.

Creditors also had the right to file an involuntary petition if the debtor disappeared and left his estate (whatever assets remained) for the creditors to dispose of. Or the creditors were permitted to file an involuntary petition if they believed this was the only course for the general creditor body.

But the debtor had to commit at least one of six acts of bankruptcy, as spelled out by the Bankruptcy Act, for any creditor or group of creditors to file involuntary proceedings against him. Insolvency alone was not enough. It had to be proven that the debtor did one or more of the following:

1. Transferred or concealed any part of his property, with the intention to hinder, delay, or defraud his creditors.

2. Made a preferential payment to a creditor *while insolvent*, within four months of the petition.

3. Permitted, while insolvent, a creditor to obtain a

lien upon his property, and did not vacate or discharge the lien within thirty days.

4. Made a general assignment for the benefit of his creditors.

5. Permitted, while insolvent or unable to pay his debts as they matured, the appointment of a receiver or trustee to take charge of his property.

6. Admitted in writing that he was unable to pay his debts and was willing to be adjudicated a bankrupt. This last act indicated that he had no objection to the filing of a bankruptcy petition but preferred that someone else do it.

Bear in mind that involuntary petitions in bankruptcy were intended for the liquidation of a debtor's estate, not to salvage it. Now, the terms of the Bankruptcy Code stipulate that an involuntary petition can be filed *at any time*, not necessarily to liquidate, although that is possible, but to rehabilitate the debtor and save his business for him. In other words, if the debtor will not or cannot propose his own plan, the creditors can do it for him, and if the plan is found feasible by the courts, it will be approved as if arrived at by agreement between debtor and creditors, even though the debtor may not actively have participated in the fashioning of that plan.

Before any creditor proceeds with an involuntary petition, however, major revisions in the law must be considered. Now, the debtor must owe a minimum of $5,000; where there are twelve or more creditors, three creditors are still required, with claims aggregating that $5,000. Where the debtor has less than twelve creditors, one creditor may file, but his claim must be at least $5,000, up from the previous $500.

As for grounds covering involuntary cases, there are now only two as opposed to the previous six, and they are not considered acts of bankruptcy. These are now the two acts representing the only grounds upon which an involuntary petition may be filed:

1. Debtor is generally not paying its debts as they become due.

2. A custodian was appointed for or took possession of the debtor's assets during a 120-day period preceding the filing of the petition.

Creditors who want to file an involuntary petition should be forewarned. Assume that three creditors, with claims totaling more than the requisite $5,000, believe that their debtor is "generally" not paying his debts on time. But they cannot know for certain exactly how many other creditors the debtor has, or know exactly the status and amount of the debts owed to these creditors.

Based upon factors such as the number and amount of the debtor's paid and unpaid debts, it is possible for the bankruptcy court to decide that the debtor did in fact "generally" pay its debts on time; the judge dismisses the involuntary petition, leaving the original three petitioners exposed to liability for costs, attorneys' fees, and worse, damages claimed by the debtor. Furthermore, if the court finds that the petition was filed in bad faith, debtor's punitive damage claims against the creditors can be sizable.

The second alternative—appointment of a custodian to take possession of the debtor's property—is far safer. (An assignment for the benefit of creditors falls into this category.) But here, too, there is a possible pitfall. The Code expressly provides that the actual taking by a third party of *less than substantially all* of the debtor's property may not serve as the basis for relief sought by petitioning creditors. So if you expect to base your petition on this second alternative, be sure you know exactly how much of your debtor's property has been taken over by someone else—that is, by a trustee, a receiver, a sheriff, etc.

Involuntary petitions can be filed either under Chapter 7, for total liquidation of the estate, or under Chapter 11, rehabilitation of the debtor. In the second instance, it is the intent of the creditors to save the business, not destroy it.

If a debtor balks at requesting an order for relief under Chapter 11, which may be recommended by some of his major creditors, the creditors themselves now have the right to file their own petition to request relief under Chapter 11. The debtor can then either move to have the court dismiss the creditors' petition, if he has sufficient grounds for making that request, or file his own petition.

In either event, the new regulations help the creditor by forcing a recalcitrant debtor who is in deep financial trouble to negotiate with the creditors under the jurisdiction of the courts. Previously, creditors had no such prerogative. All they could do was wait for a debtor to file for reorganization under Chapter XI, whenever he felt it was time to do so, which may have served only to diminish his assets; or the creditors could file their own involuntary petition to liquidate his business. This, too, may not have been the best move for them.

In this one respect, at least, the Code works to the benefit of the creditors.

Chapter 13

This chapter may not be encountered too often by the average creditor, since it deals with what used to be known as individual or personal bankruptcies. Formerly limited to wage earners, Chapter 13 has been expanded to include any individual with regular income. The Code is specific in its limitation of this chapter to individuals only, although in rare instances a husband and wife may be permitted to utilize Chapter 13, that is, if they operate what was once known as a "Mom and Pop grocery store," or similar store. But such instances will not occur too often, and not in all jurisdictions. In almost every case, the filing will have been made by an individual.

Chapter 13 can be used only on a voluntary basis; involuntary petitions cannot be filed. In other words, only the debtor can make use of this chapter, not the creditor, as he can in either Chapter 7 or Chapter 11. Also, under Chapter 13, a petition for relief is limited to those individuals whose unsecured debts total $100,000 or less. Take particular note of this last provision, for it can affect you, a general unsecured creditor. (Secured debts must total $350,000.)

Let's take an example of a hardware store, in the smaller range. You, as an electrical distributor, allow this customer regular open terms with a high credit of $5,000. This store is operated as a proprietorship, with Mr. J. Doe as the sole owner. Mr. Doe runs into trouble and has to request an order for relief. Since his "regular income" is derived from his hardware store, he is permitted to file under Chapter 13.

How does that affect you? In the long run, perhaps no more than if the petition had been filed under Chapter 11. But conceivably there *can* be a substantial difference, because under the new Chapter 13, the debtor can now propose a plan of arrangement to the court *without the participation of creditors*. And acceptance of that plan by unsecured creditors, meaning you, is not required, as long as you and other unsecured creditors receive at least as much as they would have if the business had been liquidated.

In most cases, if any of your customers utilize Chapter 13, you shouldn't be hurt too badly, inasmuch as the courts must still look out for the "best interests" of creditors, and it's not likely you'll be involved for too large a sum. But it *is* possible for you to be a sizable, if not the major creditor, as in the case of the electrical distributor selling to Mr. J. Doe. In a proceeding that involves the maximum of

$100,000, if the debtor owes you $5,000, that makes the money owing to you 1/20th of the total. Anytime your participation approaches that percentage, you have cause for concern.

But again, the plan offered to the court by your customer and eventually approved by the judge, does not have to hurt. It can be just as beneficial to you as to the debtor. On the other hand, the plan can be substantially less than it might have been if the creditors had been involved in negotiations. Since creditors cannot so participate under this chapter, all you can do is hope for the best, and hope that the court is as concerned with your interests as those of the debtor.

Summary

Whatever the chapter you or your customer have become involved in, always file a proof of claim, and file that claim as quickly as possible. If it's an out of court settlement, or an assignment for benefit of creditors, file that claim with the creditors' committee. If the proceeding takes place under Chapters 7, 11, or 13, file your claim with the bankruptcy judge or the designated party. In either event, whether the claim is filed with your creditors' committee or with the courts, always request a signature indicating receipt of your claim and date of that receipt. Send along with your claim a stamped, self-addressed postcard or a copy of your covering letter for the addressee to return to you.

Remember that you do not have to attend any creditors' meeting to participate in the ultimate dividends. Your proof of claim can do the job for you. Also, if you like, you can designate someone else to represent you—your company attorney perhaps, or an attorney specializing in collections, or a collection agency. But this representation will cost you a percentage of all monies you will receive.

Normally, if you appear on your customer's books as an unsecured creditor, the creditors' committee or the court will get in touch with you and will most likely send you a proof of claim to fill out.

Suppose, however, that noone advises you of any proceeding, whether in court or out of it. What do you do?

In the first place, once you become aware of your customer's problems, try to find out what that customer is doing about them. Has he filed a petition with the courts to request an order for relief? If so, who is handling it, and under what auspices?

Your credit agency should be able to give you this information; if you've inquired on that customer within the current year, your credit agency will probably let you know when an order for relief has been requested, or whether a meeting with creditors has been called. Or you can find out from one of your colleagues, or your group interchange. And trade papers generally carry news of insolvency or bankruptcy proceedings. Unless you're really not paying attention, there is no reason for you to be left out in the cold.

Secondly, you need not wait for a blank proof of claim to be sent to you. You can always ask your creditors' committee to send one to you (whether in court or out of court, each proceeding must have a creditors' committee), or you can buy some blanks from your local stationery store. Proofs of claim are standard forms, as shown in the accompanying illustration.

Completing this form is not at all complicated. "Consideration for this debt," as shown in paragraph 3, is "For merchandise sold and delivered," or "shipped and delivered," if you prefer. For paragraph 5, insert the date your last invoice was due, even though other invoices were due earlier, or average them. As an unsecured creditor, you won't have notes or other fiduciary documents from your debtor; paragraphs 6, 8, and 9 should therefore be answered "None." Finally, have the form notarized. Except where specifically requested, you do not have to fill in the reverse of your standard proof of claim form—the reverse is a power of attorney.

And that's it. Mail your proof of claim either to your creditors' committee or to the courts, and you're now protected.

In those matters where you do supply a power of attorney, that power of attorney, or proxy, comprises only your permission to your creditors' committee to negotiate on your behalf, but not to vote your consent or acceptance of any plan arrived at between debtor and creditors' committee. Only you, in writing, can indicate your acceptance or rejection of such a plan. If you do not vote, your vote will no longer be counted. In the past, you were considered to be against the plan if you withheld your vote. Conversely, an affirmative vote had to be indicated in writing. Under the new rules, your affirmative vote still has to be in writing, as does a negative vote. If you withhold your vote, that vote is lost.

It's also a good idea to get proofs of delivery for all open invoices and for all open chargebacks for claimed non-delivery as soon as you learn that one of your customers has taken one of the steps outlined in this section. In that way, you will be protected in the event your claim is disputed, either by the debtor or by any other designated party.

Everyday Credit Checking

UNITED STATES DISTRICT COURT FOR THE _____ DISTRICT OF _____

In re

BANKRUPTCY NO.

Include here all names used by bankrupt within last 6 years.

Bankrupt

PROOF OF CLAIM

1. **If claimant is an individual claiming for himself** The undersigned, who is the claimant herein, resides at* _____

   If claimant is a partnership claiming through a member The undersigned who resides at* _____

   is a member of _____ a partnership, composed of the undersigned and †

   _____

   and doing business at* _____

   and is authorized to make this proof of claim on behalf of the partnership.

   If claimant is a corporation claiming through an authorized officer The undersigned, who resides at* _____

   is the _____ of _____, a corporation organized under the laws of

   _____ and doing business at* _____

   and is authorized to make this proof of claim on behalf of the corporation.

   If claim is made by agent The undersigned, who resides at* _____

   is the agent of _____

   of* _____ and is authorized to make this proof of claim on behalf of the claimant.

2. The bankrupt was, at the time of the filing of the petition initiating this case, and still is indebted [or liable] to the claimant, in the sum of $ _____

3. The consideration for this debt [or ground of liability] is as follows:

4. [*If the claim is founded on writing*] The writing on which this claim is founded (or a duplicate thereof) is attached hereto [or cannot be attached for the reason set forth in the statement attached hereto].

5. [*If appropriate*] This claim is founded on an open account, which became [or will become] due on _____

   as shown by the itemized statement attached hereto. Unless it is attached hereto or its absence is explained in an attached statement, no note or other negotiable instrument has been received for the account or any part of it.

6. No judgment has been rendered on the claim except

7. The amount of all payments on this claim has been credited and deducted for the purpose of making this proof of claim.

8. This claim is not subject to any setoff or counter-claim except

9. No security interest is held for this claim except

[*If security interest in property of the debtor is claimed*] The undersigned claims the security interest under the writing referred to in paragraph 4 hereof [or under a separate writing which (or a duplicate of which) is attached hereto, *or* under a separate writing which cannot be attached hereto for the reason set forth in the statement attached hereto]. Evidence of perfection of such security interest is also attached hereto.

10. This claim is a general unsecured claim, except to the extent that the security interest, if any, described in paragraph 9 is sufficient to satisfy the claim. [*If priority is claimed, state the amount and basis thereof.*]

Dated: _____ Signed: .... **TYPE OR PRINT NAME SIGNED** ....

To

of*

POWER OF ATTORNEY

The undersigned claimant hereby authorizes you, or any one of you, as attorney in fact for the undersigned and with full power of substitution, to vote on any question that may be lawfully submitted to creditors of the bankrupt in the above-entitled case; [if appropriate] to vote for a trustee of the estate of the bankrupt and for a committee of creditors; to receive dividends; and in general to perform any act not constituting the practice of law for the undersigned in all matters arising in this case.

Dated: _____ Signed: ....

[*If appropriate*] By .... As ....

Address: ....

| STATE OF | COUNTY OF | ss.: | **ACKNOWLEDGMENT** |

INDIVIDUAL-PARTNERSHIP-CORPORATION: Acknowledged before me on

PARTNERSHIP: by   who says that he is a member of the partnership named above and is authorized to execute this power of attorney in its behalf.

CORPORATION: by   who says that he is the   of the corporation named above and is authorized to execute this power of attorney in its behalf.

....

....
official character

*State post-office address.
†Name and post-office address of each partner.

11
Letters, Data Processing, and Other Matters

Letters
    Individually typed versus the form letter
    A direct reply on the sender's letter
    Seven good will letters
    The letter writer's style
    Characteristics of successful correspondence
Writing to your salesman
    Giving him new, positive information
    Negative information
Data processing
    The EDP revolution
    Data processing services
    Hardware versus software
    Use of dual system
    Benefits of data processing for the credit manager
    The three basic products for the credit manager

Ledger cards
    Advantages and disadvantages
    Accuracy of data processing
    Simplicity for bookkeepers
Aged schedule
    Its importance to the credit manager
    Customer information provided
    Entering payments on the schedule
Statements
    Types of computerized statements available
    Their use as past due reminders
    Convenience for the customer
The two basic data processing services
    Their description
    Advantages and disadvantages of each
Field trips
Notations on a calendar pad
Summation
    Description of a successful credit manager

By the end of his working day, the average credit manager has been busy with a variety of tasks and problems. He has processed his orders, reviewed his payments, resolved complaints, replied to questions, requested proofs of delivery, pursued collections, and corresponded with customers, credit agencies, adjustment bureaus, attorneys, and so on. If he is like most of his peers, the average credit manager need not complain of dullness in his work, for there is much to occupy his time and his attention.

Letters

During the course of his day, the credit manager will unquestionably write some letters, either through his own initiative or as answers to others. Whether these letters are individually dictated or composed depends upon available personnel. Perhaps he has a secretary or assistant to whom he can give dictation, or perhaps he has to prepare all his correspondence himself.

In either event, he need not send individually written letters in every instance. Frequently, a form letter will accomplish what is needed with a minimum of effort and expense. An inquiry from a major customer with a large accounts payable department (or "vendor assistance," as some chains prefer) does not require a dictated reply, for your answer will probably reach a clerk who is interested only in what you have to say, not in how you say it.

Similarly, if you initiate the correspondence, there are times when you write to a department rather than to a specific individual. You can use a three part message form, preprinted with your company name, address, and telephone number.

You needn't dictate your message for someone else to prepare. Even if your typing skills are limited, it takes but a matter of moments to hunt and peck a few brief lines. Those who can't type at all can of course write the message by hand.

Another time-saving device is the reply directly on the sender's letter. Often you will receive a form letter from a customer asking you to reply on the form itself. Once you've answered, make a copy of the letter by running it through your photocopying machine and keep the copy for your files. And make sure your answer is dated.

Even if your customer does not suggest answering on

his letter, there's no reason why you can't do so, provided it's not an elaborate reply. You can attach a small form that says something like the following:

> So that we can respond to your correspondence more promptly, we are taking the liberty of replying to your attached letter by a marginal notation on the letter itself. We felt you would appreciate this answer by return mail rather than wait for a formal letter.

The practice is becoming more and more popular, as more and more offices recognize that formality is no longer required procedure. Again, date your reply and make a copy for your files. Impress this point upon everyone in your office who may handle correspondence. Whenever an answer is made directly upon a letter, whether it be a form letter or individually typed, a copy must be made for your files, and the date of the reply noted.

Should the credit manager use form letters of his own devising?

Yes. For example, where a customer's order contains incorrect selling or shipping terms, he can be advised of the proper terms by the use of a form letter that covers a number of possible corrections.

You can also use a form letter objecting to an unauthorized or incorrect chargeback. Or to return a check. Or to request information. Or for any other purpose that can be handled without a dictated letter. In certain cases, as with past dues, you may use a particular form often enough to warrant having it offset or printed; at other times, you can have a master typed and run it through your copying machine as you need it.

To a busy credit manager, time is a commodity in scarce supply; in certain sections of the country, so is the labor pool. Form letters can replace both and, in addition, expedite the flow of information.

Ideally, there are half a dozen or so instances where letters are advisable but are infrequently written, because the average credit manager simply doesn't have the time for them.

How many of the following letters do you send?

1. Welcoming a new customer, while advising him of your terms (this is especially useful for a marginal account).

2. Thanking an old customer for reactivating his account.

3. Thanking a new customer for his references and advising him that you will follow up on each of the names listed.

4. Assuming the references have been satisfactory, later advising the same new customer that a line of credit has been opened.

5. Welcoming a new owner of an established business with whom you had been dealing for years.

6. Thanking a new customer for a prompt first payment and suggesting he write directly to you should he encounter any problems with future shipments.

7. Thanking an old customer for continuing promptness.

While not one of these letters is absolutely essential to the operation of a credit department, each can be designed to generate good will. But don't bother with letters of this kind where very large customers are involved, for your correspondence would have to be directed to the buying and/or merchandising departments. The buyers and merchandising manager might be impressed with your sincerity, but because much of their purchasing is planned for months ahead and is often determined by computer and committee, a cordial hand extended by the credit department cannot materially affect their buying policies.

For the smaller customers, though, good will letters can be especially effective. They like to know that they're as important to you as the customers who spend ten times as much, or a hundred times more.

And bear in mind that good will letters must be individually typed. You can use the same format and same message for any number of customers, but someone in your office will have to type each letter. You want your customer to think that you've taken the time to write directly to him; a printed or offset form letter would destroy that impression.

Letter writing can be self-destructive if you approach it with trepidation. Don't let it overwhelm you; it's not a difficult procedure once you understand what your correspondence is intended to achieve. You're making a point, or supplying information, or answering someone else's questions, or requesting payment. In each instance, you're writing a business letter, not a work of art.

Don't try to be fancy or elegant. Be yourself, and be natural. Choose the style that's most comfortable for you, but above all, stay away from the stilted and the stiff; it won't hurt your cause to write your letter as if you were talking directly to the addressee.

Remember always that your addressee is as busy as you are. He has neither the time nor the patience to read, "It is indeed our humble pleasure to acknowledge with gratitude your valued order of the 18th instant." Language like that went out with the Edsel.

Here are a few other frequently used words and phrases that you ought to avoid—a simpler alternative for each is shown in the column to the right:

AVOID	USE INSTEAD
Complete, as to complete a form	Fill out
Execute, as to execute a document	Sign

AVOID	USE INSTEAD
Forward	Send
Furnish	Supply
Inasmuch as	Since
In lieu of	Instead of
Pertaining to	Of, or about
Be in a position to	Can
Due to the fact that	Since, or because
In the amount of	For or of
Make inquiry of	Ask
With reference to	About
In spite of the fact that	Although

The keynote should be simplicity and directness tempered with courtesy, consideration, and clarity. If you apply all of these criteria to your correspondence—whether it be a form letter or a letter individually dictated—you'll never go wrong.

Writing to your salesman

Another area of correspondence too often overlooked by the credit department is communicating with a salesman, particularly a road salesman who rarely visits the home office. You probably do get in touch with him if you need information on a specific customer. But what about those occasions when *you* have information for *him*? Information that can frequently mean more business, both for your salesman and your company?

You may learn that a marginal account with whom you have been dealing for some time has improved its position, and its credit rating has been upgraded from a third column or C position to a second column or B position. Both you and your salesman, in the past, moved warily with this account because of its previous marginal condition. Your salesman, in fact, no longer bothered to call upon the account, simply because the amount of business you were willing to accept did not warrant his time and/or the expense to make a costly trip to visit this customer.

To illustrate. This account had a Dun & Bradstreet rating of DD3, $35,000 to $49,000 (see Table 1, Chapter 4). As we explained in Chapter 5, your line of credit for this customer would have been at the most $3,500, or even less if your company preferred a conservative policy.

Your first order for the previous year was $2,000; you shipped on January 15th, meaning the $2,000 was due on February 10th—assuming selling terms of Net 10 EOM. But your customer did not pay when due. He paid on March 25th, 45 days past due. In the meantime, he sent you another order for $2,000.

Bear in mind that these orders came directly from your customer, without a visit from your salesman. Your salesman was aware of activity with this customer only from his commission reports, or only as the result of communicating with your sales department.

You released your customer's second order on March 25th, *after* he paid your previous, past due invoice. You shipped two weeks later, meaning the second invoice was due on May 10th. Once again, your customer paid 45 or so days later, this time not until the end of June.

Your total business, during a six month period, came to $4,000.

As for the balance of the year, both you and your salesman assumed, from your previous history with this customer, that he would place perhaps another $4,000 with your company, and would continue to pay as slowly as he had in the past.

But then you find, from a new credit agency report, that this customer's position has been considerably improved, and his Dun & Bradstreet rating, which last year was DD3, is now DC2, $50,000 to $74,999, with a much better payment record. His line of credit, therefore, can be increased to $5,000, or $7,500, or higher. Not only that, it is evident that his payment pattern has improved. No longer will he be 45 or more days past due, but will most likely pay you on time, or at the worst, fifteen days or so late.

A quick calculation will show you that now you can ship him at least three times during a six month period, instead of two, with a corresponding increase in the size of each order. It is conceivable that your business with his customer can triple, if he so desires.

Do you bother to let your road salesman know of the improvement in his customer's condition? Perhaps you don't because you feel this is the function of the sales department, assuming you have one.

That may be, but why wait for your sales manager to find out what you already know? If the protocol in your organization requires it, report this information to your sales department, and let them handle it. But if your organizational structure informally allows you to correspond directly with your road salesman, or if you have no officially designated sales department, then why not tell your road salesman what you, as the credit manager, would be the first to find out?

Conversely, new *negative* information about an account should also be transmitted either to your sales department or your road salesman. In that way, you may be saving valuable time for your salesman who may continue, in all innocence, to call upon a customer who is no longer worth the effort.

Data processing

Computers, management information systems, data communications concepts, input, output, printout, programming, hardware, software, on-line receivables.

These words and phrases are all part of a new language created by a revolution that has been taking place over recent decades. EDP (electronic data processing) has been transforming the world of commerce, to the ultimate benefit of the credit manager.

In the fifteen or so years following World War II, most of the public immediately thought of the monstrous marvel UNIVAC when anyone mentioned computers. It was a remarkable machine for the television networks on election night, or a wondrous giant for the think tanks to develop their complex formulas. But the rapidly evolving age of computerization has changed everything.

Data processing is no longer a luxury and is no longer confined to the wealthier corporations that can afford to buy their own ultraexpensive installations. Now there are minicomputers for the smaller company, or, for those who prefer a minimum of expenditure, data processing services.

The advantages of data processing are too well known for further elaboration. But perhaps you may not be as familiar with its specific benefits for you as a credit manager. The purpose of this section, therefore, is to acquaint you with (or to remind you of) the various features of data processing that can help you in your daily tasks.

We will not attempt to discuss the advantages of hardware over software. In computer language, hardware refers to the machine itself, which is installed on your premises and which your organization programs and operates; software is an off-premise or on-line service for which you pay an established weekly or monthly fee, or it refers to the program itself.

Whether your company decides to buy or rent a computer, or contract for an on-line service, depends upon how much money it can spend, or exactly what it expects to accomplish. There are many operations in your office that can be automated, but our discussion will be confined to the computerizing of accounts receivable, for it is with this area that the credit manager is primarily concerned.

Before you convert to automation, you must be prepared to employ a dual system for a number of months. Continue with your old, manual system while you're installing and breaking in the new. Do not, under any circumstances, throw away your old system until the new method is completely under your control. Using a dual system may entail extra work for a few months, but you'll find, in the long run, that it has been worth it. No matter how carefully a computerized system has been planned and programmed, something will always go wrong in the early stages.

Here are some of the principal benefits of data processing:

1. Simplicity
2. Accuracy
3. Control
4. Easy analysis
5. Comparative information

A computerized schedule is simple to read, and you can be certain of its accuracy. Computers can't think for themselves, but they always reject anything that doesn't fit. And because your automated system is simple and accurate, you have a far greater degree of control over your accounts receivable. Further, the comparative information gives you more freedom in the checking of credit.

You will have three material products resulting from your conversion to data processing:

1. Computerized ledger cards
2. An aged schedule
3. Statements of all open items

These three are the basic end result, whether your company does its own data processing with its own hardware or you lease an on-line service.

Ledger cards

A computerized ledger gives you all the information you need on a given account—name, address, zip code (and telephone number, if you so desire), credit rating, salesman number, commissionable rate payable to the salesman, discount if any, and every single transaction within your posting period as well as all open items from previous periods. The ledger card will show you date, number, and amount of invoice or credit, date of payment and invoices paid during the previous posting period, and date and amount of chargeback. You also have a cumulative balance of open items, so that the final total will show you exactly what your customer owes you at that moment.

All of this information has been fed to the computer by way of account numbers. Each customer is assigned an account number, usually in alphabetical order by account name, and this number is entered on your computer's master list together with necessary information such as name and address, credit rating, and so on. From then on, whenever you have a transaction of any kind with one of your customers, your computer reaches into its memory bank, links account number and customer together, and prints out a ledger card for that customer.

But automated ledger cards can have some disadvantages. For example, depending upon the type of service you select (see the section on "Data processing services") computerized ledger cards may not be as up to date as manually posted ledgers. If your automated posting is being done on a monthly basis, you will always be one month behind.

For the supplier whose terms are calculated on a 30 or 60 day cycle, this is not too much of a handicap; most payments will arrive in the month following shipment, and by then your postings will have been completed, so your bookkeepers should have no trouble reconciling payments to invoices. If your payment period is less than 30 days, so then will be your posting. (It is possible, with some data processing companies, to have interim ledger cards. Find out if such a service is available before settling on your data processing organization.)

Another potential disadvantage of the automated ledger card for the credit manager is the staleness of information such as credit ratings. With a manual ledger card, it's a simple matter to change a rating by hand; with an automated ledger card, you must give a new set of instructions to your computer, and you may have to wait until the following month for the revised rating to appear on your customer's card.

Any potential disadvantage of data processing, however, is outweighed by the accuracy of automated ledger sheets. The entire picture for a given account is yours at a glance—what invoices or credits are still open, when and how much he paid in the previous period, the date and amount of chargebacks.

For your bookkeepers, gone is the laborious posting by hand (or by bookkeeping machine, which in itself is arduous work). And you may find, that once your system has settled to a smooth routine, you can cut down on your bookkeeping staff. In a recent survey, slightly more than half of the companies who had converted to data processing reported decreases in the personnel of their accounts receivable departments.

Aged schedule

This is probably the single most important product of computerization for the credit manager. An aged schedule properly organized and produced can simplify your tasks to a significant degree.

With an aged schedule before you, you can tell immediately whether a given account owes you money, how much, for how long, and what the total sales are to that point for that customer. In short, you need no longer refer to your ledger cards for your experience with any account. An aged schedule can give you the necessary information, easily and quickly, and you may never have to leave your desk.

An aged schedule lists, in one convenient book, all your accounts, by both account number and name. It shows the total owed by each customer, aged by the periods you specify. It also lists the credit rating, the highest individual sale since the beginning of your posting year, the total of sales to date compared to the total of sales at the same time the year before, and the date and amount of the last payment.

All of this information on each customer will be on one line, reading across from the left to right. Each page of your schedule will have twenty or so individual customers listed; for the average credit manager, an aged schedule of this kind (which you should request be given to you bound) should not be unwieldy at all, even though it contains thousands of accounts.

When your customers' orders come in, it's a simple matter to verify current position by a glance at your schedule. And when you review their checks, why not enter the payments directly on the schedule itself? In that way, you'll always know if an account has paid you that month without having to refer to your ledger card. This procedure is particularly helpful when your automated posting is a month behind.

Statements

These are another important product of automation. You can have your statements printed out in a variety of ways—open items only, past due items only, or a single total balance. You can also have an automatic computation of service or interest charges (if your company has them), any dunning or seasonal message of your choice, and single or multiple copies.

For the credit manager who uses statements as past due reminders, multiple copies can be of some advantage, except that you may discard far more than you use. It's sometimes more economical to run a portion of your statements through your copying machine than to pay for many multiple copies that you will later throw away. (If you have your own computer, extra copies should be no problem. It's only when you lease an outside service that costs can begin to mount.)

Statements that are used as past due reminders have an additional benefit—they allow your customer to answer on the statement form itself without having to take the trouble to compose an explanatory letter. Your customer may say:

"Not yet due. I requested extra dating."
"No record of this invoice. Please send duplicate."
"No record. Please send proof of delivery [or proof of shipment]."

Don't be surprised to find handwritten messages of this kind scrawled over your statements. Everyone looks for time-saving devices, and what better way for your customer than to reply directly on a form that already has his name, address, zip code, account number, date of sale, invoice number, and amount owing? The points he's referring to are ready-made, and all that's required for a complete message is a line or two.

And if you enter payments on your aged schedule, why not at the same time cross off the comparable item on your customer's statement? You may find, after applying his check, that he has overlooked one or two invoices. You can then send him a copy of the statement showing the unpaid invoices. You won't even need an accompanying letter, but simply stamp the open items PAST DUE.

Data processing services

With these three benefits in mind—accurate and easy to read ledger cards, aged schedule, and statements—the credit manager who does not yet have automation can now begin to think of converting his accounts receivable.

In examining the type of service that would probably be most beneficial to you, we will limit our discussion to the off-premise or on-line software program, since the investment in the computer itself may be far too costly for your company, or not necessary.

If you have decided upon an on-line, software program, you can choose one of two basic types of service:

1. You send all necessary documents, including invoices, to the service organization, which then collates and processes all the requisite information and returns the documents.

2. You retain all documents in your possession, and you prepare the information to be fed to the service organization's computers.

The first method is simpler, but more expensive, since the service organization is doing most of the work.

It may be that your company does not want its invoices leaving its premises, even though you're sending duplicate copies. In that case, you will have to use the second alternative. This method can be cheaper than the first, but you will have to do much of the work. But there may not be that much extra work involved, depending upon the number of individual postings you may have during a given day—invoices, payments, credits, and so on. Also, as will be shortly explained, this second method can give you, the credit manager, extremely valuable benefits as an additional product.

For some years, utilizing the second method involved posting all required information upon a machine you either had to buy outright or lease from your data processing organization. This meant that someone in your company had to be available at all times to prepare the posting of your information, probably upon a tape, which was then sent to your data processing company.

Although this kind of machine is not all that difficult to learn or to use, someone has to know its functions. Your bookkeeper probably became the operator, and to be on the safe side, operation of the machine had to be taught to one other bookkeeper or member of the staff.

This machine has one function only—posting your ledger information for the benefit of the data processing service. The machine itself can provide nothing further for you; any additional information must be purchased from your service.

The on-line programs have now been simplified by use of a desk top terminal (or cathode ray tube). This type of terminal has a keyboard much like a typewriter's, and anyone can learn to use it. You do not have to buy this terminal; you lease it from your service or it is furnished as part of the overall package. But you—as the subscriber—will have to pay additional monthly charges to your phone company for use of a line from your terminal to the service's computer.

It is a relatively simple process to enter all your transactions for a given day on this terminal, which then transmits them to the computer, housed on the premises of your service organization. The computer collates all your material and prints out, as required, your aged schedule, your statements, and your ledger cards. It is possible, as well, to have your data processing company supply interim ledger cards, as needed, instead of having to wait until the end of your posting month.

With a terminal, your month end material should be ready for you by the next day, so that little time is lost. If you use the first method of off-premise data processing—that is, sending all necessary documents to your service organization—it may take a few days longer for the computerized material to be sent to you.

Perhaps even more important for you, the credit manager, is another by-product of the terminal. When your posting for each day has been completed, which shouldn't take all that much time, the terminal will then be available for credit information.

By entering your customer's account number on the keyboard and asking the terminal to furnish whatever information you're looking for on that particular customer—how much is currently owing, what is his manner of payment, when was the last payment received, what is his high credit, his latest credit rating, and so on—the information will come back to you instantaneously on the terminal screen. This information, which is stored in your service organization's computers, is available anytime you ask for it. Even if you have posted something on that customer only a few minutes or a few seconds before, you will have that information instantly available as well.

No longer need you wait for your aged schedule printout or your ledger cards to verify a customer's behavior or payment pattern. And changed credit ratings can be entered on the terminal as often as you choose. This, and any other information you may need on a given customer, can be yours after that at a moment's notice simply by asking your terminal to flash that information on its screen. These are advantages that may well be worth the additional expense for leasing this type of service, rather than the cheaper off-premise program.

As for automatic approvals, these can be easily computerized to give you not only the automatic approval itself, but the high credit, unshipped orders, balance owing, line of credit, and so on; a computerized system will also list exceptions for you, those accounts that have to be reviewed each time they send in an order. It may be that your system already has automatic approvals, which may now be handled manually, as are the exceptions. A leased computer can do much of this work for you, more efficiently and more accurately.

Other by-products of an on-line program, whether you use the first or second alternative, might be of interest both to you and your sales department: a salesman commission report (this will be helpful to your bookkeeping department); a comparative sales analysis; a cash application report; and a category analysis, which would summarize sales activity by product and product group, compare sales dollars and units, with percentage calculations by product, product groups, salesman, customer groups, and so on.

But for you, the credit manager, a computerized accounts receivable system will be important in four general areas you work with every day:

1. Credit checking
2. Collection activities
3. Customer deductions and adjustments
4. Answering credit interchange requests

Also, such a computerized system can help you prepare reports for management, if that's one of your normal functions.

There would probably be other benefits that may fit your needs. While most data processing companies offer essentially the same kind of service, each has something special for you, and can tailor its program for your requirements.

Investigate at least two or three data processing companies before making your final decision. And choose your data processing organization as carefully as you approve orders for your customers. Data processing companies can go out of business as quickly as anyone else. If that should happen to you, it might well be months before you can straighten out the resultant bookkeeping mess, for you could be left with noone to do your posting, at least until you find someone else to do the job for you.

Field trips

For many credit managers, field trips and personal visits to customers undoubtedly are a normal part of their routine. They interview new customers and counsel old; they gather credit information and establish a pattern of good will; or they attempt to solve problems that have become too complicated for the normal lines of communication.

The average credit manager of the smaller company, however, may not be able to take the time for regularly scheduled field trips. He has other and primary tasks that prevail. He cannot travel to interview a new customer or to obtain credit information; he cannot devote hours, or perhaps even days, to the counseling of a customer in trouble (aside from his lack of opportunity, he may not be equipped for the task, or his company may not be important enough as a supplier).

But the average credit manager ought not to ignore field trips and/or personal visits for collection purposes. If nothing else, they must be made on a limited, regional basis.

There are occasions when an account becomes too muddled for ordinary procedures. It may be that the customer, through lack of proper personnel, inefficiency, or even as the result of a deliberate management policy, is hopelessly past due. The credit manager has failed, despite his best efforts, to bring the account to a current basis. When there is enough money owing, a personal visit to the customer may be the only answer.

It's too simple to use the excuse that you don't have time for a personal visit; you'll end up wasting even more time because the account will grow progressively worse, almost to a point of no solution.

When your customer is located on the other side of the country, it may be difficult, if not impossible, for you to travel that distance. But certainly you can visit those fairly close by.

Get your pertinent papers together, arrange an appointment with someone in charge, someone who has the authority to make decisions, and set aside the few hours you'll need for traveling and discussion. A face to face and friendly confrontation with the proper person can do wonders for both of you.

Frequently, one such trip can resolve most if not all of

your problems with the account. Beyond that, your customer's personnel will begin to understand your needs and you will appreciate theirs, so that, whenever another such problem arises in the future, a phone call to the same responsible executive may be enough for a successful resolution.

For the customers who are too far away, the telephone can be a substitute. Don't rely only upon letters, especially for complicated matters or for a great deal of money or for many past dues. Place a long distance call, and make others as they may be needed. It isn't cheap, but it's far less expensive than the cost of traveling, and far more productive than the mails. And it won't take you away from your desk.

Notations on a calendar pad

We have now reached the end of the credit manager's day. Perhaps a number of matters have been put over for handling at a future date. How has be provided for them?

If he tends to forget some details from time to time, as most of us do, he at least ought to make entries on his calendar pad. Otherwise he may dig through a stack of work one day and find something buried there that should have been taken care of weeks before.

And some sort of follow-up system should be developed. Writing a single letter to a very busy customer sometimes isn't enough. Don't rely upon the other fellow to answer in time. He may not.

If the credit manager fails to send a necessary second or third letter, the item in question may never be resolved, to the eventual displeasure of the customer. Wherever the fault may lie, negligence can only harm the vendor.

Summation

In 1841, the American poet and essayist Ralph Waldo Emerson wrote:

"A man is a bundle of relations, a knot of roots, whose flower and fruitage is the world."

What Mr. Emerson wrote then can be applied to the credit manager of today, for it is the credit manager's relationship to his work, to his company, and to his customer that bears the fruit of success or failure. In his knot of roots can be found diligence, vigilance, resourcefulness, courage, caution and reason. When he has tied all of these together, and added expertise and knowledge, he can at last speak of himself as a credit manager.

Index

accountant, for creditors' committee, 225, 231
accounts:
  automatic, *see* automatic account
  average, *see* average account
  marginal, *see* marginal accounts
  non-automatic, *see* average account
  requirements, *see* requirements accounts
  semi-automatic, *see* semi-automatic account
accounts payable, 14
  as part of liabilities, 94, 95
accounts receivable:
  average collection periods, 190, 208–210
  computerization of, 259, 264
    dual system for, 259
    ledger cards, 260–262
    schedule of, 260, 262–263
    statements, 260, 263–264
  definition of, 14
  in key ratios, use of, 110–111
  limitation of, 93–94
  major categories of, 91–92
    affiliated companies, 91–92
    charge customers, 91–92
    leased departments, 91–92
  as part of assets, 89–90, 91–92
adjustments, in insolvency proceedings, 224
affiliate, 114, 115
  assets of, 92
  definition of, 15
  monies owed by, 92
agencies, credit, *see* credit agencies
aging schedule, *see* schedule
allowances:
  advertising, 45, 119, 125–126
  on back orders, 162–163
  discussion of, 124–126, 162–163
  as entries on ledger cards, 162–163
  freight, 146–147
  home office, 45, 125, 126
  new store, 31, 45, 125–126

allowances: (*cont.*)
    Robinson-Patman Act, 126–127
    as unauthorized deduction, 155
    warehouse, 45, 125
American Institute of Certified Public Accountants, 89
anticipation:
    as allowance for prepayment, 44, 155
    cutoff date of, 160–161
    definition of, 17, 160
    for extra dating, 161
    illustration of, 159–162
    rate of, 161–162
    for ROG terms, 162
Apparel Trade Books, *see* Credit Clearing House
arrangement, plan of, 229, 230, 233–234, 235–236, 239, 242
"as had," 45, 133
as of the 25th:
    definition of, 16
    discussion of, 127–128
    as extra dating, 127–128
assets:
    current, 90–93, 94
        accounts receivable, 90, 91–92
        cash, 90–91
        merchandise inventory, 90, 92–93
        securities and bonds, 90–91
    definition of, 13, 89
    fixed, 93–94, 99–101
    intangible, 94
    in key ratios, use of, 104–105, 109
    limitations of, 115
    slow, 94
assignment for benefit of creditors, 221, 226–227, 236, 240, 243
attorney:
    for collections purposes, 199, 202–206
    for creditors' committee, 225, 231
    in insolvency proceedings, 237, 243–244
    power of, *see* power of attorney
automatic account, 25–29
    in past due situation, 26–29, 187–188
average account, 33–38
    in past due situation, 33–35, 188, 189

back orders:
    allowances for, 162–163
    in customer instructions, 148
    definition of, 19
    in fine print, 145
    refused shipments of, 148, 183
bad debts, 212–216
    company policy towards, 212–213
    extraordinary loss, 215–216
    marginal accounts, relation to, 39, 40–41, 213, 215–216
    net loss, definition of, 214–215
    "normal" loss, 215
    percentage of, 214–215
    ratio of, 214–215
balance sheet, *see* financial statement
bank credit, 5
bankruptcies, 217–247
    in credit reports, 114
    debtor rehabilitation, 217–226, 228–247
    failures, causes of, 220–221
    marginal accounts, relation to, 39, 216
bankruptcy:
    assignment for benefit of creditors, 226–227, 236, 240, 243
    case history of, 69–71
    claims for, *see* claims

Index

involuntary petition in, *see* Chapter 11, of Bankruptcy Code, involuntary petition under
referee in, 232
six acts of, formerly required, 238–239
trustee for, *see* trustee
voluntary petition in, 221, 236–238, 241–243
Bankruptcy Act, 228, 229, 233, 238
   Amendatory Act of 1938, 218
   Chandler Act, 218
   Chapter X, *see* Chapter X, of Bankruptcy Act
   Chapter XI, *see* Chapter XI, of Bankruptcy Act
   Chapter XII, *see* Chapter XII, of Bankruptcy Act
   early statutes, 217–218
   history of, 217–219
Bankruptcy Code:
   Chapter 7, *see* Chapter 7, Bankruptcy Code
   Chapter 11, *see* Chapter 11, Bankruptcy Code
   Chapter 13, *see* Chapter 13, Bankruptcy Code
   consents required under, 230, 233, 234
   debtor's use, 206, 216, 221, 226, 230–231, 236–237, 241–243
   discussion of, 218–247
   history of, 218–219
   involuntary petition under, 221, 230, 238–241
   provisions of, 219–220
   size of committee under, 230, 232, 234
banks, as sources of credit information, 49, 64, 73–75
barter, 2

bill of lading:
   certification of, for non-delivery, 178
   customer's instructions for, 165
   definition of, 17–18
   for letter of credit, 131
   for shortage claims, 170
   with sight draft, 132
   for title to goods, 143
bookkeeper, as credit manager, 4, 6
bookkeeping, double entry, *see* double entry bookkeeping
books, reference, *see* reference books
bulk sale, 222
business failures, *see* bankruptcies, failures, causes of

calendar pad, notations on, 6, 270
cancellations:
   automatic, 133–134
   date of, 121, 135
   definition of, 19
   refused shipments, cause of, 147–148, 150–151, 183
capacity, 7–10
capital, as part of three C's, 7–8, 9
   as net worth, *see* net worth
capital stock, 96–97, 99
carrier, common, *see* common carrier
cash:
   in advance, definition of, 14, 130–131
   advantages of, 130–133
   before delivery, definition of, 14, 131
   as cashier's check, 131
   as certified check, 131
   on delivery, definition of, 14, 130, 132
   disadvantages of, 130–132

Index

cash: (cont.)
    as letter of credit, 131
    in letter of rejection, 43, 44–45
    as part of assets, 89–91
    sight draft, as variation of, 132
cash discount, *see* discount
CBD, *see* cash, before delivery
Chandler Act, for bankruptcies, 218
Chapter 7, of Bankruptcy Code, 230, 236–238, 240, 243
Chapter 11, of Bankruptcy Code, 219, 221, 226–227, 236, 237–238, 242, 243
    as consolidated chapter, 221, 229
    consents required for, 230, 234
    discussion of, 228–236
    involuntary bankruptcy under, 222, 230, 238–241
    new features of, 229–230
    new merchandise for debtor, 235
    plan of arrangement, procedure for, 234, 235–236
    size of committee under, 230, 232
    terms under, 235, 236
    trustee for, 222
Chapter 13, of Bankruptcy Code, 221, 230, 243
    debtor's use of, 221, 241–243
    discussion of, 241–243
    disadvantages of, for creditors, 242–243
    limitations of, 241–243
Chapter X, of Bankruptcy Act, 219, 221, 228, 229
Chapter XI, of Bankruptcy Act, 218, 219, 221, 228–229, 230–231, 233, 234, 238, 241
Chapter XII, of Bankruptcy Act, 219, 228–229
character, capacity, and capital, 7–10

chargeback:
    definition of, 21
    detention charge, 168–170
    nine general areas of, 153–184
        allowances, 155, 162–163
        anticipation, 155, 159–162
        discounts, 155–159
        freight, 155, 165–170
        non-delivery, 155, 173–182
        pilferage or damage, 155
        returns, 155, 183–184
        in shortage claims, 151, 170–171
        violation of customer instructions, penalties for, 45, 46, 118, 133, 140–142, 144, 155, 163–170
    in relation to new orders, 33
    retailer's policy towards, 164
    service charge, 164, 167–170
"cheapest way," 144
checklist of familiar terms, 12–21
checks:
    for bank name, 73
    cashier's, 131
    certified, 131
    unsigned, 157
CIA, *see* cash, in advance
claims:
    in assignment for benefit of creditors, 226–227, 243
    in Chapter 7, of Bankruptcy Code, 237–238, 243–247
    in Chapter 11, of Bankruptcy Code, 233–234, 237–238, 243–247
    in Chapter 13, of Bankruptcy Code, 242–247
    in involuntary bankruptcy, 238–239, 243–247
    for non-delivery, *see* non-delivery

in out of court settlement, 222–226, 243
for pilferage, *see* pilferage
proof of, in insolvency proceedings, 225, 233, 237–238, 243–247
against Postal Service, 180
for shortages, *see* shortages
against slow paying accounts, 202–206, 208
against trucker, 172–182
  documents for, 176–180
  time limit for, 175, 177
against United Parcel Service, 180
in voluntary bankruptcy, 237–238, 243–247
clearance, *see* interchange
COD, *see* cash, on delivery
collateral, 7
collection agencies, 198–199, 202–206, 244
  lists for subscribers, 80
  procedures of, 202–206
    free demand period, 203–204
collections:
  alternatives to final notice, 199–201
    certified letter, 200
    letter to president of corporation, 201
    mailgram, 200
    phone call to customer, 200–201
    your salesman, 199
    sight draft, 200
  final notice, 192–193, 198, 199–202
  judgment clause, 203
  letters for, 190–192, 194–199
    certified, 200
    standard printed forms, 192–193
  procedures for, 186–208
    intervals of, 190, 191–192
  schedule for, 186–187
  the statement as past due reminders, 193–194, 195–197, 263–264
committee, creditors', *see* creditors
common carrier, 140, 143, 144, 149, 165, 169, 171–178, 181–182, 184
  definition of, 18
company policy:
  accounts receivable, turnover of, 190
  anticipation, 160–162
  bad debts, 212–213
  interest, 207
  line of credit, 81
  marginal accounts, 41
  new store allowance, 126
  past dues, 35, 186–187, 189–190
  penalties for violation of instructions, 163
  rejection of orders, 43
  returns, 159, 183–184
  slow paying accounts, 39–41, 130
  unearned discounts, 156–158
computers:
  in credit granting, 3, 266–268
  as fourth C, 10
  significance of, 10–11
  for smaller companies, 10–11
confirmations, 46, 133
consolidating:
  customer instructions for, 141, 145, 165, 168
  definition of, 18
consolidators, 143
  definition of, 18
  as FOB point, 141–145, 146–147
controller, as credit manager, 4

Index

credit:
  commercial, definition of, 5
  definition of, 1–2
    evolution from Latin, 1–2
  language of, 24
  line of, *see* line of credit
  as a medium of exchange, 2
  mercantile, definition of, 5
  open terms, definition of, 14
  practice of, 5
  relationship to buyer, 5
  significance of, 2, 6
  sources of information for, 48–80
  three C's, as keystone of, 7–8
Credit and Collection Letters, 195
credit agencies, 49–56
  for bank name, 73
  interchange, sponsorship of, 69
  reliance upon, 50, 55, 84
  services of, 31, 39, 49–50, 54
credit checking:
  definition of, 14
  early days of, 9
  human element in, 3
  for marginal accounts, 41
Credit Clearing House, Division of Dun & Bradstreet:
  Apparel Trade Books, 53, 55
  rating key, 53
credit department:
  composition of, 3–4, 6
    in large corporations, 3, 4
    in smaller companies, 3, 4
  responsibilities of, 5–6
Credit Exchange, Inc., 54
credit file, 33
"credit fraternity," 124
credit granting:
  in past due situations, 26–29, 34–36, 39–41
    average accounts, 33–35
    marginal accounts, 39–41
    requirements accounts, 26–29

  semi-automatic accounts, 30–32
  procedure for, 12
credit information, *see* information
credit interchange, *see* interchange
Credit Interchange bureaus, 57, 59
credit manager:
  assessment of customer by, 8–10
  bad debts, his relationship to, 212–216
  in bankruptcy proceedings, 219
  data processing, his relationship to, 11–12
  description of, 271
  function of, 3, 4, 5, 12
  as novice or trainee, 5
  problems of, 5–6
  recognition of, 3
  responsibilities of, 5, 6, 139
  role of, in commerce, 2–3
  twin goals of, 213–214
  vigilance of, *see* vigilance, credit manager's
credit ratings, 35–36, 39, 50–53
  definition of, 14–15
  for line of credit, 55, 84–86, 256–257
  systems of, 49, 50–53, 84–85
credit reports, 9, 31, 49, 50, 54, 63–67, 113–144
Credit Research Foundation, Inc., 38, 208–209, 214
creditors, in insolvency proceedings:
  best interests of, 224, 225, 228–229, 235, 242–243
  claims of, 223, 224–225, 233, 237–238, 242–245
  committee for, 223, 225, 226, 230, 231–232, 233, 243, 244, 245
    accountant for, 225, 231
    attorney for, 225, 231

Index

chairman of, 225, 231, 232
first meeting of, 223–224, 231, 232, 237
power of attorney to, 233, 245
proof of claim to, 225, 233, 243–247
secretary to, 225, 231
meetings of, 223–225, 226, 231–232, 233, 237, 241, 243, 244
presence at, 223
credits, definition of, 21
current assets, *see* assets
current liabilities, *see* liabilities
customer:
    appraisal of, by credit manager, 8–10
    instructions from, *see* instructions, customer
    line of credit for, 84–87
    as source of information, 49, 78–79
customers, new, 33, 36–38, 216
    analysis of, 36–38
    marginal, 41, 72
    relation to bad debts, 216
cutoff date:
    for anticipation, 160–161
    for discount, 156–157
    for ROG, 129

damage:
    cartons, segregation of, 171
    claims against trucker, 171–173
    responsibility for, 171–173
data processing:
    for accounts receivable, 259, 264
        dual system for, in conversion of, 259
    ledger cards, 260–262
    schedule, 260, 262–263
    statements, 193–194, 260, 263–264
    benefits to credit manager, 258–260, 266–268
    desk top terminal, 266–267
    discussion of, 258–268
    hardware, on premises use of, 258–259
    minicomputers, 11, 258
    on-line service, 258–259, 264–268
    services, types of, 264–268
    for the smaller company, 11–12, 258
    software, off premises use of, 258–259, 264–268
dating:
    additional, *see* extra dating
    extra, *see* extra dating
days sales outstanding, 208–210
debit, definition of, 21
debit memo:
    as advice of non-delivery, 178
    definition of, 21
debtor:
    in assignment for benefit of creditors, 226–227
    Chapter 13, use by, 241–243
    character of, 9–10
    in financial difficulty, courses open to, 221–222
    general denial by, in suit, 205–206
    hazard to, in assignment, 227, 236
    in involuntary bankruptcy proceedings, 240–241
    new grounds for, 239–240
    in out of court settlement, 221, 222–226
    rehabilitation of, 217–220, 222–226, 228–247
    six acts of bankruptcy by, formerly required, 238–239
    voluntary bankruptcy by, use by, 221, 236–238

Index

Debtor and Creditor Law, 227
debtor-in-possession, 228, 229, 233, 235–236
delivery, proof of, *see* proof delivery
delivery receipt, free and clear, in pilferage cases, 171–173
depreciation, 101
detention charge, 168–170
discount:
  cash, 122–123, 155–156, 157–158
  definition of, 17, 122
  discussion of, 122–124, 155–159
  as incorrect payment, 45, 119–120, 155–157
  time, 122, 155–159
    cutoff date of, 122, 156–158
    limitation of, 156–158
  trade, 122–123, 155
  unauthorized, invoice for, 158
  unearned, 123, 156–159
  variations of, 123–124
  as violation of Robinson-Patman Act, 158
division, 114
  definition of, 15
double entry bookkeeping, 12
DSO, *see* days sales outstanding
Dun & Bradstreet, 30, 49, 53, 66
  classification of accounts, 14–15
  credit rating system, 51, 55, 84–86
  reference books, 36, 49, 50, 65, 66

EDP, *see* data processing
electronic data processing, *see* data processing
End of the Month, *see* EOM
EOM, 123–124, 128
  definition of, 16, 119
equity, *see* net worth

expansion, without adequate funding, 70–71, 112–113
extra dating, 31
  with anticipation, 161
  definition of, 16
  discussion of, 127–130
  for new stores, 125
  with ROG, 129
  for slow paying customers, 129–130, 188
  for small accounts, 32

failures, business, causes of, 220–221
Feakes Mercantile Agency, 54
field trips, 268–270
Fields, J. M., *see* J. M. Fields
final notice, in past due situations, 192–193, 198, 199–202
  alternatives to, 199–201
    certified letter, 200
    letter to president of corporation, 201
    mailgram, 200
    phone call to customer, 200–201
    your salesman, 199
    sight draft, 200
financial affairs, trend of, 34–35, 86–87, 112–113, 220–221
financial statement, 84–113
  accountant's disclaimer, 88–89
  composition of, 87
  definition of, 13, 24
  from new customer, 37
  validity of, 87–89
fine print, 118, 132–134, 145, 166
fixed assets, 89, 93–94, 100–101
FOB:
  consolidator, 141
  definition of, 17, 139–140
  point of, 139–141, 143–144
    destination, 139–140

Index

shipping, 140–141, 143–144, 172
follow-up letters, 121, 270
Food Fair, 29, 41, 114–115
form letters, 120–121, 251–254
   for collections, 190–192, 194–199
   for proofs of delivery, 176–179
   for references, 77–78
fourth C, *see* computers
franchise operation, 134
fraud, 114, 220, 226, 229, 237
free and astray:
   in claim for non-delivery, 174, 175
   definition of, 19
free and clear delivery receipt, 171–173, 174
free demand, in collection procedure, 203–204, 205
Free on Board, *see* FOB
freight:
   allowances for, 146–147
      double charge, 146–147
      free area, 146–147
   chargebacks for, 139, 141, 155, 165–170
   collect, 139–142
   customer's instructions, 165–168
      service charge, 167–168, 169
      in traffic guide, 165–168
      violation of, 165–168
   via parcel post, 140, 142
   prepaid, 142, 143–144, 146
   transit insurance for, 173, 180–182
   United Parcel Service, 142

general ledger, 20
Grant, W. T., *see* W. T. Grant
group interchange, *see* interchange, group
guide, traffic, *see* traffic guide
gum tape, 150

high credit, definition of, 14

inflation, 110, 161, 169
information:
   computerized, 266–267
   negative, *see* negative credit information
   non-financial, 113–115
   sources of, 48–80
      banks, 73–75
      credit agencies, 49–55
      your customer, 78–79
      interchange groups, 57–63, 67–73
      NACIS reports, 63–67
      references, 77–78
      your salesman, 75–76
insolvency, 202
   definition of, 21
   discussion of, 217–247
instructions, customer:
   for invoicing, 46, 163–164
   multiplicity of, 163–165
   for shipping, 147–150, 165–170
   violation of, 31, 45, 118, 163–170
insurance, transit, 173, 180–182
interchange:
   definition of, 16
   industry reports, local, 49, 67–73
      advantages of, 69–71
      bankruptcy, illustration of, 69–71
      information from, 68–69
      preparation of, 68–69
   industry reports, national, 49, 56–63, 64–67
      advantages of, 57
      disadvantages of, 57
      information from, 58–63
      preparation of, 59–63
   local groups, 67–69
      meetings of, 67
      membership of, 67

interchange: (cont.)
  NACIS, see NACIS reports
  NACM national groups, 67
    meetings of, 67
    membership of, 67
    as references, 69
interest, 27–28, 160, 203, 206–207, 263
Interstate Commerce Commission, 175, 181–182
inventory, merchandise:
  appraisal of, 93
    lower of cost or market, 93
  assets, as part, 89, 92
  computation of, 93
    first in, first out, 93
    last in, first out, 93
  in key ratios, 105–107, 109
  limitation of, 92–93
  tax on, 148
  turnover of, 105–107, 125
investment credit, 5
invoices:
  certification of, for non-delivery, 178
  definition of, 19–20
  instructions for, 46, 131, 132–133, 148–149
  skipped, see skipped invoices
involuntary bankruptcy, see Chapter 11, of Bankruptcy Code, involuntary bankruptcy under

Jewelers Board of Trade, Red Book, 52
J. M. Fields, 41, 114
judgment clause, 203

key ratios:
  collection period for receivables, 111
  computation of, 102–103
  current assets to current liabilities, 104–105
  debt to net worth, 108
  fixed assets to net worth, 109
  illustration of, 104–111
  inventory turnover, 106–107
  inventory to working capital, 109
  liquid or quick, 105
  net profit to net worth, 110
  net profit to sales, 110
  other, 111
  sales to inventory, 105–107
  sales to net worth, 107–108
  sales to receivables, 110–111
  value of, to credit manager, 102–104
K mart Corporation, 26

last resort, the, see collection agencies
leased departments, 92
ledger, definition of, 20
ledger cards, 33, 35
  computerization of, 260–262, 266, 267
    advantages of, 260–262
    disadvantages of, 261
ledger experience, 20, 54, 56, 58, 68, 69, 268
legal digests, see negative credit information
letter of credit, 131
letters:
  certified, 200, 202
  collection, 187, 190–192, 194–199
  discussion of, 251–257
  follow-up, see follow-up letters
  form, see form letters
  good will, 253–254
  for references, 78
  for rejection of orders, 42–45
  reply to customer's, 251–252

to your salesman, 255–257
style of, 252, 254–255
liabilities:
  capital stock, 96–97, 99
  current, 94–95
    accounts payable, 94–95
    accruals, 94
    notes payable, 94–95
  definition of, 13, 94
  in key ratios, use of, 104–105, 108
  long term, 94, 95–96
  net worth, 96–99
  retained earnings, 96, 97, 99
line of credit, 34–35, 80–82
  for A-rated accounts, 35
  definition of, 14
  percentage method for, 84–86
    based on net worth, 85
    based on working capital, 85
  for requirements account, 81
  for semi-automatic account, 30
liquid ratio, 105
losses, *see* bad debts
Lumbermen's Credit Association, 54

mailgram, 200
"man's confidence in man," 1–2
manifest, definition of, 18
marginal accounts:
  bad debts, relation to, 40, 45, 213, 215–216
  bankruptcies, relation to, 39, 216, 220–221
  characteristics of, basic, 38, 221
  credit ratings of, 38–39, 55, 255–257
  definition of, 15, 38–39, 216
  in improved condition, 255–257
  interchange on, 58, 72
  as a new customer, 41, 72
  in past due situation, 39–41, 188, 189
  rejection of orders from, 42–45
  risk factors of, 38–39, 220–221
merchandise, ownership of, 17, 138–139, 140, 142–144
mercantile credit, 5
minicomputers, *see* data processing
Montgomery, Ward, 26
Morris, Robert, early victim of bankruptcy, 217–218

NACIS reports, 58, 63–67
  for bank name, 73
  business directory, 63, 65
  client security, 65
NACM, *see* National Association of Credit Management, services of
National Association of Credit Management, services of:
  adjustments, 224
  in bankruptcy legislation, 218, 219
  collections, 195–199, 204–205
    bureaus for, 204–205
    letters for, 195–199
  correspondence courses, 12
  interchange, 16
    local, 67–69
    NACIS reports, 63–67
    national, 64–67
National Collection Service, 205
National Credit Information Service, *see* NACIS reports
National Credit Interchange system, 56–63, 64, 66
National Institute of Credit, 12
negative credit information:
  collection agency lists, 80
  legal digests, 80
  for your salesman, 257

net:
  definition of, 16–17, 119
  discussion of, 119–121
net worth:
  capital stock, 96–97, 99
  definition of, 13, 96–99
  illustration of, 97–98
  in key ratios, 107–110
  as a liability, 96–99
  for line of credit, 84–85
  retained earnings, 96, 97, 99
non-automatic account, *see* average account
non-delivery:
  chargeback for, 155, 171–173, 174–175
  complete, 174, 177–178
  debit memo as advice of, 178
  filing claim for, 174–182
    documents for, 176–180
    indemnification, 178
    parcel post forms for, 178, 180
    standard form for, 176–179
    time limit for, 175, 177
  partial, 171–173, 174, 175
  proof of delivery, 174–179
    form letter for, 176–179
    methods for request, 174–175
    requests for, 174
    service charge for, 174–175
notes payable, as part of liabilities, 94, 95–96

open terms, definition of, 14
order for relief, 231, 244
orders:
  automatic approval of, in computerization, 267
  confirmations of, 46, 133
  infrequent, 34, 188
  rejection of, *see* rejection of orders
  shipping order to order, 40, 216
  signatures on, 133
  stamping the back of, 135
  unsolicited, 31, 33, 41, 70
out of court settlement, *see* settlement, out of court
overtrading, 106, 107, 108

packing slip, definition of, 20
parcel post, 140, 142, 143, 175, 178–180
partnership, liability limitation of, 115
past dues:
  average account, 33–36, 187–189
  classifications of, 188–189
  collection procedures for, 186–208
    form letters, 194–199
    standard printed forms, 192–193
    statements, 193–194, 263–264
  company policy towards, 34, 186–187, 189–190
  definition of, 21
  discussion of, 185–210
  field trips for, 269–270
  final notice, alternatives to, 199–201
    certified letter, 200
    letter to president of corporation, 201
    mailgram, 200
    phone call to customer, 200–201
    your salesman, 199
    sight draft, 200
  interest for, 203
  marginal account, 39–41, 188, 189
  partial payment of, 197–198
  reminders, 187, 192, 193, 203, 263–264
  requirements account, 26–29, 187–188

percentage method, for line of credit, 84–86
personal opinion:
   definition of, 15–16, 24
   for semi-automatic accounts, 31
pilferage, 151, 155
   cartons, segregation of, 171
   claims against trucker, 171–173
   responsibility for, 171–173
P.O., *see* personal opinion
policy, company, *see* company policy
Postal Service, 142, 180
power of attorney, in insolvency proceedings, 223, 233, 245
prepayment, *see* cash
pro forma, definition of, 18–19
pro no., definition of, 19
Produce Reporter Company, Fruit and Produce Book, 52
profit and loss, statement of, 101–102
   components of, 102
profit, net, as used in key ratios, 110–111
proof of claim, in insolvency proceedings, *see* claims, proof of, in insolvency proceedings
proof of delivery:
   for collection agency, 208
   from common carriers, 174–179
      notice of intent to file claim against, 176–177
   customer's request for, 26, 133, 143, 174, 176, 178, 207, 264
   definition of, 19
   for insolvency proceedings, 245
   for parcel post, 175
      insured, 175
      uninsured, 175
   service charge for, 175–176
   for skipped invoices, 133, 175, 207–208
proprietorship, liability limitation of, 115
proximo, definition of, 123–124
proxy, creditor's, 233, 245

quick ratio, 105

rating systems, *see* credit ratings
ratios, 87, 104–111, 190
   key, *see* key ratios
   for line of credit, 85
Receipt of Goods, *see* ROG
receivables, *see* accounts receivable
receivables, turnover rate of, 208–210
recommendations, by credit agencies, 14–15, 37, 49, 50, 54
referee in bankruptcy, 232
reference books, 36, 49, 50, 53, 54–55, 63, 65
references:
   advantages of, 77–78
   disadvantages of, 77
   information from, 49, 77–78, 253
   supplied by interchange group, 69
refused shipments:
   lapsed cancellation date, 150–151
   reasons for, 147–151, 183
   redelivery charges, 151
rejection of orders, 42–45
   company policy, 43
      letter of rejection, 42–43
   partial prepayment, 44–45
requirements accounts:
   amounts to ship, 81
   as automatic account, 25–26, 267
   definition of, 15, 24
   in past due situation, 26–29, 187–188

retained earnings, 96, 97–99
returns, 155, 183–184
Robinson-Patman Act, 126–127, 158
ROG:
  with anticipation, 162
  cutoff date for, 129
  definition of, 17
  as extra dating, 128–129
routing guide, see traffic guide

sales:
  average collection period, 111, 208–210
  in key ratios, use of, 105–108, 110, 111
salesman, your:
  information for, 255–257
  in past due situation, 199
  as source of credit information, 9, 49, 75–76
schedule, 33, 35
  computerization of, 260, 262–263, 266, 267
    advantages of, 262–263, 264
  definition of, 20
secretary to creditors' committee, 225, 231
Sears, Roebuck, 26, 30
S. E. C., see Securities and Exchange Commission
Securities and Exchange Commission, 228
selling, terms of, 31, 117–134
semi-automatic account, 30–32
  investigation of, for unusually large orders, 30–31
service charge:
  for proofs of delivery, 175–176
  for return of defective merchandise, 183, 184
  for violation of instructions, 164, 167–170

settlement:
  common law, 222
  out of court, 221, 222–227, 229
shipment, proof of, 143
shipments, refused, see refused shipments
shipping:
  back orders, 145
  charges for, 17, 19, 138, 165–170
  cheapest way, 144
  customer's instructions, 165–170
    in traffic guide, 165
    violation of, 45, 165–170
  parcel post, 140, 142, 143
  routes, 144–145
  terms of, 45, 137–151
    collect, 140–142, 168
    prepaid, 142, 143–144, 146, 168
  United Parcel Service, 142
  weight, as defense against shortage claims, 170
shipping memo, see packing slip
shortages:
  customer's claims of, 170–171, 173–176
  defense against, 170–176
  hidden, 171
sight draft:
  for collection purposes, 200
  as prepayment, 132
signature, on orders, 133
skipped invoices, 26–29, 72, 133, 175–176, 187, 188, 207
Small Business Administration, 79
statements:
  computerization of, 260, 263–264, 266
    advantages of, 263–264
  definition of, 20–21
  as past due reminders, 193–194, 195–197, 263–264
subordination, 95

subsidiary, 114–115
  definition of, 15
suppliers, number of, 85, 86

tact, in letter writing, 42–43
terms:
  payment, 45
  selling, 31–32, 117–135
  shipping, 137–151
  variations of, 45
30x, *see* extra dating
three C's, 7–8
trade debts, *see* liabilities
trade discount, *see* discount
traffic guide, 144, 164, 165–166, 167, 168
trend of financial affairs, *see* financial affairs, trend of
trial balance, *see* schedule
trustee, 222, 228, 237, 240
TRW Business Credit Services, 64, 65, 66–67

undertrading, 107, 108
Uniform Commercial Code, 219
United Parcel Service, 142, 180
UNIVAC, 258
UPS, *see* United Parcel Service

vigilance, credit manager's, 31–32, 46, 71, 72, 163, 220, 271
violations, penalties for, *see* chargebacks, violation of customer instructions, penalties for
voluntary bankruptcy, *see* bankruptcy, voluntary petition in

without exception, *see* free and clear delivery receipt
working capital:
  definition of, 13–14, 99
  illustration of, 99–101
  in key ratios, use of, 109, 111
  for line of credit, 85
W. T. Grant, 29, 41